Beyond the Anarchical Society

Edward Keene argues that the popular idea of an 'anarchical society' of equal and independent sovereign states is an inadequate description of order in modern world politics. International political and legal order has always been dedicated to two distinct goals: it tries to promote the toleration of different ways of life, but at the same time it promotes one specific way of life that it labels 'civilization'. The nineteenth-century solution to this contradiction was to restrict the promotion of civilization to the world beyond Europe. That discriminatory way of thinking has now broken down, with the result that a single, global order is supposed to apply to everyone, but that has left us with an insoluble dilemma as to what the ultimate purpose of this global order should be, and how its political and legal structure should be organized.

EDWARD KEENE is Tutor in Politics at Balliol College, Oxford, and has previously taught at the School of Oriental and African Studies in London and at the Georgia Institute of Technology in Atlanta. With Eivind Hovden he co-edited the journal *Millennium*, and *The Globalization of Liberalism* (2002). He is the author of *International Society as an Essentially Contested Concept* in Michi Ebata and Beverly Neufeld (eds.), *Confronting the Political: International Relations at the Millennium* (2000) and *The Reception of Hugo Grotius in International Relations Theory* (Grotiana).

D1596628

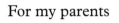

For my parents

Beyond the Anarchical Society

Grotius, Colonialism and Order in World Politics

Edward Keene
University of Oxford

CAMBRIDGE
UNIVERSITY PRESS

PUBLISHED BY THE PRESS SYNDICATE OF THE UNIVERSITY OF CAMBRIDGE
The Pitt Building, Trumpington Street, Cambridge, United Kingdom

CAMBRIDGE UNIVERSITY PRESS
The Edinburgh Building, Cambridge CB2 2RU, UK
40 West 20th Street, New York, NY 10011-4211, USA
477 Williamstown Road, Port Melbourne, VIC 3207, Australia
Ruiz de Alarcón 13, 28014 Madrid, Spain
Dock House, The Waterfront, Cape Town 8001, South Africa

http://www.cambridge.org

First published 2002

Printed in the United Kingdom at the University Press, Cambridge

Typeface Plantin 10/12 pt   *System* LaTeX 2_ε [TB]

A catalogue record for this book is available from the British Library

ISBN 0 521 81031 0 hardback
ISBN 0 521 00801 8 paperback

Contents

Preface

As anyone who has studied international relations will probably be aware, the title of this book is a reference to Hedley Bull's famous work, *The Anarchical Society: A Study of Order in World Politics*. My use of a similar language is intended in part as a tribute to the power and insight of Bull's argument, and in part as a criticism of its limitations. Before I present my own perspective on order in world politics, then, I want to explain briefly why I attach so much importance to Bull's approach, and where I think he went wrong.

To my mind, the most attractive feature of Bull's work is his lucid defence of the view that in certain respects international relations are social relations, and that order in world politics should therefore be conceived as a form of social order. Bull developed this position primarily to challenge the popular belief that international relations should be understood in 'Machiavellian' or 'Hobbesian' terms. In other words, he was taking issue with the argument that, because the international system is anarchic, all states have to obey the brutal logic of *Realpolitik* and must devote themselves to the pursuit of their own national interests. Bull acknowledged that this perspective captures some aspects of international relations, as does an alternative 'Kantian' perspective that highlights the importance of transnational or ideological solidarity and conflict, but he insisted that neither tells us the whole story. In particular, they underestimate the importance and frequency of cooperation and regulated intercourse among states, based on the norms, rules and institutions of the modern 'anarchical society' of equal and independent sovereign states. While it is important to explain how the logic of anarchy influences the behaviour of states, it is just as important to understand the normative structure of the order that has been created in this international society. As well as having to explain how states respond to the anarchical nature of the international system, theorists must also make sense of the relationship between the goals that are promoted by the existing order in the society of states and alternative goals that might conceivably be regarded as attributes of justice in world politics. Here, one of the key themes in

Bull's work was the claim that, although it often falls short with regard to certain principles of 'human' or 'world justice', the society of states nevertheless represents a valuable achievement in terms of its realization of 'interstate' justice; it sustains an order where ethnic, cultural and political differences are tolerated through the norm that states should respect each other's sovereignty. This goal, Bull argued, should not lightly be dismissed in the attempt to build a more liberal or cosmopolitan world order.

The bulk of the academic commentary on Bull's theory, whether critical or supportive of his views, has concentrated on these rather general claims about the normative character of international order and its relationship to different conceptions of justice. For many years, the main debates were centred on the questions that Bull himself raised about whether or not an international society exists, whether or not the order sustained by the society of states can provide for a satisfactory conception of justice in world politics, and what is happening to the traditional pattern of international order as it is forced to deal with contemporary developments in world politics. More recently, international relations theorists have also begun to address certain questions that are more internal to his approach, applying insights from social theory to refine Bull's often rather vague, and now rather dated, functionalist ideas about precisely how normative principles are established in international society and how they come to play a constraining role on the behaviour of states. The range of these enquiries has been as diverse as social theory itself: various post-structuralists, critical theorists, historical sociologists and social constructivists have all produced significant treatises on where the norms, rules and institutions of the modern society of states came from, why they look the way they do and how they condition the conduct of international actors.

I recognize that these controversies about Bull's account of order in world politics raise serious issues that demand attention, and that his conception of social order needs to be supplemented with more sophisticated analyses of social theory. However, I do not think that these are the most serious problems with Bull's work, and in this book I am going to explore another weakness in his argument that I regard as much more pernicious. This may surprise some readers, because my approach will not really engage with the main debates that have occupied international relations theorists since *The Anarchical Society* appeared in the late 1970s. I will not, for example, join realists and cosmopolitans in asking whether the kind of norm-governed order that Bull described is a significant or desirable feature of world politics. Nor will I ask which kind of social theory offers the best chance for making sense of how the modern pattern of order in the society of states was established, how it works and what its future prospects are. My argument is directed at a completely different question: is Bull's account of the anarchical society, founded on the principle of states' mutual respect for each other's territorial sovereignty, an adequate description of the norms, rules and institutions that have characterized order in world politics since around the middle of the seventeenth century?

As the title of this book suggests, my answer is no. I believe that Bull's chief mistake was to underestimate the dualistic nature of order in world politics. My position is that there have always been two patterns of modern international order, each of which was dedicated to its own goal, and therefore possessed its own unique normative and institutional structure. Bull's work provides a description of only one of these: the pattern of order that developed in the European states-system, through relations between European rulers and nations. He almost completely ignored the other pattern of order, which developed roughly simultaneously in the colonial and imperial systems that were established beyond Europe. As is exemplified by Bull's conception of interstate justice, the main purpose of the European order was to promote the toleration of ethnic, cultural and political differences; the extra-European order, however, was dedicated to the goal of promoting a particular idea of civilization, transforming 'uncivilized' cultures and social, economic and political systems along the way. This divergence is manifested in the very different international political and legal arrangements that were established in the two contexts. The European order of toleration was predicated on the principle that states should respect each other's territorial sovereignty, and hence their equality and independence. By contrast, the extra-European order was based on the principle that sovereignty should be divided across national and territorial boundaries, creating hierarchical institutions through which colonial and imperial powers transmitted the supposed benefits of their civilization to the rest of the world.

This is a crucial omission from Bull's work, since the world we live in today contains the legacy of both of these patterns of modern international order. As Bull was well aware, the principles of toleration and mutual respect for sovereignty outgrew their European roots in the twentieth century, gradually being extended to cover all the peoples of the world. But because he lacked a proper understanding of the extra-European order of civilization that had also existed in modern world politics, he failed to realize that its basic norm of dividing sovereignty to promote good government and economic progress had also persisted into the new global political and legal order that was constructed after 1945. And because subsequent scholars have not properly investigated this weakness in Bull's theory of the anarchical society, they have also failed to appreciate the long-standing tension between toleration and civilization that has always lain at the heart of order in modern world politics. Instead, they have consistently misrepresented the contemporary practice of dividing sovereignty as an unprecedented, 'post-modern' or 'post-Westphalian' phenomenon.

Before I develop this argument, I want to make one final remark about its scope. I have chosen Bull as my critical foil because his work has been exceptionally influential in contemporary international relations theory. So many scholars today use Bull's description of the modern society of states as a starting point for their own work that I regard it as absolutely crucial to demonstrate the shortcomings of his thesis. However, the position that I am attacking is not just Bull's alone. On the contrary, what I will call the orthodox theory of order in world politics has been a central part of mainstream thinking about international relations and international law for roughly two hundred years; in a sense, Bull's work is just the latest re-statement of a much older position, up-dated to suit the specific problems and dilemmas of international relations in the late twentieth century, but substantially unchanged in its fundamentals. In criticizing Bull, then, I am really attacking one of the most popular and long-standing points of view on international political and legal order that there is. Obviously, this is an ambitious project, and I suspect that it takes more than a single book to challenge an academic orthodoxy that has become so deeply entrenched over the last two centuries that even many 'critical' and 'dissident' scholars working today still accept its core claim about the centrality of the society of sovereign states to the modern world. Nevertheless, the orthodox theory is so badly flawed that it acts as a major hindrance to our ability to comprehend the nature of the dilemmas that we face today, and it is of the first importance that we begin to call its basic assumptions into question. At the very least, I hope that my argument will illustrate the seriousness of its shortcomings, and thus encourage others to adopt a fresher perspective on order in modern world politics, whether or not they agree with the interpretation that I will present here.

Acknowledgements

I have been mulling over the argument of this book for about ten years, and if I was to acknowledge all the people who had contributed to the ideas presented in it, I would have to list practically everyone with whom I have had any sustained engagement in my undergraduate, postgraduate and professional careers. You know who you are, and you have my heartfelt gratitude for all the advice and suggestions you have given me. That said, there is a smaller group of people who have been especially important to the development of my work, and I would like to offer them more direct thanks here.

My biggest intellectual debt is to Justin Rosenberg, who supervised the Ph.D. thesis on which this book is based. Justin was an invaluable source of expertise and encouragement while I was writing the thesis, and he has been a model of thorough and imaginative scholarship as I have tried to take the next step to presenting my ideas to a wider public. Close behind him in their importance are Andrew Hurrell and Fred Halliday. Andrew engaged my interest in international relations theory while I was an undergraduate, and his thoughtful, learned questioning has been a constant stimulus ever since. Fred probably has more responsibility than anyone else for my decision to pursue an academic career; his charismatic approach to the study of international relations gave me both a sense of vocation and an abiding affection for everything that the London School of Economics (LSE) has traditionally represented. As well as Justin and Fred, I have benefited hugely from the other members of the International Relations Department at the LSE, particularly Michael Banks, Mark Hoffmann and Peter Wilson, but it is no disrespect to them if I say that I probably learnt even more from my fellow Ph.D. students. I had the good fortune to find myself in a vibrant and friendly community of scholars, which gave me an experience to cherish and had a profound impact on my work: my particular thanks go to the members of the Modernity workshop, my colleagues at *Millennium* and above all to Eivind Hovden, not just for helping me to develop my thoughts on international relations, but also for keeping me cheerful during the often lonely business of writing a thesis.

Completing the Ph.D., though, was really only half the battle. Since then I have received a great deal of help from numerous scholars, and I would like to thank them for their comments, criticisms and encouragement. As I moved into my first proper job, I was lucky enough to find myself at SOAS, surrounded by the same kind of intelligent and convivial community that I had just left at the LSE: Kathryn Dean, Sudipta Kaviraj, Charles Tripp, Tom Young, and most of all Stephen Hopgood have been excellent friends and colleagues. I am extremely grateful to my Ph.D. examiners, Andrew Linklater and James Mayall, for their penetrating analysis of my thesis, and to the readers of the initial manuscript that I sent in to Cambridge University Press. I think, and I hope they will agree, that their excellent suggestions have led to real improvements in both the content and presentation of my argument. Considerable thanks are also due to Margot Light, who encouraged me to submit my thesis to this series and has been wonderfully sympathetic and helpful as I have slowly gone about the nerve-wracking task of turning a Ph.D. that I knew no-one would ever read into a more public statement of my position. Finally, I am no less grateful to the several experts who have taken the time to read parts of the manuscript and have saved me from numerous errors, among whom Peter Borschberg and Nicholas Onuf have my special thanks for their extraordinary intellectual generosity and perception. Of course, it would be asking too much of anyone to spot all the mistakes that I have made, and I take responsibility for the remaining ones that have made their way into print.

Although these intellectual debts are considerable, they pale besides the constant and loving support of my family. Since 1999, I have been in the enviable position of having two families, one in Georgia and one in London, and consider myself doubly blessed. My wife, Molly, has shown me unstinting tenderness and compassion, and her gentle strength has sustained me during the writing of this book. I have always drawn upon my sister Harriet's unconditional love. But most of all it is my parents, Gillian and David, who have given me the rare opportunity to follow my vocation, as well as a perfect foundation from which to pursue it. I am profoundly moved by their generosity of spirit, and it is but a small recompense to dedicate this book to them.

Introduction

This book is about the patterns of political and legal order that have characterized international relations since the seventeenth century. On seeing that opening statement, one might well expect a large part of the book to be devoted to explaining how the modern world came to be organized as a 'Westphalian system', or to the closely related idea that modern states collectively form an 'international society' that preserves their mutual independence and maintains a degree of peaceful coexistence in their relations with one another. It would also be perfectly reasonable to expect my analysis to go on to ask whether or not this society of states can provide for justice in the world today; or how international relations are presently being transformed as a result of the emergence of a quite different kind of 'post-Westphalian' order that is founded on new normative principles and embodied in new international legal rules and institutions.

But these are well-trodden paths and I do not intend to go down them again, other than to say where I think they are misleading. We already have a shelf full of excellent books on the international society of sovereign states, of which one of the best contemporary works, certainly one of the most lucid, is Hedley Bull's hugely influential account of *The Anarchical Society*.[1] I will pay a considerable amount of attention to how Bull's argument was put together, but it would hardly be worthwhile just to repeat what he has already said about order in the modern society of states, even with the addition of a few extra historical, philosophical or sociological flourishes to give his vision of the anarchical society a little more depth. Nor will I look to build upon the extensive literature that has been devoted to identifying what justice means in an international context, or the more recent, but already sizeable, body of scholarship on the idea that a new kind of world order is developing.[2] In my view, this work operates

---

[1] Hedley Bull, *The Anarchical Society: A Study of Order in World Politics* (London: Macmillan, 1977).

[2] On contemporary thinking about justice and international society, see David Mapel and Terry Nardin (eds.), *International Society: Diverse Ethical Perspectives* (Princeton University Press, 1998). It would be premature to identify coherent schools of thought on the idea of

within excessively restricted parameters because it unthinkingly accepts conventional assumptions about the modern pattern of international political and legal order. Far too many 'critical' enquiries into contemporary world politics are conducted by asking questions about what is, or should be, happening to the same old society of states. It hardly needs saying, for instance, that the increasingly popular idea of a post-Westphalian order does not make much sense unless one begins from the proposition that the modern pattern of international order was itself Westphalian. Very few analyses of contemporary world politics have managed to break free from this conventional way of thinking about international relations in the past, and that significantly limits their capacity to think about the present and the future in a genuinely original way.

My intention is to explore these issues by taking a less travelled road, one indeed that has practically disappeared from the map in the last fifty years or so and is now in an alarming state of disrepair. My starting point will be the account of the law of nations that was developed in the early seventeenth century by the Dutch lawyer, Hugo Grotius. In view of my claim that we need to liberate ourselves from conventional wisdoms about modern international relations, that might seem like an odd place to begin, because scholars today usually see Grotius as one of the principal authors of the utterly conventional idea of a society of equal and independent, territorially sovereign states. Grotius, the argument goes, lived precisely at the time when this pattern of international order was emerging: his main work, *De Jure Belli ac Pacis*, was first published in 1625, little more than twenty years before the modern system began to take shape with the signing of the Peace of Westphalia in 1648. Commentators have therefore assumed that what is significant about his work is its anticipation of the problems that result from the decentralized nature of the Westphalian system, and that his prominence in the history of international legal thought derives from his having been one of the first to suggest how the binding force of the law of nations could be preserved in such an anarchic and pluralistic environment. Other themes in his work that do not fit in with the logic of the states-system are usually explained away as hang-overs from medieval theory and practice, which had not

an international transformation, but a few prominent and heavily cited works are David Held, *Democracy and the Global Order: From the Modern State to Cosmopolitan Governance* (Cambridge: Polity Press, 1995); Andrew Linklater, *The Transformation of Political Community* (Cambridge: Polity Press, 1998); Gene Lyons and Michael Mastanduno (eds.), *Beyond Westphalia? State Sovereignty and International Intervention* (Baltimore: Johns Hopkins University Press, 1995); and John Gerard Ruggie, *Constructing the World Polity: Essays in International Institutionalization* (London: Routledge, 1998). A number of different approaches are collected in Eivind Hovden and Edward Keene (eds.), *The Globalization of Liberalism* (London: Palgrave, 2001).

yet been decisively rejected in Grotius's day; or they are interpreted as
well-intentioned but rather idealistic proposals about how the quality of
order in the modern society of states might be improved, if only states
could be persuaded to work together in the common interest of international society as a whole, pay more respect to the rights of individuals,
act collectively to enforce international law and so on.[3]

I think that this point of view overlooks important ways in which the
unorthodox elements of Grotius's account of the law of nations were relevant to modern world politics, albeit with respect to certain features
of modern international order that for the most part developed outside
the European society of states, and are often ignored or dismissed as
'anomalies'.[4] In particular, I want to highlight two key propositions in
Grotius's theory about the rights that public authorities and private individuals possess in the law of nations. The first is that the sovereign prerogatives of public authorities are divisible from one another, such that it
would be possible for sovereignty to be divided between several institutions within a single political community, or, to put it in a more obviously
international context, it would be possible for a state to acquire some of
the sovereign prerogatives that had originally belonged to another and
exercise them on its behalf. The second proposition is that under certain
conditions individuals have a right in the law of nations to appropriate
unoccupied lands; furthermore, if no established political authority acts
to protect their rights, the individuals themselves may conduct a 'private
war' in their defence and would be justified by the law of nations in so
doing. Neither of these claims can safely be dismissed as nostalgia for
medieval Christendom or as an idealistic proposal for the reform of the
existing society of states. On the contrary, they have a striking proximity
to the practices of colonialism and imperialism that Europeans adopted
in the extra-European world. A proper account of the relationship between the Grotian theory of the law of nations and modern world politics
should make an analysis of his ideas of divisible sovereignty and private

[3] An important contemporary statement is Hedley Bull, 'The Grotian Conception of
International Society', in Herbert Butterfield and Martin Wight (eds.), *Diplomatic Investigations: Essays on the Theory of International Politics* (London: George Allen and Unwin,
1966), pp. 51–73. Of course, this interpretation of Grotius is not originally Bull's. On the
contrary, it has been around for well over a hundred years, and can be found in almost
any late eighteenth or nineteenth-century textbook on international law: for an example,
chosen more or less at random, see William Manning, *Commentaries on International Law*
(London: Sweet, 1839), pp. 20–2.
[4] For a number of these 'anomalies', some of which speak directly to extra-European international politics (especially the British Commonwealth and the East India Company),
see Bull, *The Anarchical Society*, pp. 274–5. Again, this observation does not originate
with Bull. His point echoes Lassa Oppenheim, *International Law: A Treatise*, 2nd edition,
2 vols. (London: Longmans, 1912), especially vol. I, pp. 111–15.

appropriation its central themes, and ought to include an examination of the colonial and imperial systems of governance that represented a distinctive pattern of modern international political and legal order based on these principles.[5]

Admittedly, Grotius's ideas about the divisibility of sovereignty and individuals' rights in the law of nations look rather peculiar in comparison with the conventional understanding of modern international legal thought, where sovereignty is supposed to be indivisibly packaged up in territorial bundles, and where individuals are supposed not to have any international personality at all. That might tempt some to assume that Grotius's ideas were almost immediately discarded by later scholars and practitioners of international affairs, and that my interest in them is merely archaic; but that assumption would be quite wrong. Over the last fifty years or so, we have lost sight of these notions as part of modern international legal and political discourse because experts on international relations seldom read the authors who continued to use them or pay attention to the contexts in which they were expressed. Few realize, for instance, that even in the late nineteenth century it was still perfectly reasonable for an extremely prominent and influential British international lawyer to argue that the doctrine that sovereignty is indivisible 'does not belong to international law', and that 'sovereignty has always been regarded as divisible'.[6] And, as for individuals' private rights to property, the mere fact they were seldom explicitly mentioned in modern discussions of public international law does not imply that they were completely absent from the prevailing international legal order. On the contrary, as one international lawyer put it in the early twentieth century, the express stipulation of the principle that individuals' property rights

---

[5] Richard Tuck's recent book on *The Rights of War and Peace: Political Thought and the International Order from Grotius to Kant* (Oxford University Press, 1999) includes an excellent treatment of Grotian thinking about property and its relationship to colonialism, and see also L.C. Green and Olive Dickason, *The Law of Nations and the New World* (Edmonton: University of Alberta Press, 1989). Meanwhile, James Muldoon's equally good *Empire and Order: The Concept of Empire, 800–1800* (London: Macmillan, 2000) contains several important insights into the political theory of divided sovereignty (although not so much in the Grotian context) and its relationship to imperial governance in North America, as does Richard Koebner, *Empire* (New York: Grosset and Dunlap, 1965). To the best of my knowledge, though, no-one has put these themes together to offer a sustained analysis of the general pattern of political and legal order that developed out of the Grotian theory of the law of nations and the practices of European colonialism and imperialism. Nor has anyone yet properly analysed how such an enquiry would impact upon orthodox theories of order in modern and contemporary world politics.

[6] Henry Sumner Maine, *International Law: The Whewell Lectures of 1887*, 2nd edition (London: John Murray, 1915), p. 58, and an 1864 minute for the British government by the same author, in Adrian Sever (ed.), *Documents and Speeches on the Indian Princely States*, 2 vols. (Delhi: B.R. Publishing, 1985), Document 65.

were inviolable was widely seen as 'unnecessary by reason of the universal recognition and adoption' of the principle among all the members of the society of states.[7]

This interpretation of the Grotian theory of the law of nations and its relationship to the practices of colonialism and imperialism leads to what are really the central propositions in my argument: that there has been a long-standing division in the modern world between two different patterns of international political and legal order; and that the world we live in today is a combination of both, and an extremely awkward and unstable combination at that.[8] The main problem with the orthodox account of modern world politics is that it describes only one of these patterns of international order: the one that was dedicated to the pursuit of peaceful coexistence between equal and mutually independent sovereigns, which developed within the Westphalian system and the European society of states. I am happy to concede that the detailed analysis of these arrangements represents a valuable contribution to our understanding of modern international politics and international law, but it is really only telling half of the story. Orthodox theorists have paid far too little attention to the other pattern of international order, which evolved during roughly the same period of time, but beyond rather than within Europe; not through relations between Europeans, but through relations

[7] Alexander Fachiri, 'Expropriation and International Law', *British Year Book of International Law*, 6 (1925), 169, and see also Konstantin Katzarov, *The Theory of Nationalisation* (The Hague: Martinus Nijhoff, 1964), especially pp. 284–7. As an aside, I might add that even Bull described respect for property as an 'elementary, primary and universal goal of social life', and therefore (presumably) he saw this principle as part of the normative structure of modern international order (*The Anarchical Society*, p. 3). For all Bull's attachment to a pluralist conception of international society and positivist theories of international law, the notion of 'elementary, primary and universal' goals looks to me suspiciously like a poorly disguised version of classical arguments from natural law. It is interesting, and not, in my view, coincidental, that this lapse into naturalism should have occurred precisely on the issue of individuals' rights to life and property.

[8] This is a different claim from the popular line of argument that the political and legal order of the states-system should be juxtaposed against the pattern of social relationships characterized by the capitalist world economy. I do not dispute the latter's existence, nor do I deny that it has been an extremely significant feature of the modern world, but the trouble with the bulk of this literature is that it has continued to treat modern international politics and law in terms of the conventional idea of a society of states, asking how global capitalism represented the real sociological basis of that form of political order, or how both sprang from a shared conceptual outlook on the part of modern Europeans: see, for example, Justin Rosenberg, *The Empire of Civil Society: A Critique of the Realist Theory of International Relations* (London: Verso, 1994), and Kurt Burch, *'Property' and the Making of the International System* (Boulder: Lynne Reinner, 1998). My point, by contrast, is that modern international political and legal order was *not* exclusively defined by the norms, rules and institutions of the society of states, irrespective of its relationship to modern forms of socio-economic organization.

between Europeans and non-Europeans.[9] Instead of being based on a states-system, this pattern of order was based on colonial and imperial systems, and its characteristic practice was not the reciprocal recognition of sovereign independence between states, but rather the division of sovereignty across territorial borders and the enforcement of individuals' rights to their persons and property.

Grotius himself can hardly be assigned all the responsibility for the different ways in which international order developed within and beyond Europe after the seventeenth century. He provided an account of the law of nations that was used by Europeans to legitimize their behaviour towards non-European peoples, but Grotius himself did not conceive of the world as divided in two, with one political and legal order for Europeans and another for non-European peoples. He tended to think of international legal order in universal and broadly non-discriminatory terms: his idea of the divisibility of sovereignty, in particular, was directed as much at public authorities within Europe as at ones outside.[10] During the eighteenth and nineteenth centuries, however, Europeans began to be more discriminating in their international relations, adopting one kind of relationship, equality and mutual independence, as the norm in their dealings with each other, and another, imperial paramountcy, as normal in their relations with non-Europeans. Grotius's original scheme of the law of nations underwent a dramatic change in the process, particularly through the introduction of a new idea of civilization, which comprehensively radicalized the application of his ideas about how sovereignty should be divided and how individuals' private rights should be acquired and protected in the extra-European world.

The concept of civilization performed two roles in international legal thought: it defined the border between the two patterns of modern international order, and it described the ultimate purposes that the extra-European order was for. This vision of a bifurcated world was fully

---

[9] Some paid more attention than others. There are a couple of throw-away comments from Bull that vaguely gesture in the right direction, while even more suggestive hints of the pattern of order I am describing can be found Martin Wight's writings, unsurprisingly given his early interest in British colonialism and imperialism. Among the original members of the English school, though, Adam Watson probably went furthest in his analysis of imperial systems as representing the other end of the 'spectrum' of order in world politics to states-systems, although in his study of order in modern world politics he tended to stick fairly closely to the orthodox idea of a society of states. See chapter 1 for a fuller discussion.

[10] One important qualification to this claim is that, as we will see in chapter 2, he did say that the indigenous inhabitants of America lived in a condition of natural simplicity, a claim of great significance for the future development of theories about colonial appropriation. Otherwise, however, Grotius was fairly even-handed in his depiction of non-European peoples and rulers, and, aside from property, he only made a clear distinction between the law of nations in Christendom and the law of nations beyond on a few rather marginal issues, such as postliminium.

developed by the middle of the nineteenth century, and one can see in international legal texts from that period a widely accepted distinction between the family of civilized nations and the backward or uncivilized world beyond (although that is not to say that such distinctions had never been made before then).[11] In the family of civilized nations, the main point of international political and legal order was understood as being to encourage respect for the equality and independent sovereignty of individual states or nations; its ultimate purpose, simply put, was to promote the toleration of cultural and political differences between civilized peoples so as to allow them to live together in peace. Outside the family of civilized nations, however, other forms of international political organization and different legal rules were deemed appropriate, in keeping with the belief that here the central purpose of international order was to promote the civilization of decadent, backward, savage or barbaric peoples.[12] Non-European rulers were very seldom denied sovereignty altogether, but they were usually permitted to retain only those prerogatives which they were deemed competent to exercise, and certain specific prerogatives were nearly always vested with a European (or, in the United States, the federal) government in order to ensure the promotion of commerce, technology and good government, as well as the establishment and protection of individuals' rights, especially to property; civilization, in other words.[13] While, say, a nineteenth-century British diplomat would have found it inconceivable that he might claim a right to exercise any sovereign prerogatives over the French, his counterpart in the colonial service would have thought it perfectly appropriate to take over some of the sovereign prerogatives that an Indian prince possessed, even ones guaranteed by prior treaties, if that was what it took to facilitate progress or to stamp out corruption and barbarism.

By the mid to late nineteenth century, then, the world was clearly divided in two for the purposes of international political and legal order: an order promoting toleration within Europe, and an order promoting civilization beyond. Very quickly, however, the distinction began to break

[11] This distinction was endemic to nineteenth-century international law, but an exemplary statement is James Lorimer, *The Institutes of the Law of Nations: A Treatise of the Jural Relations of Separate Political Communities*, 2 vols. (reprint of the 1883 Edinburgh Edition by Scientia Verlag Aalen, 1980).
[12] These terms and others like them were so important to the intellectual framework of modern international law that I will be using them a lot, and it would clutter up the text if I were to put them in inverted commas all the time. My unqualified use of this language should not be understood as an endorsement of this way of discriminating between European and non-European peoples.
[13] A classic treatise, which captures these various dimensions of the concept, is John Stuart Mill, 'Civilization', in *Collected Works, Volume 18: Essays on Politics and Society* (London: Routledge, 1977), pp. 119–47, especially p. 120. (First published in 1836.)

down, and one of the hallmarks of world politics in the twentieth century
has been a prolonged effort to merge the two patterns of modern international order into a single, all-encompassing world order, despite
the profound differences in their normative principles, legal rules and
institutional arrangements. Most of the scholarship on how this 'universal international society' was created has concentrated on the expansion
of the society of states, which is hardly surprising given that most scholars
concentrate exclusively on the society of states the rest of the time. The
construction of a global international order is therefore usually conceived
solely in terms of the spreading practice of the reciprocal recognition of
sovereignty and the entry of new states into what had previously been a
European club. Occasionally, since attention is now, often for the first
time, focused on the geographical margins of the European society of
states, theorists have glimpsed the importance of the concept of civilization as a standard that had to be attained before recognition would be
granted.[14] But because they still insist on thinking about modern international order in terms of the society of states, this insight has not been
developed into a detailed analysis of where the concept came from; or
of how it had been structuring relations between European and non-
European peoples for at least fifty years before the latter's entry into
international society really became an issue; or of the particular legal
and institutional arrangements, such as divided sovereignty in systems of
imperial paramountcy, that had been developed in the extra-European
world to promote civilization.

Furthermore, because they do not realize that a distinct pattern of
international order already existed in the extra-European world before
the expansion of the society of states, orthodox theorists cannot grasp
the crucial fact that the construction of a global political and legal order was a two-way process. Of course, the extension of recognition to
non-European peoples was very important, but it was not the only factor
at work. At the same time, the principle of civilization that had previously structured international relations beyond Europe began to creep
into the European political system itself. While the toleration of political and cultural difference was becoming a more important aspect
of relations between European and non-European peoples, the promotion of civilized values was becoming a more important feature of relations between European states. A defining moment in this latter process

---

[14] This is often where ideas about 'Western values' and the 'culture of modernity' creep into
the picture, but the most detailed analysis is Gerrit Gong, *The Standard of Civilization in
International Society* (Oxford: Clarendon Press, 1984); one of the first statements of the
orthodox position here is Oppenheim, *International Law*, pp. 32–3.

was the first world war. Many wars had previously been fought for the purpose of civilizing the indigenous peoples of America, Asia and Africa, but the 'Great War for Civilization' was principally fought against other Europeans. During the first half of the twentieth century, Europeans gradually became accustomed to the idea that they should be more respectful of the very different political and cultural systems of non-European peoples, while becoming increasingly open to the possibility that their fellow Europeans could be guilty of barbarism and might need to be civilized themselves. The struggle against Nazism was the high point of this development, since now not only were other Europeans seen as the single greatest threat to civilization, but also civilization was being defended against a version of the racist ideology that had previously given it much of its legitimacy as a way of demarcating the boundary between the two modern patterns of international order.

By 1945, the capacity of European states to maintain their imperial and colonial systems had evaporated, and the intellectual framework within which diplomats and international lawyers operated had undergone a transformative change; these developments resulted in a number of crucial legal and institutional developments that took place over the next fifteen to twenty years. The practice of recognizing non-European peoples as equal and independent members of the society of states became much more open and inclusive, as the old standard of civilization, in the sense of a certain level of economic, political and judicial advancement, was largely abandoned in favour of a broader idea that every nation has a right to self-determination.[15] The toleration of different ways of life has thus become an absolutely central principle in the new global political and legal order. But the old idea that one of the purposes of order in world politics is to promote civilization has by no means been abandoned. As well as encouraging respect for the equality and independence of all sovereign states, the United Nations is also supposed to facilitate economic and social progress, and it is intended to protect the fundamental human rights of individuals, as Article 55 of the Charter makes clear. In contemporary phenomena such as international agencies for economic development, international humanitarian law, the articulation of a code of peremptory and non-derogable principles of *jus cogens*, pressure to democratize domestic political systems and the increasing centralization of decision-making processes through supranational organizations, the lingering influence of eighteenth and nineteenth-century thinking about how the world should be organized so as to promote civilization can still be seen at work in

[15] For example, John Dugard, *Recognition and the United Nations* (Cambridge: Grotius Publications, 1987), especially p. 78.

international relations today. We thus live in a world which is supposed to have a single, global political and legal order for everyone, but one that is dedicated to two very different, indeed often contradictory, purposes.

Therein lie the horns of the principal dilemma that we are struggling with at the moment. It is incorrect to describe our problem in terms of the difficulty that the society of states has in providing for justice in world politics, or that we are witnessing a painful and confusing process of transformation as a new kind of 'post-Westphalian' order gradually emerges to supplant the old Westphalian one. Our central problem is that we still think in the same dualistic way as nineteenth-century international lawyers and diplomats about the purposes of order in world politics, but we have abandoned the discriminatory method that they used to resolve the resulting contradictions. The central question for international political and legal theorists today, then, is whether it is possible to sustain both of those purposes and still have a coherent pattern of international order, without recourse to the old method of discriminating between advanced and backward peoples. We are stuck, in other words, with the fundamental modern problem of having to choose between toleration and civilization as purposes of international order, but we now have to work out a completely different way of deciding how that choice ought to be made. Can we maintain the modern dualism about the goals of international order through the adoption of a new 'post-modern' way of reconciling them? Or do we have to abandon at least one (and possibly both) of the long-standing modern beliefs about what international order is for if we are to have a consistent and non-contradictory order in world politics today, albeit one that will probably be unsatisfactory to many of the people who live in it? Before anyone wades through the details of my argument, I ought to admit that I do not have any clear answers to these questions, but I think that the orthodox way of thinking about order in modern world politics in terms of the Westphalian system and the society of states is so misleading that it obscures their real nature. A necessary first step to working out the right answer is to pose the right question, and I hope that my analysis will at least make a small step towards that goal.

As a jumping-off point for my argument, in chapter 1 I will begin by asking why so many scholars today think of order in modern world politics in terms of the existence of an international society of mutually independent sovereign states. Although this point of view has enjoyed great popularity for around two hundred years, I will concentrate on a group of theorists who have been extremely influential in presenting the idea of the society of states to contemporary audiences. These scholars are often known as the 'English school', and their main focus was the British Committee for the Theory of International Politics (which was originally formed in the late 1950s).[16] I will explain how the English school came to be so attached to the idea that order in modern world politics should be understood by analysing the norms, rules and institutions of the society of states, and how they came to associate this position with a 'Grotian tradition' of international theory. Having explained the limitations of the English school's account of modern international order and Grotianism, I will then go on to outline how the Grotian theory of the law of nations should be understood; how it was relevant to the practices of colonialism and imperialism; how those practices led to the creation of a distinct extra-European pattern of international order, founded on the principle of civilization; and how this order mingled with that embodied by the society of states to produce the internally contradictory global order that we live in today.

---

[16] For an overview of the English school's work, including a discussion of the importance of the British Committee, see Timothy Dunne, *Inventing International Society: A History of the English School* (London: Macmillan, 1998). The shortcoming of Dunne's otherwise excellent treatment, in my view, is that he does not place the English school into its deeper historical context: his contextualization of the school's work does not really go much further back than E.H. Carr; whereas I think that the main influences on the school's view of order in modern world politics have to be located much earlier, in the early nineteenth-century reaction to the French Revolution.

1   The orthodox theory of order in world politics

Nowadays, order in modern world politics is usually described in terms of the norms, rules and institutions of the European society of states. The distinguishing characteristic of this international society is that it acknowledges the existence of different political systems and cultures in the world, and attempts to facilitate their peaceful coexistence with one another by promoting toleration. It tries to achieve this goal through the normative principle of the reciprocal recognition of sovereignty: each state is supposed to recognize the independent sovereignty of the others within their territorially defined spheres of domestic jurisdiction. Thus no state is allowed to interfere in the internal affairs of another, and each has the space to develop its own way of life as it chooses. Numerous implications for the structure of international order follow from this starting point. Because each state is an independent sovereign, there is by definition no central authority that can lay down and enforce international law, maintain peace and security, or compel the members of international society to act in ways that are contrary to their national interests. The institutions of the society of states therefore have to be able to cope with extreme decentralization, even anarchy. For example, the integrity of the system and the independence of its individual members are primarily maintained by the highly flexible and voluntaristic institution of the balance of power, albeit sometimes with the addition of a special managing role for the great powers. Another important example is the distinctive character of modern international law: in line with positivist doctrines, and in contrast with theories of natural law, the only foundation for legally binding rules in international society is the volition of states, and the scope of international law is therefore restricted to rules to which states have given their consent.

At the risk of stating the obvious, the theory that order in modern world politics is built upon a society of states like this rests on two propositions: that the modern international system is composed of states, in other words that it is a 'states-system'; and that in their relations with one another, states do indeed constitute something that can reasonably be described as a 'society'.[1] Both of these propositions have a long history in political and legal thought. The idea of a states-system originated about 200 years ago. In its current form, as a description of a system of mutually independent states who recognize each other's territorial sovereignty, it was developed by late eighteenth and early nineteenth-century conservative historians who wanted to present a picture of European public order that would legitimize their efforts to contain the French Revolution and undermine the Napoleonic imperial system; they worked out the notion of a states-system (*Staatensystem*) to achieve that end. The proposition that international relations can be described as a society is even older. This idea was first developed in the sixteenth and seventeenth centuries, by legal scholars who tried to describe the binding force of the law of nations (*ius gentium*) in terms of a society of nations (*societas gentium*). As one would expect, their understanding of society was heavily coloured by their jurisprudential interests: the crucial evidence for the existence of a society, on this view, is the existence of an authoritative legal order, and international society is synonymous with an order of binding norms and rules that applies to all rulers and peoples.

The theory of the modern society of states that scholars use today is a combination of these two strands of thought: the political-historical concept of a states-system and the legal concept of a *societas gentium*. But it is important to notice that current scholarship typically *begins* with the idea of a states-system, and only then adds the proposition that an international society exists, suggesting that having established a systematic pattern of relations with one another, states then go on to constitute a society by making a collective commitment to observe certain shared norms, obey general rules and participate in common institutions.[2] Ironically, that is a reversal of the chronological order in which the concepts actually emerged in political and legal thought, where the idea of a *societas gentium* preceded the idea of a states-system by over one hundred years. It should immediately be obvious that this transposition might lead to problems. In the first place, the contemporary theory of order in modern world politics relies on an account of the historical development of European public order that is highly polemical, having been designed by reactionaries to suit their needs in the struggle against Revolutionary France and the Napoleonic Empire. Secondly, it offers an interpretation of sixteenth and seventeenth-century legal thought about international society that is largely carried out in terms of a pattern of order and a set of normative principles that were, for the most part, quite unknown to

---

[1] One of the clearest examples of this argument is Hedley Bull, *The Anarchical Society: A Study of Order in World Politics* (London: Macmillan, 1977), ch. 1.
[2] *Ibid.*, p. 13.

the theorists concerned; it refracts earlier theories through the prism of later ones. The current conventional wisdom about the society of states is therefore suspect both in its description of the pattern of order in the modern international system and in its treatment of the concerns of earlier legal theories of international society.

Unfortunately, most people take the orthodox theory of order in modern world politics at face value. Few have investigated the sources for its concept of the states-system to ask what might have been left out by the counter-revolutionaries who invented the idea; nor have many scholars questioned the accuracy of the prevailing interpretation of the older legal concept of international society. I will explore both of these issues here, with the intention of demonstrating the limitations of the orthodox theory. Like the conventional approach, I will begin with the concept of a states-system, explaining exactly where this idea came from, and what was left out of it, deliberately or otherwise; I will also look at how the concept has been developed in contemporary theories of the society of states, where despite considerable additions the most serious original flaws of the concept have not been corrected. Then I will look at orthodox accounts of the concept of international society, charting the confusions and distortions that have been created by the effort to fit sixteenth and early seventeenth-century legal theories into the context of eighteenth and nineteenth-century political debates. As I indicated in the introduction, throughout this chapter my focus will be on the 'English school' (or the British committee on the theory of international politics), and especially Hedley Bull, whose theory of the 'anarchical society' of states has been hugely influential in contemporary international relations theory, and which I consider to be a reasonable proxy for the entire contemporary literature on modern international society. Nevertheless, it is worth repeating that the English school should in no way be thought of as having originally developed this way of thinking about order in modern world politics: the orthodox theory that I am describing here has been a part of mainstream scholarship for over a hundred and fifty years, as the influence of the new counter-revolutionary history of the states-system began to make itself felt among both political and legal theorists.

The origins of the idea of a states-system

When the members of the English school began to construct a theory of international relations, they agreed that their work ought to include an historical analysis of the distinctive characteristics of modern world politics. To bring that element into their research programme, they decided to focus on the comparative history of states-systems. In many ways, that was the obvious choice. One of the British committee's leading members, Herbert Butterfield, had great respect for the original authors of the concept of a states-system – the 'Göttingen' or 'German historical school' – whom he saw, with good reason, as the founders of modern historiography.[3] Their thesis that the distinction between the medieval and modern worlds can be understood in terms of the development of a decentralized system of mutually independent sovereign states, a *Staatensystem*, has exercised a pervasive influence on historical, sociological and political theoretical scholarship over the last 200 years, and continues to do so today; the English school are hardly alone in having fallen under its spell.[4] And, in any case, the members of the English school firmly believed that by studying the European states-system they could uncover phenomena of general and lasting significance for contemporary world politics, if only because, as Bull observed, Europe's long period of global dominance had attached a unique importance to that particular way of organizing international affairs.[5]

Nevertheless, we should not lose sight of the fact that the decision to focus on states-systems had serious implications for the orientation and unfolding of the English school's research programme. In adopting this idea as their organizing concept, the British committee were aware that they were committing themselves to a particular theory of modern history that had been developed in the late eighteenth and early nineteenth centuries by scholars who were 'apologists or protagonists' for the European states-system at a time when it was facing a mortal threat from the French

---

[3] Herbert Butterfield, *Man on his Past* (Cambridge University Press, 1955). See also Butterfield, *The Origins of History* (London: Eyre Methuen, 1981). The most famous member of the German historical school, and the most influential in terms of the development of modern historical method, was Leopold von Ranke, but on the idea of a states-system the key thinker was A.H.L. Heeren. So far as the English school's historical research programme was concerned, the *Ur*-text, so to speak, was Heeren, *Manual of the History of the Political System of Europe and its Colonies, from its Formation at the Close of the Fifteenth Century to its Re-Establishment upon the Fall of Napoleon*, translated from the 5th German edn, 2 vols. (Oxford: D.A. Talboys, 1834) (the 1st edn was published in 1809). See Bull, *The Anarchical Society*, p. 12; Martin Wight, *Systems of States* (Leicester University Press, 1977), pp. 20–1; Adam Watson, 'Hedley Bull, States Systems and International Societies', *Review of International Studies*, 13 (1987), 147–53; and Watson, 'Systems of States', *Review of International Studies*, 16 (1990), 99–109.

[4] For an interesting historical attack on this widespread assumption, albeit one that follows a rather different tack from my own, see Nicholas Henshall, *The Myth of Absolutism: Change and Continuity in Early Modern European Monarchy* (London: Longman, 1992).

[5] Hedley Bull, 'The Emergence of a Universal International Society', in Bull and Adam Watson (eds.), *The Expansion of International Society* (Oxford: Clarendon Press, 1984), p.124; on its relevance to contemporary world politics, see also Watson, *The Evolution of International Society* (London: Routledge, 1992), p. 196. I ought to add that I strongly disagree with Bull on that point, as will become clear in due course.

Revolution.[6] The idea of a states-system was originally developed as part of the attempt to justify certain normative principles as the authentic basis for order in modern world politics; for all the merits of the concept as a way of highlighting genuinely important dimensions of modern and contemporary international relations, its initial purpose was to stigmatize the French Revolution, and especially the Napoleonic imperial system, as unlawful in terms of the 'traditional' principles of European public law and order. Like all good propaganda, the historical concept of the states-system contained a substantial kernel of truth, but presented in a distorted way. It exaggerated the significance of some aspects of modern world politics, while down-playing or even ignoring others that were not so helpful to the counter-revolutionary cause. Such distortions may well be inherent in any historical narrative, and the reactionaries were no less scrupulous than their opponents, but I submit that it is unacceptable to take their history for granted as an objective description of order in modern world politics.

Although several scholars have complained about the problems that flow from conceptualizing modern world history in terms of the idea of a states-system,[7] the reasons *why* the orthodox perspective is a distorted one are not fully appreciated at present because far too little attention has been paid to the sources that the counter-revolutionaries used to construct their account of the modern states-system. It is therefore impossible to understand what they were including and, just as importantly, what they were leaving out. The trouble here is that most scholarship on pre-revolutionary thought has concentrated overwhelmingly on speculation about natural law and the law of nations as the root of modern thinking about the European political system, usually tracing a path from Hugo Grotius, through Samuel Pufendorf, to Emerich de Vattel. Certainly, Pufendorf was one of the first to use the idea of a states-system, although he meant something completely different by that term from the way it is now understood. It must also be acknowledged that Vattel's description of the European political system looks remarkably like the orthodox conception of international society in use today:

The constant attention of sovereigns to all that goes on, the custom of resident ministers, the continual negotiations that take place, make of modern Europe a sort of Republic, whose members – each independent, but all bound together by a common interest – unite for the maintenance of order and the preservation of

---

[6] Bull, *The Anarchical Society*, p. 12.
[7] For a recent discussion of this point, and in my view a very perceptive one, see the introduction to James Muldoon, *Empire and Order: The Concept of Empire, 800–1800* (London: Macmillan, 2000).

liberty. This is what has given rise to the well-known principle of the balance of power.[8]

That does sound familiar, but for all the apparent similarities, Vattel was *not* the main source for the idea of the states-system that the English school put at the centre of their historical research programme. To suppose that he was is to overlook a crucial element of his conception of the European political system and its legal foundation. The early modern legal theorists mentioned above were primarily trying to discern, through rational speculation, principles of natural law that could be used as a general normative framework for the family of nations. By the middle of the eighteenth century, as illustrated *par excellence* by Vattel, this approach was increasingly linked to the belief that revolutions were justifiable if a ruler had violated the fundamental principles of natural law, and that interventions in support of revolutions in other states might be justified on the same grounds.[9] Of course, that was precisely the conclusion that the counter-revolutionaries wanted to avoid, and in consequence they were wary of adopting the natural lawyers' conception of the European political system. They occasionally acknowledged Grotius's reputation, but did not use his or any other earlier theories of natural law to any great extent.[10]

Nevertheless, with the French revolutionary armies in the ascendant and with the prospect of Napoleonic hegemony looming, the reactionaries were more desperate than ever for an account of European public law that would justify the principle that the liberty of individual states should be respected; their problem was that they needed an argument that would support this point without jeopardizing monarchical dynasticism. The solution lay in a quite distinct, and now somewhat neglected, literature on the law of nations that had also been developing since the mid-seventeenth century. In contrast with the more abstract, rationalist approach of the natural lawyers and the *philosophes*, this literature was based on the empirical analysis of treaties: a typical work would present a collection of the texts of some important agreements, with a commentary on the negotiation process that had led to them and an analysis of the implications of their provisions for the rights and duties of individual rulers.[11] With

[8] Emerich de Vattel, *The Law of Nations or the Principles of Natural Law Applied to the Conduct and to the Affairs of Sovereigns*, trans. C.G. Fenwick (Washington: Carnegie Institution, 1916), p. 251.

[9] *Ibid.*, p. 340. As I will explain in more detail in chapter 2, Grotius had developed a completely different way of justifying resistance, and arguably a rather more opaque one, based on the divisibility of the sovereign power rather than appeal to natural law.

[10] See, for example, Heeren, *History of the Political System of Europe*, vol. I, p. 173.

[11] For example, Frederic Leonard, *Recueil des Traitez de Paix . . . depuis pres de Troi Siecles*, 6 vols. (Paris, 1693); 'S.W.', *A General Collection of Treatys . . . from 1648 to the Present*, 4 vols. (London, 1710–32); Jean-Yves de Saint-Prest, *Histoire des Traités de Paix . . . depuis*

only a few exceptions, the treaties in question had been made by dynastic rulers, and usually involved the transfer of specific prerogatives from one family to another. They thus served the counter-revolutionary purpose well in so far as they trapped France, like other states, in a restraining web of treaty obligations, while reinforcing the claim that European public order as a whole rested on the principle of respect for the lawful rights of dynastic rulers codified in the treaties.[12] This led easily enough to the conclusion that the European system had traditionally been a 'system of predominant monarchies', which, the reactionaries added, had performed a valuable function by limiting the potential for disorder and conflict by 'preventing the people from taking a more active part in public affairs'.[13] The republicanism of the French revolutionaries, their interventions on behalf of revolutions elsewhere and their 'sophistical' notion of popular sovereignty, could be labelled not merely as subversive and unlawful, but as destructive of the sensible 'cabinet policy' that had been an indispensable element of order in the European system over the preceding century and a half.[14]

Although it reinforced the rights of dynastic monarchs, the mere analysis of treaties was not quite enough, however. Unfortunately for the counter-revolutionaries, the historical literature on prior agreements between European rulers did not fully endorse the idea that the basic principle of the European legal order was the preservation of the mutual independence of the members of the states-system. On the contrary, the close reading of treaties often pointed towards patterns of overlapping rights and privileges, more a system of mutual dependency than the reverse. An excellent example was the constitution of the Holy Roman Empire as codified by the Peace of Westphalia, a subject particularly dear to the heart of the historians at the University of Göttingen (arguably,

---

la Paix de Vervins, 2 vols. (Amsterdam, 1725); Jean Dumont, Corps Universel Diplomatique du Droit des Gens . . . depuis le Regne de l'Empereur Charlemagne, 6 vols. (Amsterdam, 1726); and G.F. de Martens, Summary of the Law of Nations, Founded on the Treaties and Customs of the Modern Nations of Europe, trans. William Cobbett (Philadelphia, 1795). Martens, incidentally, was a professor at the University of Göttingen, which perhaps provides an institutional connection explaining the importance of this line of argument to the counter-revolutionaries, and especially Heeren. For some biographical details, see Arthur Nussbaum, A Concise History of the Law of Nations (New York: Macmillan, 1947), pp. 163–77.

12 For an interesting early version of this line of argument, which almost anticipates the later fusion of treaty obligations with the balance of power made by the counter-revolutionaries, see Jean Dumont, Les Soupirs de l'Europe, Or the Groans of Europe at the Prospect of the Present Posture of Affairs, anonymous translator (1713), especially pp. 32, 75 and 84ff. Dumont was one of the most highly respected international legal historians of the eighteenth century.

13 Heeren, History of the Political System of Europe, vol. I, p. 9.

14 Ibid., vol. I, p. 10 and vol. II, p. 162.

the leading centre of counter-revolutionary historical scholarship). At the core of the imperial constitution was the idea of 'territorial sovereignty' (*Landeshoheit*), which defined the specific bundles of prerogatives – often known as the 'German liberties' – that were held by the imperial electors, princes and so on, in contrast to the 'reserved rights' held by the emperor himself. Of course, this was not 'territorial sovereignty' as we would understand it today, and it certainly did not equate to outright independence. One of the pre-revolutionary Göttingen experts on the subject, Johann Stephan Pütter, maintained that the Westphalian settlement had not simply worked against imperial despotism, but also served to prevent the estates from abusing their limited rights of territorial sovereignty by claiming to be completely independent entities. In this respect, he likened the imperial constitution to arrangements in other carefully balanced 'compound' bodies with mixed constitutional systems, such as the United Provinces of the Netherlands and the United States of America.[15] That posed a serious problem for the later counter-revolutionary scholars: if the French could establish their own set of 'reserved rights' through treaties, the new imperial system (or 'federal' system, as the French preferred to call it) might even be legitimized as the successor to the old one.[16] Ostensibly, the counter-revolutionaries wanted to present themselves as the defenders of the traditional liberties of the German and other states, but they were hardly going to commit themselves to that role if it merely meant replacing the Habsburg dynasty with a Napoleonic one at the head of a revitalized European empire.

Not unlike Vattel's fusion of the theory of natural law with the practice of the balance of power, the solution was to build a bridge between

[15] Johann Stephan Pütter, *An Historical Development of the Present Political Constitution of the Germanic Empire*, trans. Josiah Dornford, 3 vols. (London, 1790), vol. II, pp. 168ff.

[16] Although not articulated in quite these terms, something like this argument was made by the French themselves, who argued that they were actually *restoring* the traditional European pattern of law and order after its destruction by the expansiveness of Russia and Prussia, and by the rival commercial and maritime system established by Great Britain: Alexandre Maurice Blanc de Lanautte, Comte d'Hauterive, *De l'Etat de la France à la Fin de l'An VIII* (Paris: Henrics, 1800). The power of Hauterive's thesis is evident from the fact that one of the first counter-revolutionary responses was to deny that the Peace of Westphalia had created a general European system at all: Friedrich von Gentz, *On the State of Europe before and after the French Revolution; Being an Answer to the Work Entitled De l'État de la France à la Fin de l'An VIII*, trans. John Charles Herries, 2nd edn (London: Hatchard, 1803). This argument ran perilously close to ruling out the idea of a traditional legal order that the Revolution was subverting, and in later counter-revolutionary works the central position of the Westphalian settlement as the foundation of the European balance of power was largely restored. For an interesting discussion of some of the international legal issues raised by the Napoleonic system, and an illustration of how quickly the counter-revolutionary position found its way into mainstream textbooks on international law, see William Manning, *Commentaries on the Law of Nations* (London: Sweet, 1839), ch. 10.

the empirical studies on European treaties and the numerous pre-revolutionary books on the strategic nature of the European system, which had long argued that it was in the common interest of all rulers to operate a balance of power that would guarantee their mutual independence.[17] A vital early text in the counter-revolutionary arsenal by C.W. Koch[18] (subsequently revised by his colleague F. Schoell) made precisely this move, producing an account of the modern European political system that captures the core elements of current thinking about international society in a way that has undergone remarkably little change in the 200 years since the book first appeared. From a starting point rooted in the empirical-historical analysis of European treaties, Koch developed a much more wide-ranging analysis of the underlying principles of the balance of power and mutual independence in the European system as a whole than was usually the case in earlier historical works, which had tended to focus on the details of individual treaties. His central point was that:

> The object of this system is to maintain public order, to protect the weak against the strong, to put obstacles in the way of the ambitious projects of conquerors, and to prevent dissensions that might lead to the calamities of war. Uniting the different sovereigns of Europe in a common interest, it commits them to sacrificing their individual desires to the general good, and creates, so to speak, one family.[19]

Unlike Vattel's thesis, however, Koch's account of this system rested not upon natural law but upon the normative and legal order furnished by treaties. The system's foundation, he argued, was the Peace of Westphalia, which had established the basic conventions of modern international affairs and had been 'constantly refreshed by all the subsequent treaties up to the French Revolution': the Peace was thus 'the turning-point of

---

[17] The early works on the balance of power had typically been nervous about the threat from Spain: the leading example is Henri, Duc de Rohan, *A Treatise of the Interests of the Princes and States of Christendom*, trans. 'H.H.' (Paris: Thomas Brown, 1640). By the late seventeenth century, Spain had been replaced by France as the likely candidate for world monarchy: see François Paul de Lisola, *The Buckler of State and Justice* (London: James Fisher, 1667); Slingsby Bethel, *The Interest of Princes and States* (London: John Wickins, 1680); and John Campbell, *The Present State of Europe, Explaining the Interests, Connections, Political and Commercial Views of its Several Powers*, 3rd edn (London: Longman, 1752).

[18] Koch's attitude to the Revolution was more complex than some of the other counter-revolutionaries. He was a deputy *extraordinaire* to the French National Assembly (seeking recognition for the rights of Protestants in Alsace, for which the Peace of Westphalia may well have been an important touchstone), was imprisoned during the terror, and briefly served in the Tribunate before its suppression by Napoleon, when he retired from public life to return to academia in Strasbourg.

[19] C.W. Koch and Frederic Schoell, *Histoire Abrégé des Traités de Paix, entre les Puissances de l'Europe, depuis la Paix de Westphalie*, revised edition (Paris: Gide, 1817), p. 3; this and the following citations are my translation (1st edn published *c.* 1797).

modern politics'.[20] Its unique significance was asserted on the grounds that the Westphalian treaties had confirmed the German states 'for ever in the exercise of their territorial supremacy [*supériorité territoriale*] and in the other rights, prerogatives and privileges that they had hitherto enjoyed'; it had thus set them up as 'a barrier against the other powers', and hence as the foundation of the balance of power in Europe as a whole.[21] At a stroke, Koch had provided exactly what the counter-revolutionaries needed: an account of the traditional pattern of public order in the European political system that highlighted the importance of the balance of power between mutually independent sovereigns, but derived the legitimacy of that system from agreements between dynastic rulers rather than abstract principles of natural law.

Koch's description of the development of the European political system from its Westphalian origins was one of the principal sources for the book that eventually became the starting point for the English school's own historical research programme: A.H.L. Heeren's *Manual of the History of the Political System of Europe* (originally written in German).[22] Apart from his observations about the importance of monarchical government to maintaining political order in general, to which I have already alluded, Heeren's main claim was that the 'essential property' of the European states-system was its 'internal freedom; that is, the stability and mutual independence of its members'.[23] Like Koch, he saw a considerable role for Westphalia in this respect: while he admitted that the Peace had not dealt with all the important political relations on the European continent, it was 'by settling the leading political maxims that the Peace of Westphalia became the foundation of the subsequent policy of Europe'.[24] Crucially, the Peace had attached a new importance to the imperial constitution

---

[20] *Ibid.*, p. 6, my translation. The same affirmation about the significance of the Westphalian treaties was also made in C.W. Koch, *Table des Traités entre la France et les Puissances Étrangères, depuis la Paix de Westphalie jusqu'a nos Jours*, 2 vols. (Basle: Decker, 1802), p. 5, and Koch, *History of the Revolutions in Europe*, including additions by Schoell, trans. Andrew Chrichton, 3 vols., *Constable's Miscellany*, 33–5 (Edinburgh: Constable, 1828), pp. 63ff. Few other treaty historians had attached so much significance to the Peace; most, indeed, tended to go back to much earlier treaties as their starting point, and regarded Westphalia as part of a continuum, although it was acknowledged as special because of the widespread participation of so many different rulers.

[21] Koch and Schoell, *Histoire Abrégé*, pp. 6 and 182.

[22] Heeren quite rightly described Koch's *Histoire Abrégé* as 'very important, and indeed, indispensable' to his own work: Heeren, *History of the Political System of Europe*, vol. II, p. 262. It was the only source to which he referred for his account of the crucial period from the death of Frederick the Great in 1766 to the French Revolution. For the English school's discussions of the importance of Heeren, see note 3 above. If any one person invented the orthodox history of modern Europe in terms of the evolution of the states-system, Koch has as good a claim as any; one might almost call the English school's theory of international society a Koch and Bull story.

[23] Heeren, *History of the Political System of Europe*, vol. I, p. 6.

[24] *Ibid.*, vol. II, p. 162.

as the linch-pin of European order, 'indissolubly connected with the maintenance of the balance of power', and this had been achieved by ensuring that '[t]he imperial power was now constitutionally restricted within the narrowest limits; the princes were in the fullest sense rulers of their respective states'.[25] Pütter's earlier point about the proximity between the empire and mixed republican systems like the United Provinces or the United States was grudgingly acknowledged in the admission that the empire was 'a federation under a limited sovereign', but really Heeren saw the imperial constitution in a quite different light, as an example for all of Europe of how a states-system should be organized on the basis of mutual independence and respect for those rights of territorial sovereignty which rendered the princes effectively independent rulers.[26]

The states-system in the English school's research programme

The English school derived its core historical proposition about the normative structure of modern international society from Heeren: that it rests on a system of states, the character of which is defined by the principle of internal freedom, established by agreements between states that reflect their common interest in mutual independence. 'It is this feature', Heeren had argued, 'which distinguishes such a system from one of an opposite class, that is, where an acknowledged preponderance of one of its members exists.'[27] Or, as Adam Watson put it, reflecting on the British committee's choice of an historical research programme: 'The European system since Westphalia – that is, during most of its existence – has theoretically been a society of independent states who all recognize each other as such. The committee accepted the theory.'[28]

---

[25] *Ibid.*, vol. II, p. 160–1.

[26] *Ibid.*, vol. II, p. 161. Heeren was contemptuously dismissive about the Dutch Republic, describing it as an 'imperfectly formed' polity that would lead to no republican enthusiasm in the rest of Europe (*ibid.*, vol. II, p. 114). As for the Americans, he remarked (in, I imagine, something of a sneering tone) that 'the state of society in these colonies' inevitably led to a 'considerable leaven of republicanism' (*ibid.*, vol. I, p. 182). On the other hand, he thought that the German Empire was a wonderful arrangement that showed how small states could coexist with large ones (*ibid.*, vol. I, p. 12). Gradually, partly thanks to Heeren's influence, international lawyers began to move from the rather restricted imperial concept of territorial sovereignty contained in the idea of *Landeshoheit*, to a more broadly applicable notion of *Staatshoheit*: see Jean Louis Klüber, *Droit des Gens Moderne de L'Europe*, 2 vols. (Stuttgart: Cotta, 1819), p. 40, and, for his reference to Heeren, see pp. 27–8n.

[27] Heeren, *History of the Political System of Europe*, vol. I, p. viii.

[28] Watson, 'Systems of States', 103. Note the slip here in labelling this theory in terms of the concept of *society*. As I have shown, the idea of the states-system and the idea of a *societas gentium* really originated from completely distinct literatures.

Of course, the English school realized that they could not simply re-peat Heeren's point of view and leave it at that. Quite a bit had happened in the 150 years since Heeren produced his argument, to put it mildly, and they dedicated the bulk of their efforts to trying to bring his concep-tion of the modern states-system 'down to the present'.[29] In up-dating Heeren, the English school added two new strands to the original his-torical narrative of the states-system. First, as I mentioned earlier, they adopted Wight's suggestion that they should focus on the *comparative* study of states-systems in different periods and places. Wight's view of the importance of comparison undoubtedly reflected the influence upon him of Arnold Toynbee, whose efforts had been directed at a massive comparative study of the different civilizations of the world. In effect, the English school substituted Heeren's conception of the states-system for Toynbee's idea of civilizational systems; as they saw it, this gave their work more of a specifically international flavour.[30] They produced a host of studies of different states-systems – such as the Greek city-state system or the Chinese system of 'warring states' – and, again for purposes of com-parison, a series of contrasting studies of fundamentally different ways of organizing international relations – such as the Islamic system. Many of these discussions were eventually pulled together in Watson's work on *The Evolution of International Society*, which envisioned a 'spectrum' of different forms of international political systems, ranging from rela-tively centralized and hierarchical imperial systems to the more anarchi-cal states-systems based on the mutual independence of their members.[31] This conceptual scheme, somewhat richer than Heeren's, allowed Watson to chart the 'swings of the pendulum' in world politics between the impe-rial and the mutual independency ends of the spectrum of international political organization. In his view of modern world politics, however, Watson tended to stick quite closely to Heeren's original thesis, arguing that, despite occasional movements towards imperialist centralization and hegemony, the modern states-system has on the whole remained firmly in line with the principle of mutual independence.

The second new theme that the English school introduced was a study of the changes that had taken place to the European system in the years since its 're-establishment' after the fall of Napoleon. Within Europe it-self, the most important change involved the abandonment of Heeren's cherished beliefs that legitimacy in the system rested on the 'sacred-ness' of the principle of dynastic succession. Instead, and as one of the

---

[29] Watson, 'Hedley Bull, States Systems and International Societies', 150.
[30] Arnold Toynbee, *A Study of History*, 11 vols. (Oxford University Press, 1954).
[31] Watson, *The Evolution of International Society*, and see also the numerous unpublished papers on these topics in the *British Committee Papers* at the RIIA Library.

lingering after-effects of the French Revolution, the nineteenth century witnessed the establishment of a new principle of legitimacy: national self-determination.[32] The old society of absolutist monarchical states gave way to a new society of nation-states. Although this provoked serious disagreements about how the territorial boundaries around the different national units should be drawn, ultimately leading to another great crisis of the states-system in the twentieth century over the 'German question', the basic principle that the independence of states should be respected was not fundamentally challenged by this development. The English school also paid a great deal of attention to another change in the scope of the states-system: its expansion to the world beyond Europe, with the recognition of non-European peoples as sovereign states during the late nineteenth and twentieth centuries. Again, this posed profound questions for the pattern of order that the states-system embodied, especially by suggesting that in practice its internal harmony may to a certain degree have depended on cultural values and understandings that were so deeply shared by its original European members that there had never been much need to make them explicit parts of the states-system's formal legal and institutional structure. The English school confronted this issue by examining how a standard of civilization was established as a criterion for the acceptance of new members to the society of states, requiring them to undergo certain changes to their domestic political and legal systems before they would be granted recognition as equal and independent sovereign states.[33]

The imposition of the standard of civilization did not solve all the problems involved in the expansion of international society to embrace a much more multicultural membership. As Bull argued, once non-European states had been incorporated into the society of states, they began to question various other aspects of its internal organization, leading to what he called a 'revolt against the West', particularly as non-European states began to insist upon more comprehensive rules governing racial discrimination, uniting the international society against the apartheid regime in South Africa. More controversially, they also developed a radical conception of a 'New International Economic Order' that actively promoted greater equality in the global distribution of wealth. Bull pointed out that the non-European states were not always subversive, however; even the 'revolt against the West' had in some respects reinforced the traditional structure of the states-system, since the new states were generally keen to

---

[32] James Mayall, *Nationalism and International Society* (Cambridge University Press, 1990).

[33] As well as Bull, *The Anarchical Society*, a more sustained discussion is offered in Gerrit Gong, *The Standard of Civilization in International Society* (Oxford: Clarendon Press, 1984).

assert their prerogatives as equal and independent sovereigns as the basis for sustaining or enlarging their influence in world politics.[34] Neverthe-less, Bull still believed that the survival of the states-system and society of states in contemporary world politics would ultimately depend on its ability to create a genuinely cosmopolitan culture, not one based solely on Western values and the 'culture of modernity', that would be able to attract support from both European and non-European peoples.

It would be quite unfair to underplay the importance of these addi-tions to the original theory of the states-system, but it would be wrong to suppose that they are enough to give us a proper account of order in modern world politics. The counter-revolutionary description of the development of European public order does not just need up-dating; it needs to be expanded with respect to its description of early mod-ern world politics. There are two crucial gaps that ought be addressed. First, its hostility to the French Revolution reflects a general antipathy towards republican forms of government, expressed through the con-tention that the European system was a system of monarchies, where republics like the Dutch achieved little more than grudging recognition. Several contemporary historians have noted that this is a serious un-derstatement of the importance of republicanism to the development of modern European politics, and have attempted to recover a sense both of the role that republics played in early modern Europe, and the relevance of republican political ideas to modern international thought as well.[35]

A second gap, and if anything a more serious one, is the lack of a proper account of the development of international political and legal order be-yond Europe. Heeren certainly did not neglect the colonies; indeed they were a central feature of his book. But what is crucial is that he viewed the possession of colonies and the control of extra-European trade merely as material ingredients within the European balance of power. The norma-tive character of relations between European and non-European peoples, or between European governments and their colonial settlers, did not interest him. This could be explained in several ways. It may well have been the case that he simply did not see it as relevant to the central

---

[34] Hedley Bull, 'The Revolt against the West', in Bull and Watson, *The Expansion of International Society*, pp. 217–28, and see also Robert Jackson, *Quasi-States: Sovereignty, International Relations and the Third World* (Cambridge University Press, 1990).

[35] Some works on the Dutch Republic, notably Marjolein 't Hart, *The Making of a Bourgeois State: War, Politics and Finance during the Dutch Revolt* (Manchester University Press, 1993), have gone a long way to dispelling some of Heeren's myths about the weakness and ineffectiveness of that form of government on the European stage. On republicanism in Europe more generally, see Robert Oresko, G.C. Gibbs and H.M. Scott (eds.), *Royal and Republican Sovereignty in Early Modern Europe* (Cambridge University Press, 1997), and on international relations theory, Nicholas Onuf, *The Republican Legacy in International Politics* (Cambridge University Press, 1998).

question he was trying to address, namely the legal basis of European public order, as threatened by Napoleon. But there may have been less straightforward reasons: he was trying to stigmatize the Napoleonic imperial system within Europe, and it hardly would have suited that purpose to call attention to the increasingly consolidated British imperial system in the world beyond Europe. Indeed, some French apologists had already accused the British of undermining the Westphalian order precisely on those grounds, and the counter-revolutionaries were anxious to defuse that criticism by treating the colonies as essentially irrelevant to questions about order and legitimacy in world politics altogether.[36] Heeren may also have been mindful of the republican sympathies that the British colonies in America had already had great success in defending: he would have been loath to grant their dangerously radical beliefs any formative role in the structure of modern international legal order.

The English school did not ignore the extra-European world either, but they only turned their attention to it in the later nineteenth century in order to depict the process of the expansion of international society. To all intents and purposes, they accepted Heeren's focus on the European states-system in the earlier period, adding no reflections on how relations between European and non-European peoples had developed over the centuries before questions about the latter's entry into the society of states came on to the agenda. In so doing, however, they had to respond to a very perceptive criticism of the orthodox history of the states-system that was advanced in the 1960s by Charles Alexandrowicz. Alexandrowicz was interested in a contemporary dispute about the treatment of non-Europeans as 'new' states: many of them, he argued, had enjoyed full recognition of their sovereignty in the sixteenth and seventeenth centuries, as evidenced by their treatment in the works of scholars on the law of nations such as Grotius. He took this to imply the existence of a universal family of nations in the early modern period, based on natural law. During the eighteenth and nineteenth centuries, he continued, the new school of positivist international lawyers shrank the family of nations, effectively evicting non-Europeans from membership, and forcing them to apply for readmission on less favourable terms, or subjecting them to outright imperial subjection.[37]

Wight did not reject this argument out of hand, and cautiously agreed that it might be plausible to treat Grotius as having offered a 'dualistic or

[36] This is a key theme in the dispute between Hauterive, *De L'Etat de la France*, and Gentz, *On the State of Europe*.

[37] Charles Alexandrowicz, *An Introduction to the History of the Law of Nations in the East Indies* (Oxford: Clarendon Press, 1967), and also 'Empirical and Doctrinal Positivism in International Law', *British Year Book of International Law*, 47 (1974–5), 286–9.

concentric conception of international society', with a universal family of nations surrounding a core of European states in Christendom.[38] Bull, however, was much more hostile. He attacked Alexandrowicz's position on the grounds that the natural law conception of a universal international society was merely hypothetical, and that in any case relations between European and non-European states were not carried on in such a way as to constitute a 'society' because 'they were not united by a perception of common interests, nor by a structure of generally agreed rules setting out their rights and duties in relation to one another, nor did they cooperate in the working of common international institutions'.[39] Bull contended that natural law was merely asserted unilaterally by the Europeans as a rationale for their exercise of colonial and imperial domination over non-European peoples, and he added that it is simply a matter of fact that Europeans have been the dominant military and commercial actors in modern world politics, so it is quite right and proper to devote the bulk of our attention to the arrangements that they worked out in their own society of states.[40]

Although other scholars appear to have been convinced by Bull's argument here,[41] I think it is extremely weak. The first part of the argument is so perfectly circular that it could have been written with a compass: Bull asserts that the natural law position was hypothetical because no international society existed beyond Europe; then, because natural law is only hypothetical, he uses a positivist conception of what an international society is to show that no international society existed beyond Europe. His observation, which in any event is empirically highly debatable, that European and non-European peoples were not united by common interests, a structure of 'generally agreed rules' and collective participation in common institutions, could hardly be of interest to a natural lawyer, who would see a *societas gentium* arising in a quite different way, from the already binding force of a normative and legal code that is a given feature of the natural order of things, and applies to all peoples and rulers whether they agree to it or not. All Bull is really doing here is accusing the natural lawyers of not being positive international lawyers; while that is true enough, it is hardly a compelling criticism of their position.

---

[38] Wight, *Systems of States*, p. 128. His own earlier interests in British colonial administration may well have led him to look favourably on Alexandrowicz's argument, but his works on that topic do not seem closely relevant to the position: see Wight, *The Gold Coast Legislative Council* (London: Faber and Faber, 1947), and *British Colonial Constitutions* (Oxford: Clarendon Press, 1952).

[39] Bull, 'The Emergence of a Universal International Society', p. 117.

[40] *Ibid.*, p. 124.   [41] For example, Gong, *Standard of Civilization*.

Secondly, Bull's point that natural law was a rationale for colonialism and imperialism seems to undermine his contention that it was merely hypothetical. Clearly, in fact, natural lawyers were saying something very important indeed about the practices that European states were engaged in outside Europe; to dismiss them as abstract metaphysicians who were increasingly out of touch with the real world of modern politics seems hardly fair, if at the same time we are to blame them for providing the justification upon which two of the most significant forces shaping the modern world were founded. Nor do I find it particularly disturbing that they were asserting this rationale unilaterally and without regard for the wishes of non-European states. As I have already noted, that risks presupposing a positivist doctrine that international society rests on the consent of its members, but it is also worth bearing in mind that the European states-system was asserted in a unilateral way with respect to those groups who were excluded from it, such as the old supranational institutions of medieval Christendom or, in its original context, the French revolutionaries and builders of the Napoleonic imperial system.

The third problem with Bull's argument is that it is a non-sequitur to say that the fact of European dominance means that, whether we like it or not, we should devote the bulk of our attention to the evolution of the European states-system. Since, as Bull obviously realized, European dominance was primarily exercised through practices of colonialism and imperialism, rationalised through natural law arguments, we should devote the bulk of our attention to the forms of international governance that Europeans created in their colonial and imperial systems. To the extent that the fact of European dominance ought to dictate what our research programme on order in modern world politics should be, it directs us *away* from the European states-system, not towards it. Bull was therefore inadvertently supplying as good a reason as one could wish for to justify a study of order in modern world politics completely at odds with his own: an examination of the links between natural law theory and the extra-European political and legal order based on colonial and imperial systems. That does not mean that I am embracing Alexandrowicz's position and completely rejecting Bull's. In his anxiety to load all of the blame for colonialism and imperialism onto the positive lawyers and the Göttingen historians of the European states-system, Alexandrowicz adopted far too rosy a view of early modern natural law. Bull was quite right, in my view, to insist on the importance of natural law to extra-European international politics in its colonial and imperial periods. In a sense, they were both right, since colonizers and imperialists were not particularly choosy as to whether they got their justification from the one legal doctrine or the other; the eclectic approach of Grotius suited them perfectly in that respect.

I think that that is sufficient to illustrate some of the historiographical problems that are created by the orthodox idea that order in modern world politics is fundamentally defined by the European states-system. But, as we have just seen, the English school, and especially Bull, usually talked about the legal concept of an international society, rather than the notion of a states-system as such. I want to turn now to asking how this blend was achieved, and with what consequences for our understanding of early modern international legal thought, and that of Grotius in particular.

The concept of international society and the 'Grotian tradition'

The second strand of the English school's research programme was an analysis of the history of political and legal thought about international relations, particularly in an effort to identify and develop the special *via media* that they saw as integral to 'Western values'.[42] To locate this middle way, Wight distinguished between three different traditions of 'international theory' (realism, rationalism and revolutionism), each of which had its own particular conception of international society, theory of mankind, theory of war, theory of ethics and so on.[43] Bull tentatively suggested that this scheme of three traditions may have been derived from Otto von Gierke.[44] Gierke had argued that, as early modern theorists of natural law progressively moved away from medieval conceptions of world monarchy, they began to use instead a novel idea of a society of nations (*societas gentium*) to preserve a belief in the efficacy of the law of nations. They were attacked from two sides as they did so: exponents of a strictly absolutist or unitary conception of sovereignty, such as Thomas Hobbes, denied the existence of a *societas gentium* because they found it illogical to place any constraints on the independent will of the sovereign; at the same time, though, there were several thinkers who felt that the idea of a mere society of nations was insufficient, and argued for the creation of a new world-state or empire to replace the old medieval *dominus mundi*.[45]

---

[42] Martin Wight, 'Western Values in International Relations', in Herbert Butterfield and Wight (eds.), *Diplomatic Investigations: Essays on the Theory of International Politics* (London: George Allen and Unwin, 1966), pp. 89–131.

[43] Martin Wight, *International Theory: The Three Traditions* (Leicester University Press, 1991).

[44] Hedley Bull, 'Martin Wight and the Theory of International Relations', in Wight, *International Theory*, p. xviii.

[45] Otto von Gierke, *Natural Law and the Theory of Society*, trans. Ernest Barker (Boston: Beacon Press, 1957), p. 85.

This gives rise, then, to a picture of three traditions of international political thought, contrasting theorists of absolute state sovereignty with theorists of a world-state and, in between these two extremes, theorists who uphold the idea of a *societas gentium* as a pragmatic way of defending the efficacy of moral principles and legal rules in international affairs, without insisting on the need for a single *dominus mundi*.

Gierke's brief statement of this line of argument may well have provided, as Bull suggested, the 'germ' of Wight's more elaborate treatise, and it certainly informed Bull's own version of the three traditions, as we will see in a moment.[46] But it is surprising, and revealing, that Bull did not mention another important source for Wight's scheme: histories of international legal thought. Another tripartite distinction appears, for example, in T.J. Lawrence's classic textbook on *The Principles of International Law*, to which Wight frequently referred in his main published essay on the history of international thought.[47] This is important because Lawrence's version differed from Gierke's in a crucial respect. Like most other international lawyers, Lawrence was interested in a disagreement that did not result from the controversy surrounding the concept of a *societas gentium*, but rather from the fact that the more narrowly jurisprudential idea of the *jus gentium* (law of nations) had come to have two distinct senses in the early seventeenth century. On the one hand, Lawrence argued, in its classical Roman sense it was little more than another term for natural law; on the other, it gradually came to be associated with volitional or positive law, established through agreements between states.[48] He maintained that modern juristic debates subsequently revolved around this disagreement about the sources of the *jus gentium*. Some, most famously Samuel Pufendorf, clung to the old view that the law of nations was simply a part of natural law; others, like Richard Zouch, adopted the positivist position and argued that the *jus gentium* depended entirely upon the consent of states.[49] In between, there was an 'eclectic' position, often called Grotian because Grotius was its most celebrated exponent, although run a close second by Vattel, which attempted to derive international legal obligations from both natural law and state volition

---

[46] Bull, 'Martin Wight and the Theory of International Relations', p. xviii.

[47] Wight, 'Western Values in International Relations', pp. 101, 102, 112n and 120n. By contrast, Wight did not refer to Gierke once in that essay, although he did use language which clearly reflects a Gierkean influence. To his credit, Bull confessed himself unsure as to whether or not Wight had indeed read the relevant passage in Gierke's book. See also T.J. Lawrence, *The Principles of International Law*, 5th edn (Boston: D.C. Heath, 1910).

[48] Lawrence, *The Principles of International Law*, p. 39.

[49] Zouch is often used as an example in the literature. Nevertheless, in my view the most important architects of legal positivism were the historians of European treaties that I discussed in the previous section, especially Jean Dumont and G.F. de Martens.

simultaneously.[50] The key point here is that students of legal thought like Lawrence generally did not see this as a dispute about whether or not an international society existed, or whether or not the existing international society should be replaced by some kind of world-state. The disagreement, as they saw it, was essentially *internal* to the *societas gentium*, and was sustained by differing views on the sources, and to a degree also the content, of the normative principles and legal obligations that they all agreed were binding upon its members.

I think that the distinguishing characteristic of Wight's history of ideas is that is was neither purely Gierkean nor purely jurisprudential, but sought to combine both. His intention was to unify these two approaches to the study of international relations, an ambitious goal that he hinted at by coining the new label, 'international theory'. Wight used this rather vague term to describe his subject matter because he did not want to commit himself to the historical study of either political or legal thinking about international relations in isolation. On the contrary, his goal was to overcome the 'unhappy partition' that had previously arisen to divide those 'philosophically minded international lawyers' that Lawrence had talked about from the 'internationally minded political philosophers' like Machiavelli, Hobbes and Althusius, with whom Gierke had primarily been concerned.[51] Wight's project was to treat both groups as involved in the development of a single field of 'international theory', to show how they had furnished international relations with its political philosophical foundations, while simultaneously acknowledging that the bulk of speculation explicitly concerned with international affairs had, at least until the twentieth century, been conducted more or less exclusively in jurisprudential terms about the law of nations.[52]

The main problem with Wight's scheme is that this purpose, however admirable it may have been in itself, entangled him in all sorts of difficulties when he tried to explain precisely what was at stake in the debate between the three traditions. At the most fundamental level, the exceptionally broad scope of his enquiry raised the question of whether the three traditions were involved in a disagreement in the wider Gierkean sense about the existence of a *societas gentium*, or in the rather narrower legal sense about the precise sources of the *jus gentium* within a *societas gentium* that everyone took for granted. Wight oscillated between the two. On the one hand, he argued that each tradition had its own distinctive

---

[50] For example, Amos Hershey, *The Essentials of International Public Law* (New York: Macmillan, 1912), p. 62.

[51] Wight, *International Theory*, p. 3.

[52] *Ibid.*, p. 1, and Martin Wight, 'Why Is There No International Theory?', in Butterfield and Wight (eds.), *Diplomatic Investigations*, pp. 18–19.

conception of international society, suggesting a certain proximity to the three classic schools of legal thought: positivism, naturalism and 'eclectic' Grotianism. His description of the traditions' contrasting views on international society did not, however, exactly correspond to the orthodox version of the three traditions of legal thought.[53] The major difference was that Wight identified both positivist and naturalist jurisprudence with the realist tradition of international theory because both regarded international society as a society of states enjoying an originally perfect liberty: the positivists held that states could subsequently be bound by rules to which they had given their consent, thus providing what Wight called a 'general, conventional or inductive' form of realism; the naturalists made an analogy between the position of states in international society and that of individuals within the state of nature, and so gave a 'deductive' analysis that stressed the importance of natural law in furnishing a right to political independence.[54] This picture gets even more confusing if we note that Wight saw the revolutionists as having most strongly emphasized the element of international society in world politics, but they believed that it rested on transnational relationships between individuals, underpinning the appearance of a society composed of distinct and independent sovereignties.[55] Finally, we have the 'eclectic' position that international society is based on relations between both states and individuals. This, Wight agreed with the textbook legal histories, was the distinctively Grotian conception of international society, where international law could be derived from both natural and positive sources simultaneously (although it is logical to suppose that that would make Grotianism, ironically enough, a form of realism).[56]

At the same time, however, one can see a thread of the Gierkean argument interwoven with this account of the three conceptions of international society. For realists – and now we are talking about the more extreme 'Hobbesian' realists – international society does *not* exist, since international relations are a gladiatorial arena in a constant and asocial state of war. Among revolutionists, on the other hand, the idea of an international society is understood to imply a 'super-state' that existing international arrangements ought or are destined to become.[57] Again, this suggests that revolutionists do not believe that an international society actually does exist at present, but uphold the concept as an ideal into

[53] Wight, *International Theory*, p. 233.
[54] *Ibid.*, pp. 14, 36, 130–1 and 233–5. On the naturalists' analogy between the liberty of states and individuals, see also the classic interpretation in Edwin Dickinson, 'The Analogy between Natural Persons and International Persons in the Law of Nations', *Yale Law Journal*, 26 (1916/17), 564–91.
[55] Wight, *International Theory*, pp. 7–8 and 48, and Wight, 'Western Values in International Relations', p. 93.
[56] Wight, *International Theory*, pp. 36–7.   [57] *Ibid.*, pp. 32 and 48.

which the currently imperfect condition of international relations should be transformed. In short, rather perversely in view of his earlier remarks about the debate between the three traditions' different conceptions of international society, Wight also appears to concur with Gierke's idea that it is only the moderate 'rationalists' who believed in the existence of an international society, which they are defending against both realist scepticism and the revolutionist belief in a future world-state, empire or community of humankind.

Several other ambiguities arose as a result of Wight's attempt to blend the two earlier historical perspectives on international legal and political theory. As I have already mentioned, both legal positivists and naturalists were to be found in Wight's realist tradition, a tradition that, in its more extreme form at least, is also represented as denying the existence of a *societas gentium*, and hence, one has to conclude, a *jus gentium* as well. This leads to the somewhat peculiar (although not completely absurd) outcome that two of the major schools in the history of international legal thought are identified with a political philosophical position that is most famous for denying the efficacy of international law altogether. Meanwhile, the revolutionists – the tradition that Wight described as having most strongly emphasised the importance of the concept of international society – apparently have no roots whatsoever in the classic schools of international legal thought, if only for the reason that none of those schools are left to inform the revolutionist perspective: positivism and naturalism had already been placed in the realist tradition, while Grotianism had to be located elsewhere. Wight therefore grounded the revolutionist theory of international law in the argument that law is merely ideological and does not rest on any natural or fundamental normative principles.[58] That, however, is an odd way to describe a tradition that is also supposed to include the Huguenot monarchomachic author of the *Vindiciae contra Tyrannos*, or Kantian philosophers for that matter, and to which Wight credited the belief that interventions might be legitimate on the grounds that 'the inviolability of frontiers is subordinated to the illimitability of truth'.[59] It is hard to see how one can uphold the 'illimitability of truth' and yet maintain that there are no natural or fundamental principles upon which to ground a code of international legal obligations.

Most important of all, though, is the ambiguity that surrounds Wight's picture of the rationalist tradition, especially in its relationship to the 'eclectic' Grotian school of international legal thought. Theorists since Wight have generally concluded that these two traditions are more or less interchangeable, and rationalism and Grotianism are commonly depicted

[58] *Ibid.*, p. 236.
[59] Wight, 'Western Values in International Relations', p. 113.

as one and the same.[60] It should already be clear, however, that such a conclusion is impossible if Wight's argument is to be taken seriously. In the classic legal sense, Grotians had occupied the middle ground between the positivist and the naturalist schools. By collapsing the latter two into the realist tradition of international theory, Wight was inevitably changing the nature of the debate with regard to the similarly moderate position taken up by the rationalists. The point is an obvious one: if you change the poles of a debate, you must be altering the terrain between them. To his credit, Wight recognized this, admitting that Grotianism and rationalism were not synonymous. Where this left the old legal Grotian tradition was, however, totally unclear. Wight did not want to abandon altogether any idea of a link between Grotianism and rationalism, since he saw both of them as crucial to defining the vital category of the *via media* in international theory and Western values, but he twisted himself into knots trying to explain how Grotians were similar to rationalists, while at the same time retaining a sense of the differences between the two traditions, as was logically required by his treatment of the schools of international legal thought whence the idea of a 'Grotian tradition' originally came.[61]

I am afraid that I will have to leave Wight tied up like that, because I cannot see a way in which his extraordinarily ambitious attempt to provide an account of the whole of 'international theory' can be made coherent, which may be one reason why he never published his lectures on the subject (their publication was posthumous). The only way, in fact, of making it work is simply to ignore all the ambiguities it contains; that, in a nutshell, was Bull's solution. He cut the Wightian knot through the drastic device of reducing 'international theory' to international political thought, spotlighting Gierke's idea of a debate about the existence of the *societas gentium* and pushing the legal debate about the *jus gentium* into the shadows.

Bull did not make any real distinction between Wight's rationalist tradition and the legal Grotian tradition. He understood both as defending the concept of international society against the extreme perspectives of those who believe that only international anarchy exists, on the one hand, and against those who uphold the idea of a universal community of humankind, on the other. Grotians are not, as the lawyers would have had it, defending a middle point between two different conceptions of the sources for obligations in international society, and to some extent different theories of the membership of international society. Bull's

[60] Bull, 'Martin Wight and the Theory of International Relations' and, for a more recent example, see Andrew Linklater, 'Rationalism', in Scott Burchill, Linklater *et al.*, *Theories of International Relations* (London: Macmillan, 1995), pp. 93–118.
[61] Wight, *International Theory*, pp. 233–4.

is a plausible idea of the moderate character of the Grotian tradition of thought, but it is clear that it is a considerable departure from the conventional point of view in international law. It is also a departure from Wight's position, to the extent that conventional legal positivists and naturalists would now presumably be in the Grotian-rationalist tradition rather than being forms of realism.

Bull's argument also rested on the proposition that the concept of international society is identical with the concept of a society of states. Since he was beginning from the concept of a state and states-system, this was more or less inevitable, although neither Wight nor the early international lawyers were quite so committed to the statist membership of the *societas gentium*. Indeed, Bull's argument implied the somewhat bizarre conclusion that the conventional Grotian position in international law, with its eclectic theory of international personality, actually lacks a properly defined concept of international society. Moreover, Bull's view of the concept of international society was not simply statist; it adopted a positivist theory of the sources for the rules of international law. Bull famously asserted that an international society is created when states '*conceive themselves* to be bound by a common set of rules in their relations with one another, and share in the working of common institutions . . . they *regard themselves* as bound by certain rules in their dealings with one another'.[62] The crucial point here is that international society is dependent on the will or volition of states to submit themselves to a set of rules, and that is an essentially positivist position. This comes through very clearly in Bull's discussion of the question of whether natural law theories of the sixteenth century (including Grotius's own) constituted a universal international society during that period, which I discussed earlier.

One reason why Bull was able to get away with this argument was that his idea that it is *only* Grotians who conceive of international relations in terms of the idea of an international society relaxed the pressure to maintain the old position that Grotians formed a distinctive school of thought by virtue of their eclectic theory of international personality. Instead, while he began using the concept of international society in a very narrow way, a certain looseness entered into his understanding of the idea of a Grotian tradition. As Bull commented in a revealing footnote in *The Anarchical Society*: 'I have myself used the term "Grotian" in two senses: (i) as here, to describe the broad doctrine that there is a *society of states*; (ii) to describe the solidarist form of this doctrine, which united Grotius himself and the twentieth-century neo-Grotians, in opposition to the pluralist conception of international society entertained by Vattel

---

[62] Bull, *The Anarchical Society*, p. 13, emphases added.

and later positivist writers.'[63] Even the 'solidarist' conception of international society, which is presumably intended as an attempt to give a more authentic representation of Grotian and neo-Grotian legal thought, is located within a 'broad doctrine' that equates international society with a society of states. This tends to lead to the idea that the specifically Grotian conception is really about solidarity *between states*, and that its eclectic theory of international personality is merely a normative claim that individual well-being is the ultimate criterion for determining the worth of actually existing international arrangements.

Consequently, there was little to prevent Bull from depicting Grotius himself as committed to an absolutist conception of sovereignty and a 'Hobbesian' premise about the membership of international society.[64] Wight, by contrast, tended to link Grotius more closely to liberal thinkers like John Locke on the grounds that both adopted a view where natural law could continue to have some force even in the context of an established civil society, and suggested that this was the basis for their view of international relations as an 'institutionally deficient' but still 'quasi-social' condition, where both natural and man-made positive law applied.[65] Bull represented Grotius's 'institutionally deficient' view of international society simply as a medievalist hangover, a consequence of the fact that '[i]n Grotius' time these institutions existed only in embryo; the international society he describes is an ideal or normative one, for which there was as yet little concrete historical evidence'.[66] There was little awareness on Bull's part of the political theoretical significance of this 'institutional deficiency', nor of the way in which Wight had used the connection between Grotius and Locke to open rationalism out to a more voluntaristic theory of political obligation.

Of course, that shows that Bull realized that Grotius's work contained a 'domestic model', even if it was only to be dismissed as a 'medieval residue'. One of the crucial features of Bull's argument is that he *did* retain a sense of Grotian dualism and eclecticism; but within a new set of parameters that, in my view, drastically limit its scope. This was contained in Bull's distinction between the pluralist conception of international society held by positivist international lawyers, and a solidarist conception, preferred by Grotius and especially by the twentieth-century 'neo-Grotians', like Hersch Lauterpacht. Bull describes the solidarist position as making two main claims about international society. First, it assumes 'the

[63] *Ibid.*, p. 322n.
[64] *Ibid.*, p. 26, and Hedley Bull, 'The Importance of Grotius in the Study of International Relations', in Bull, Benedict Kingsbury and Adam Roberts (eds.), *Hugo Grotius and International Relations* (Oxford: Clarendon Press, 1992), pp. 84–5.
[65] Wight, *International Theory*, pp. 38–9.   [66] Bull, 'Importance of Grotius', p. 90.

solidarity, or potential solidarity, of the states comprising international society, with respect to the enforcement of the law', in contrast to the pluralist belief that 'states are capable of agreeing only for certain minimum purposes which fall short of the enforcement of the law'.[67] This seems to be essentially a procedural point, relating to the question of how international law is enforced, rather than anything to do with the actual content of international law, and hence of the normative principles underpinning international order. It generally refers to the degree of consensus among the members of international society and the extent of their commitment to international law, maybe even against their own immediate self-interest.

The second solidarist claim is that 'the members of international society are ultimately not states but individuals'.[68] The point here is that, although international society is institutionally composed of states and the enforcement of law depends on the degree of solidarity among them, the *legitimacy* of this international society of states is derivative from 'the universal community of mankind'.[69] In other words, the value of international society is determined in terms of its contribution to the well-being of individual human beings (and, rather problematically, presupposes some rough consensus among states about precisely what that involves). This contrasts with the pluralists' view that the primary purpose of international society is to maintain peaceful coexistence between states with radically different cultural and political systems, and that consequently it is justifiable for states to adopt a 'convention of silence about the place in their society of their human subjects'.[70] Unlike pluralists, solidarists would tend to regard a state that was violating the rights of its subjects as a pariah, against which all the other members of international society would be justified in adopting interventionist or coercive policies.

Bull recognized the normative attractiveness of the solidarist conception of international society, but he had serious reservations about it, not the least of which was his concern that it did not take proper account of the actual circumstances of modern international relations. He was worried that the degree of consensus it required did not exist, partly because of cultural pluralism, and that assertions of the common purposes of states in international society would likely be self-interested and to the detriment of weaker states, for which sovereignty was an important asset: 'If a right of intervention is proclaimed for the purpose of enforcing standards of conduct, and yet no consensus exists in the international community governing its use, then the door is open to interventions by

[67] Bull, 'Grotian Conception', p. 52. [68] *Ibid.*, p. 68.
[69] *Ibid.* [70] *Ibid.*

particular states using such a right as a pretext, and the principle of territorial sovereignty is placed in jeopardy.'[71] This did not mean Bull was ruling out solidarism for ever. Towards the end of *The Anarchical Society*, for example, he put forward a powerful argument to the effect that the future of international society depended on cultivating precisely the kind of 'cosmopolitan culture' that could underpin genuine solidarity among states, 'rooted in societies as well as in their elites' and which 'may need to absorb non-Western elements to a much greater degree if it is to be genuinely universal'.[72] As things stood, however, Bull regarded the modern international society that actually existed as one that was more pluralist than solidarist, and had become increasingly so as it had expanded to include non-European states and hence a greater range of cultural diversity. Even in one of his last, and most solidaristically inclined, works, Bull still warned that '[t]he cosmopolitan society which is implied and presupposed in our talk of human rights exists only as an ideal and we court great dangers if we allow ourselves to proceed as if it were a political and social framework already in place'.[73] Grotian solidarism, then, is attacked on two different fronts: it is vulnerable to the accusation of being nostalgic, because it contains a 'medieval residue'; and it can be criticized for being utopian, because it prematurely asserts the existence of a genuinely cosmopolitan culture in modern international society.

Often without realizing it, the numerous scholars today who use concepts like the 'Westphalian system', the 'Grotian tradition' and the 'society of states', or who base their work on Bull's definitions of international society and solidarism, are therefore committing themselves to a peculiarly narrow and twisted perspective on order in modern world politics. The very idea of a society of states is itself something of a hybrid, and it is quite incorrect to suppose, as so many do, that it accurately reflects a Grotian tradition of thought about international political and legal order that goes back to the dawn of the modern era in the seventeenth century. The theory that we have today squeezes Grotius's extremely eclectic and wide-ranging account of the law of nations into a small box that was constructed in the early nineteenth century for the specific purpose of defending the independence of dynastic monarchs against the onslaught of the French Revolution and Napoleonic imperialism. One result of this is that we have a warped picture of early modern international legal thought that simply does not do justice to many of the central issues that animated Grotius and his successors. Another result is that we have an historical narrative of the development of political and legal order in the

---

[71] *Ibid.*, p. 71.   [72] Bull, *The Anarchical Society*, p. 317.
[73] Hedley Bull, *The Hagey Lectures*, University of Waterloo, *Mimeograph*, 1984, p. 13.

modern world that is blinkered in its outlook, not by any real considera-
tion of what is significant to us today, but rather in accordance with the
needs of nineteenth-century reactionaries. In chapter 2, I will try to take
Grotius out of that box. I will look more closely at his account of the law
of nations and try to discern what his central propositions were without
making the standard assumption that anything that does not fit in with
the logic of the states-system is clearly nostalgic, idealistic and, either
way, 'un-modern'. This will, I hope, open up a new set of possibilities for
our understanding of the nature of order in modern world politics, which
I will then go on to explore in the rest of the book.

2   The Grotian theory of the law of nations

Among theorists of international relations today, Hugo Grotius is more famous for having defended the existence of an international society than for any substantive propositions he made about what it looks like or how it operates.[1] As I explained in chapter 1, a major reason for this attitude is the way in which the 'Grotian tradition' has come to be understood in the context of Martin Wight's 'international theory' and Hedley Bull's reflections on the Grotian conception of international society. Over the last thirty years or so, the historical analysis of Grotianism by theorists of international relations has moved away from debates about the sources, content and scope of international law within a *societas gentium*, and has instead concentrated on debates about the nature of international politics within a states-system. Consequently, the Grotian position is now normally juxtaposed against two alternative political theories of international relations: Machiavellian or Hobbesian realism, and Kantian

---

[1] The same criticism could not be made, at least not without serious qualification, for historians of political and legal thought more generally. For excellent analyses of Grotius, see in particular Richard Tuck, *Natural Rights Theories: Their Origin and Development* (Cambridge University Press, 1977); *Philosophy and Government, 1572–1651* (Cambridge University Press, 1993); and *The Rights of War and Peace: Political Thought and International Order from Grotius to Kant* (Oxford University Press, 1999). Other notable works are Stephen Buckle, *Natural Law and the Theory of Property: Grotius to Hume* (Oxford: Clarendon Press, 1991); David Kennedy, 'Primitive Legal Scholarship', *Harvard International Law Journal*, 27 (1986), 1–98; Karl Olivecrona, 'Appropriation in the State of Nature: Locke on the Origin of Property', *History of Ideas*, 35 (1974), 211–30; and Olivecrona, 'Locke's Theory of Appropriation', *Philosophical Quarterly*, 24 (1974), 220–34. Peter Borschberg's editorial introduction to Hugo Grotius, *'Commentarius in Theses XI': An Early Treatise on Sovereignty, the Just War and the Legitimacy of the Dutch Revolt*, trans. Borschberg (Berne: Peter Lang, 1994) is extremely good. Unsurprisingly, the journal *Grotiana* includes numerous detailed and insightful studies of Grotius: see especially Cornelis Roelofsen, 'Grotius and the "Grotian Heritage" in International Law and International Relations: The Quarcentenary and its Aftermath', *Grotiana*, 11 (1990), 6–28, and another good essay is Ben Vermeulen, 'Discussing Grotian Law and Legal Philosophy: Marginal Notes to Some Recent Articles on Grotius', *Grotiana*, 6 (1985), 84–92. I make no apologies for the fact that in developing my own understanding of Grotius's theory of the law of nations I have made extensive use of these and other interpretative commentaries on Grotian thought.

cosmopolitanism. This leads to the popular view that the most important distinguishing feature of Grotianism is its commitment to the idea of a society of states, in contradistinction to the Hobbesian denial of such a society and the Kantian insistence on a world community of humankind. According to the defenders of contemporary 'Grotianism', this offers a valuable way of thinking about international politics because it is more sensitive to questions about world justice than the realists, while at the same time being more sensitive to the problems of anarchy and pluralism than the cosmopolitans.

On the whole, I agree that speculation about international society is an excellent way of studying international relations. But the conventional wisdom that we ought to concentrate on the development of a society of states in modern Europe is too restrictive a conceptual framework, because it commits us to the idea of a states-system as defining *the* pattern of order in the modern world and prevents us from taking other forms of international order, such as imperial systems, as seriously as we should. Moreover, the failure to pay attention to the actual content of Grotian thinking about the law of nations has inadvertently cut us off from an alternative way of thinking about modern international law that could help us to understand some of those aspects of order in world politics that look 'anomalous' from the perspective of the states-system. To begin repairing some of the damage, in this chapter I am going to take a closer look at Grotius's theory of the law of nations. For the reasons outlined above, my account will differ from much of the existing work on this subject in the literature on international relations, because I will concentrate less on his general attitude towards the issue of sociability in international relations, and more on the details of how he understood the specific rules of the law of nations in force at the time.

Before proceeding with this enquiry, I ought to acknowledge that another reason why so little attention is now paid to the details of Grotius's work is that his style is often obscure. Much of what he had to say about the law of nations will probably strike an audience today as completely pointless. When reading Grotius, it is sometimes difficult not to sympathize with Voltaire's acid remark that 'he is very learned... but what has circumcision to do with the laws of war and peace?'[2] I am certainly not going to attempt to cover *all* the details of Grotius's work, although it ought to be noted that sometimes arguments with a wider significance do spring from unlikely parts of the text. Instead, I am going to focus on two main issues that he discussed at great length in his major works on

---

[2] Voltaire, *Political Writings*, trans. David Williams (Cambridge University Press, 1994), pp. 87 and 89.

the law of nations, and to which he obviously attached cardinal importance: the sources and operation of public authority, and the acquisition
and defence of private property. This distinction between public rights of
sovereignty and private rights of ownership is one of the main organizing
devices in Grotius's account of the law of nations, and it is crucial to
understanding how he dealt with each topic in its own way and how he
viewed the relationship between the two. In addition, I should admit that
I have not just chosen these two themes because they are so prominent
in Grotius's work, but also because I think that a closer study of them
is essential to my wider project of developing a new picture of order in
modern world politics.

Grotius on public authority in the law of nations

Like most of his contemporaries, Grotius conceived of public authority
in terms of a number of rights to do specific things: to declare war, conduct foreign relations, raise taxes, make laws and so on.[3] Unlike many
of his contemporaries, however, Grotius's main concern was not to specify which particular institution, or group of institutions, should possess
these prerogatives in order to create the best possible political community. Grotius undoubtedly had views on this issue, but he was not particularly explicit about them. It is striking, for example, that in his major
work, De Jure Belli ac Pacis, Grotius did not bother to give a general argument for any particular kind of political system. His interests lay in
other, more narrowly legalistic, questions about public authority, since,
as he even-handedly remarked, 'in matters of government there is nothing which from every point of view is quite free from disadvantages; and
a legal provision is to be judged not by what this or that man considers
best, but by what accords with the will of him with whom the provision
originated'.[4]

That apparently rather bland comment is interesting because it reveals
one of the most characteristic and important features of Grotius's analysis
of political authority. He was not engaged in a philosophical enquiry into
the best form of government, so much as an enquiry into existing legal and
constitutional arrangements, centred on the attempt to discover exactly
what provisions had been made, by whom and with what intentions;
his project was not to determine what prerogatives people *should* hold,

---

[3] For a good discussion about the flexibility of early modern thinking about sovereignty in
general, see Julian Franklin, 'Sovereignty and the Mixed Constitution: Jean Bodin and
his Critics', in J.H. Burns (ed.), *The Cambridge History of Political Thought, 1450–1700*
(Cambridge University Press, 1991), pp. 298–328.

[4] Hugo Grotius, *De Jure Belli ac Pacis Libri Tres*, trans. Francis Kelsey *et al.* (Oxford:
Clarendon Press, 1925), p. 124.

but rather to identify those which in fact they *did* hold.[5] Of course, the latter enquiry had important political implications, since Grotius believed that it was proper to do what was lawful; in his scheme of things, the mundane notion of respect for the law usually trumped more grandiose and speculative attempts to demonstrate the inherent rightness of, say, princely absolutism or popular sovereignty. Assuming that legal rights had been established through correct procedures, Grotius understood them to define the parameters within which political relationships were to be conducted, setting the boundaries of autonomy, obligation and justifiable violence. Grotius's work, with all its apparent contradictions and evasions, is only intelligible if we begin from this understanding of the very specific character of the questions with which he was concerned.

In applying this approach, Grotius was certainly aware of the theory of sovereignty that Jean Bodin had recently advanced. Indeed, he began his analysis of public authority in *De Jure Belli ac Pacis* with a general definition of the concept that looks very Bodinian: 'That power is called sovereign (*summa*) whose actions are not subject to the legal control of another, so that they cannot be rendered void by the operation of another human will.'[6] He also appears to have appreciated the force of Bodin's observations about how the sovereign power should be organized within a political community. Bodin had pointed out that his definition of the concept logically required a strong distinction to be made between the sovereign and the subject. If to be sovereign means to be free from subjection to any other human authority it must be impossible, he argued, to be both a sovereign and a subject simultaneously. It would therefore be a mistake to treat any prerogative as a true mark of 'sovereignty' if it could be shared between a ruler and his or her subjects at the same time; the only authentic mark of sovereignty, he concluded, was the prerogative to make law through an act of independent will, which must by its very nature be vested in a single person or a single institution within a political community.[7] Grotius seemed to concur with this reading of the logical consequences of treating sovereignty as independence from other

---

[5] The inherent conservatism of this approach provoked Jean-Jacques Rousseau's famous jibe that Grotius could have used 'a more consistent method, but none more favourable to tyrants': Rousseau, *The Social Contract and other Later Political Writings*, trans. Victor Gourevitch (Cambridge University Press, 1997), p. 42. Note, however, that on the whole Grotius would only endorse existing arrangements that had been justly arrived at (an important exception will be discussed below), and that the method of deriving the law from facts only supports tyrants if they are truly empowered by the *status quo*; if existing arrangements are not, in fact, favourable to tyrants, then neither is Grotius's method, as we will see in moment.

[6] *Ibid.*, p. 102; compare with Jean Bodin, *On Sovereignty: Four Chapters from the Six Books of the Commonwealth*, ed. and trans. Julian Franklin (Cambridge University Press, 1992), p. 11.

[7] Bodin, *On Sovereignty*, p. 49.

judicial controls and wills, agreeing that 'sovereignty (*summum imperium*) is a unity, in itself indivisible'.[8]

One always has to be careful about these apparently clear-cut statements with which Grotius often began his discussion of complex legal questions. On the question of *summum imperium*, while apparently endorsing Bodin's conception of sovereignty as indivisible, Grotius proceeded to offer a series of exceptions to the general definition that, to all intents and purposes, nullified it. Having just said that sovereignty is indivisible, he immediately added a crucial 'but': when jurists discuss sovereignty 'a division is sometimes made into parts designated as potential and subjective', and he conceded that that may well be an accurate terminology because 'it may happen that a people, when choosing a king, may reserve to itself certain powers but may confer others on the king absolutely (*pleno jure*)'.[9] This is typical of Grotius: he asserts that in principle sovereignty is indivisible, but then shows that in both theory and practice it is often divided, and goes on to provide a whole series of illustrations of such *summitatis divisio*, without for one moment decrying them as dangerous or illogical absurdities (as Bodin unquestionably would have done).

In the course of this discussion Grotius certainly did not rule out the possibility that an individual monarch might be an absolute sovereign, holding all of the marks of sovereignty without any sharing or division involved. Indeed, his best-known example of how a people might confer powers on a king is a notorious endorsement of absolutist rule: since individual men may enslave themselves, he reasoned, 'would it not be permitted to a people having legal competence to submit itself to some one person, or to several persons, in such a way as plainly to transfer to him the legal right to govern, retaining no vestige of that right for itself?'[10] And, as if that claim by itself was not enough to attract the angry attention of subsequent generations of political theorists, Grotius underlined the point by appealing to the now infamous Aristotelian doctrine of natural slavery: 'some men are by nature slaves ... so there are some people so constituted that they understand better how to be ruled than to rule'.[11]

---

[8] Grotius, *De Jure Belli ac Pacis*, p. 123.   [9] *Ibid.*   [10] *Ibid.*, p. 103.
[11] *Ibid.*, p. 105. It is tempting to assume that he had non-European peoples in mind here. He may well have done, but if he was thinking about Americans, Asians or Africans in this context, he had ample opportunities to develop the point more explicitly here and elsewhere, and did not do so. It is conceivable, although I would be hesitant about committing myself to the point, that the Aristotelian thesis might have suited European circumstances. Perhaps he was making a comparison between the freedom-loving Dutch and the similarly inclined ancient Greeks, in contrast with those European peoples who, like Aristotle's Persians, found it easier to bear the yoke of absolutist despotism, such as the Spanish. In any case, it is also plausible to think, especially given the context

This is undoubtedly the most spectacular of Grotius's examples of how sovereign prerogatives are transferred from one holder to another, and its celebrity has helped foster the widespread belief that Grotius himself was committed to an absolutist position. But it is important to bear in mind that it was just one among several different examples that he gave of how political authority may be organized; there are, moreover, good reasons for thinking that it was not the most significant one in Grotius's own mind.

For a start, Grotius pointed out that in several instances it was quite wrong to begin from the assumption that the ruler held sovereignty in an absolute form: 'In cases of kingships which have been conferred by the will of the people the presumption is . . . that it was not the will of the people to permit the king to alienate the sovereign power [one of the pre-conditions of absolutist sovereignty]'.[12] That shifted the burden of proof to would-be absolutists, and it was a crucial qualification because it will be recalled that, in interpreting a legal provision, Grotius attached overwhelming importance to the will of the person or people who had originally made it. To amplify the point yet further, Grotius went on to specify three typical ways in which a people might grant sovereignty less than absolutely: in some cases, a ruler might hold all the prerogatives of sovereignty, but with the qualification attached that he or she remained 'responsible to the people'; sometimes, on the other hand, 'sovereign power is held in part by the king, in part by the people or the senate'; and sometimes 'in the conferring of authority it has been stated that in a particular case the king can be resisted'.[13] Public authority is organized differently in each of these instances, and it is in the second, where the power is held only 'in part by the king', that we have a clear-cut case of divided sovereignty.

That particular example is interesting for the light it sheds on the original sources of Grotius's thinking about public authority and the divisibility of the sovereign power. In an early work, the *Commentarius in Theses XI*, he had used the particular way in which the Dutch people had transferred their legal rights to justify their war against the Spanish, often labelled (rather misleadingly from a Grotian perspective) as the Dutch Revolt.[14]

of the argument, that his main goal in using this argument was to dispute the popular monarchomachic theory that the general condition of natural liberty endowed all peoples with a set of rights that they could never lose to a ruler, and which therefore provided a permanent justification for resistance against tyranny.

[12] *Ibid.*, p. 123.   [13] *Ibid.*, pp. 156 and 158.

[14] Grotius, '*Commentarius in Theses XI*': An Early Treatise on *Sovereignty, the Just War and the Legitimacy of the Dutch Revolt*. Borschberg's introduction and commentary on this text offers an excellent analysis of the development of Grotius's thought about sovereignty, upon which I have drawn heavily. See also (in English) Borschberg, 'Grocio y el Contracto Social: Un Estudio Preliminar de las Inéditas

Grotius's approach to justifying this conflict represented a departure from what was, at the time, the more common way of thinking about the Dutch action: a form of early modern resistance theory, known as constitutionalism or monarchomachism, which relied on two main claims. The first was that, before forming political societies, people had originally lived in a condition of 'natural liberty', which endowed them with a series of inalienable rights that marked the limits beyond which even the most absolute ruler might not trespass without becoming a tyrant. Fearful, perhaps, of the radical implications of the natural liberty argument, and mindful of their constituency in the French nobility, Huguenot resistance theorists had added a second claim, to the effect that the right to take up arms in defence of the people's natural liberties was not vested in the people themselves, but in an intermediary class of public officials above the ordinary people, but below the level of the monarch: 'inferior magistrates'.[15] Many Dutch political theorists made use of this argument as well, although sometimes, possibly because of the much greater level of popular support for the revolt against Spain in the Netherlands, possibly because of the more radical influence of Calvinism, they bypassed the idea of 'inferior magistrates' altogether, to argue that ordinary people had the right to use violence in defence of their natural liberties.[16]

In the *Commentarius*, however, Grotius declined to adopt either the monarchomachic line or its more populist Dutch variant (which he was undoubtedly too conservative to support). Instead, he used a quite different approach, treating the Dutch as involved in a just public war rather than an act of resistance *per se*. The crucial proposition in his argument was one with which we are now familiar: sovereignty is divisible, such that 'it may be possible for some marks [of sovereignty] to reside . . . with persons or assemblies, while others do not'.[17] Here, with his immediate purpose of justifying the Dutch cause in mind, he illustrated the point by referring to the right of the States of Holland to raise taxes, a right

---

Theses LVI', *Revista de Estudios Políticos*, forthcoming, where Borschberg discusses an early unpublished essay that reinforces the anti-Bodinian nature of Grotius's theory of sovereignty, as well as the flexibility of the Grotian theory, which has room for absolutist rulers without making absolutism a necessary condition of the sovereign power.

[15] For a seminal account, which treats this line of argument as of pivotal importance to the development of modern political theory in general, see Quentin Skinner, *The Foundations of Modern Political Thought, Volume 2: The Age of Reformation* (Cambridge University Press, 1978).

[16] See, for example, E.H. Kossmann and A.F. Mellink (eds.), *Texts Concerning the Revolt of the Netherlands* (Cambridge University Press, 1974), p. 152, and Martin van Gelderen, *The Political Thought of the Dutch Revolt, 1555–1590* (Cambridge University Press, 1992), p. 119. There may also have been good constitutionalist reasons for the relative populism of Dutch resistance theory.

[17] Grotius, *Commentarius*, p. 227.

which had never been transferred to Philip II of Spain. The 'Revolt' could therefore be justified on the grounds that Philip's representative in the Netherlands, the duke of Alva, had usurped this prerogative by levying taxes on his own initiative, and the Dutch States were entitled to defend their prerogative by waging a just public war against the Spanish.[18] If, in the course of waging this war, the Dutch were to succeed in inducing Philip to grant them further rights of sovereignty, even leading to their outright independence (which is what did indeed happen, after Grotius's death, in a treaty of 1648), that could be regarded as a legitimate spoil of a just war.

For fairly obvious reasons, this ingenious defence of the Dutch war with Spain does not appear in such an explicit form in *De Jure Belli ac Pacis*; but its basic components are still there. This is seldom appreciated, because again the attention of most readers has been fixated on Grotius's blunt rejection of the possibility of legitimate resistance and his extended critique of monarchomachic theories, which has led many people to assume that by the time of writing his later work he had more or less abandoned the Dutch cause and come around to a more monarchical way of thinking. Certainly, it is quite correct to say that Grotius offers a very negative view of resistance in *De Jure Belli ac Pacis*. He asserts, for instance, that 'as a general rule rebellion is not permitted by the law of nature', nor, for good measure, is it defensible under Hebraic law, the Gospel or early Christian practice.[19] He then went on systematically to demolish the central propositions of the monarchomachic position. I have already noted his attack on the idea that natural liberties are inalienable because a people may voluntarily enslave itself, but he also added a refutation of the belief that 'inferior magistrates' had somehow acquired special rights that make them the defenders of the peoples' freedoms. Grotius was unusually direct in his attack on this point: 'from the point of view of those possessing higher authority [inferior magistrates] are private persons. All governmental authority possessed by public officials is in fact so subordinated to the sovereign power that whatever they do contrary to the will of him who holds it is divested of authority and is, accordingly, to be considered as a private act.'[20]

The assumption that seems to colour many interpretations of Grotius's political views is that, since he was so hostile to the monarchomachic resistance theory, he must have been committed to its natural opposite: the theory of princely absolutism. But that is quite incorrect, since it ignores that what Grotius had earlier done was to produce a justification of the Dutch war with Spain that denied princely absolutism without recourse

[18] *Ibid.*, pp. 219 and 281–3.   [19] Grotius, *De Jure Belli ac Pacis*, pp. 138–46.
[20] *Ibid.*, p. 146.

to monarchomachism, or even the idea of resistance. Instead, all Grotius needed in *De Jure Belli ac Pacis* was the fairly uncontroversial proposition that 'a public war ought not to be waged except by the authority of him who holds the sovereign power'.[21] What that does is bring us to what, for Grotius, is always the really crucial question: who holds the sovereign power? Or, to put it more precisely: since the sovereign power may be divided, who holds which bits of the bundle of prerogatives and rights that collectively constitute *summum imperium*? Ownership of just a fragment of sovereignty may prove to be a sufficient basis for the prosecution of war since, as Grotius also remarked in *De Jure Belli ac Pacis*, 'whoever possesses a part of the sovereign power must possess also the right to defend his part'.[22] With that simple observation he hinted again at his old justification of the Dutch 'Revolt' as a form of just public war, because of the way in which the marks of sovereignty had been transferred among princes, representative institutions and the people. Moreover, he had validated this cause without lurching into what he clearly regarded as the immoderate and ill-founded position of the monarchomachs. While I do not mean to denigrate Grotius's intellectual integrity, it is perhaps worth noting that both the French and Swedish governments must have been absolutely delighted with an account of the law of nations that denied generally applicable theories of resistance, while being flexible enough to allow the Dutch to continue their conflict with Spain, a strategic concern of the highest order in the context of the Thirty Years War.

Before we leave the issue of divisible sovereignty, it is important to consider a related topic that is pregnant with significance for our understanding of the relevance of Grotius's work to modern world politics. As I have just explained, the most obvious backdrop to the treatment of sovereignty in *De Jure Belli ac Pacis* is the question of the legitimacy of the Dutch Revolt, to which Grotius had devoted considerable attention in his early career, and where he had already worked out a theory of the just war, rather than resistance, in terms of divided sovereignty. But another equally important context, especially in his later work, for the idea of divisible sovereignty was the case of 'unequal treaties' (*inequali foedere*). As Grotius put it, such an agreement was one that 'by the very character of the treaty, gives to one of the contracting parties a permanent advantage over the other; when, for example, one party is bound to preserve the sovereignty and majesty of the other'.[23] The classical examples he used were agreements between the Romans and their euphemistically titled

[21] *Ibid.*, pp. 100–1. It should be noted that Grotius only refers to 'public war' in this context; 'private' war could be carried on under certain circumstances without the need for the invocation of sovereign power at all. I will return to this point in the next section.
[22] *Ibid.*, p. 158.   [23] *Ibid.*, p. 130.

'friends and allies', or between Greek cities and their colonies, which were legally independent but nonetheless obliged to honour the mother city and show 'customary signs of respect'.[24]

Grotius made two main points about unequal treaties and their implications for political authority. In the first place, he argued that the mere fact of being the inferior party in such an agreement did not in itself compromise a state's sovereignty:

> a state (*populum*) is independent (*liberum*) which is not subject to the power (*potestati*) of another, even though a stipulation may have been made in a treaty of alliance that this state shall use its good offices to maintain the dignity of another state. If, therefore, a state bound by such a treaty remains independent, if it is not subject to the power of another, the conclusion follows that it retains its sovereignty (*summum imperium*).[25]

It seems to me that Grotius's line of thinking here is consistent with his general definition of sovereignty, in that if a state commits itself to any kind of inferior relationship that falls short of rendering it subject to the will of another state, then it can be understood as still being fully sovereign, even if its own freedom of action is curtailed.

As with Grotius's earlier discussion of the general concept of sovereignty, however, this idea is swiftly qualified by his second observation about unequal treaties: that, in practice, they very often lead to some division of the sovereign power, to the benefit of the superior party, because 'he who has the vantage in a treaty, if he is greatly superior in respect to power, gradually usurps the sovereignty properly so called'.[26] Although Grotius describes this development as a usurpation, he adds that if the people in question, or their rulers, do not offer resistance, in time 'the part of the weaker passes over into the right of ruling on the part of the stronger ... then either those who had been allies become subjects, or there is at any rate a division of sovereignty (*partitio fir summi imperii*)'.[27] Grotius was not particularly enthusiastic about the justifiability of resistance even against an act of usurpation. He was worried, ostensibly at least, about the possible dangers of using violence against one's own state, people and native land, and argued that a usurper should only be resisted if his position was maintained by force, if a pre-existing law specifically permitted resistance under those circumstances, or if resistance was mandated by the original and true owner of the sovereign prerogative in question.[28] Those specifications were, of course, sufficient to justify Dutch activities, where it would have been entirely plausible to argue that all three conditions applied against Spanish usurpations. Nevertheless, it

---

[24] *Ibid.*   [25] *Ibid.*, p. 131.   [26] *Ibid.*, p. 135.
[27] *Ibid.*, p. 136.   [28] *Ibid.*, pp. 159–62.

is worth bearing in mind that the mere fact of a usurpation is not sufficient to legitimize a war of resistance.

Although it is not, strictly speaking, an example of an unequal treaty, it is interesting to consider a specific case from Grotius's early work which reflects some similar issues concerning how, in practice, the division of sovereignty might work: the alliance between the Dutch and the king of Johore against the Portuguese. This issue is an important part of Grotius's treatise on the law of prize, *De Jure Praedae Commentarius*, of which only the excerpt justifying the freedom of the seas was published during his lifetime (the entire text was not published until its rediscovery in the nineteenth century). Grotius's purpose in writing this book was to provide a justification for the seizure by the Dutch of a Portuguese ship, the *Santa Catarina*. The bulk of the text is taken up with a discussion of the grounds for the Dutch war with the Portuguese, the thrust of which is to disprove that the Portuguese could ever have acquired sovereignty over the high seas or an exclusive right to trade with the East Indies, and that the Dutch were merely defending their own rights in that respect through the only recourse available to them: i.e., force. Moreover, Grotius argued, the other party in the war, the king of Johore, was a sovereign ruler in his own right, and therefore perfectly entitled to engage in a public war against the Portuguese, since they had offended his sovereign prerogatives; the Dutch had done nothing wrong in allying themselves with him because 'alliances and treaties with infidels may in many cases be justly contracted for the purpose of defending one's own rights'.[29]

Grotius, in short, could offer two main justifications for the seizure of the *Santa Catarina*, to suit two different points of view on the legal context of the war. In so far as judicial recourse was lacking, the Dutch were entitled to engage in a private war against the Portuguese, and were entitled to the prize as recompense for the injuries they had suffered. (I will look at this line of argument in more detail in the next section.) His second argument relied on the sovereign authority of the king of Johore. What probably first catches the attention here is Grotius's positive attitude towards the rights of this non-European ruler. Not only did Grotius assert the validity of treaties with heathens, he went further to praise the rationality and sagacity of the 'Indians of the Orient', and warned about the way in which 'shameless lust for property was wont to take cover under the excuse of introducing civilization into barbaric regions'.[30] He further argued that the Johorian king's decision to go to war against the Portuguese was clearly a just one: 'what could be more inequitable

---

[29] Hugo Grotius, *De Jure Praedae Commentarius*, trans. Gwladys Williams (Buffalo: William S. Hein, 1995), p. 315.
[30] *Ibid.*, p. 222.

than a prohibition imposed by a mercantile people upon a free king to prevent him from carrying on trade with another people? And what would constitute interference both with the law of nations and with the distinct jurisdictions of different princes, if such a prohibition does not?'[31]

These arguments have led numerous scholars to praise Grotius's enlightened attitude towards non-European peoples.[32] I will return to that idea, which does indeed have some merit, later; for now, though, I merely want to point to a somewhat different aspect of the argument in *De Jure Praedae* which was dealt with towards the end of the book in a rather suspiciously off-hand way. It is entirely understandable that Grotius was so anxious to praise the king of Johore and affirm his sovereign rights. He was, after all, a strategically important Dutch ally in a war against the Portuguese that was a matter of life and death for two maritime powers whose wealth depended on trade. Nevertheless, in giving the king this glowing report, Grotius created a problem for himself in terms of the legitimate ownership of the prize in question. The Dutch may have won it lawfully from the Portuguese, but, if they were fighting a public war on behalf of Johorian authority, it was clear, as Grotius acknowledged, that 'by natural law that prize was vested in the ruler of Johore himself'.[33]

Of course, the Dutch had hardly gone to all the trouble of capturing the *Santa Catarina* only to turn it over to another ruler, no matter how good an ally he was. The difficulty was swiftly solved, to Dutch satisfaction, through a couple of neat legal arguments that they and other Europeans (especially the British) would use time and again as they established their position in the East Indies. Although the prize was technically the property of the king of Johore, Grotius argued,

it was also capable of becoming a Dutch right through a grant on his part. Moreover, since war was waged on his behalf by means of ships belonging to the East India Company, at the Company's expense and at its peril...as well as by the exertions of the Company's servants, without any formal agreement as to compensation, the commonly accepted usages of war, confirmed by natural equity, clearly indicate that the prize in question was acquired *ipso iure* for the... [East India] Company.[34]

Grotius was not saying anything here that was out of keeping with his broader views on sovereignty. Kings, peoples and other institutions could, as we have seen, transfer their legal rights to one another if they so chose; they could transfer all of their rights or just a few of them; they could attach whatever conditions they liked in the process. If such transfers could

[31] *Ibid.*, p. 315.
[32] An excellent example is Charles Alexandrowicz, *An Introduction to the History of the Law of Nations in the East Indies* (Oxford: Clarendon Press, 1967).
[33] Grotius, *De Jure Praedae*, p. 316.   [34] *Ibid.*

be made between Europeans, why should they not also be made between Europeans and non-Europeans? After all, as Grotius had argued, the latter were no different in terms of the rights they originally possessed, nor did they lack the sagacity or rational capacity to make the appropriate decisions for themselves. If they wanted to transfer some of their sovereign prerogatives to, say, a European trading corporation in exchange for military services or a generous loan, what was a humble lawyer to do but record the transaction?

Grotius on private property in the law of nations

As this discussion of the seizure of the *Santa Catarina* has indicated, Grotius did not only talk about 'public wars' between the holders of sovereign powers. He was also interested in 'private wars' between individuals or corporations who lacked sovereignty, but nevertheless held certain rights that they were entitled to defend by violence if judicial recourse was denied or unavailable to them. The latter topic was really to the fore of his commentary on the law of prize, his reflections on the public authority of the king of Johore notwithstanding, and it remained a key theme in *De Jure Belli ac Pacis*.[35] The crucial point here is that the law of nations was not, in Grotius's scheme, exclusively a law *for* nations; it included rights and duties, albeit limited ones, for individuals and private corporations. While he conceptualized the rights of public authorities in terms of their possession of marks of sovereignty, the main vehicle that Grotius used to think about the rights of private individuals and bodies was the concept of property ownership. To complete our picture of the Grotian law of nations, then, I want to look more closely at his theory of how individuals may acquire property, and under what circumstances they are entitled to defend their rights with force.

Grotius's analysis of private property rights drew heavily on classical Roman law to identify two different kinds of ownership in the law of nations, each of which was acquired in its own way.[36] His account rested on a distinction between the original acquisition of property, before the

[35] The distinction is made clear in Grotius, *De Jure Belli ac Pacis*, p. 91, where Grotius also talks about mixed wars (i.e., ones between public authorities and private corporations). Although only a 'lawful authority' may wage a public war, private and mixed wars are not, *ipso facto*, illegitimate.

[36] Roman law dealt with many other forms of property and ways of acquiring it. *Occupatio* and *dominium* aside, however, Grotius argued that these were not part of natural law or the law of nations properly understood, but were contained within civil law. Other aspects of property rights were relevant only to 'each particular people in a state of peace', and it was therefore improper to describe them under the heading of the law of nations: Grotius, *De Jure Belli ac Pacis*, p. 295. For a general discussion, see W.W. Buckland, *A Manual of Roman Private Law*, 2nd edn (Cambridge University Press, 1947).

establishment of civil societies; and the institution of private property within civil society, founded on the consent of its members. According to Grotius, the first of these operated according to the principle of *occupatio*, which can be understood as appropriation; in the second context, property is called *dominium*, which is probably nearest to what we would call ownership today. The key to *occupatio* is the proposition, which Grotius had first advanced in *De Jure Praedae*, that everyone has a natural right to self-preservation. He began from an idea of individual self-ownership, observing that individuals already hold some rights even before the creation of the civil societal institution of *dominium*, because 'life, limbs and liberty would in that case be the possessions belonging to each, and no attack could be made upon these by another without injustice'.[37] He also claimed that at this early stage in human history all property in the world was held in common, with no individual ownership of land or things. And, since individuals were entitled to do what they must for survival, their rights to life, limbs and liberty were therefore extendable in this natural state through appropriation, such that 'each man could at once take whatever he wished for his own needs, and could consume whatever was capable of being consumed'.[38]

The right to appropriate through occupation, however, exists only as a natural right. Grotius argued that at some point in human history, as population levels increased and people began to form themselves into social associations, they transformed their naturally acquired possessions into a publicly recognized institution, *dominium*, regulated by laws made by the appropriate public authority. This fundamental change in the character of property could not, in Grotius's view, justly be the product of acts of individual will, 'for one could not know what things another wished to have, in order to abstain from them, and besides several might desire the same thing'.[39] It therefore had to come from 'a kind of agreement', and he supposed that, once the idea of community ownership had been abandoned and further unilateral appropriation was no longer allowed, the members of society simply decided to confirm each other in their ownership of what they had already occupied: 'all agreed, that whatever each one had taken possession of should be his property'.[40]

As we saw in the previous section, the idea of a pre-social condition of natural liberty was already well established in early modern thought,

---

[37] Grotius, *De Jure Belli ac Pacis*, p. 54.
[38] *Ibid.*, p. 186. In the *very* early history of mankind, 'when the human race could assemble' as a whole, community of property could coexist with the general *division* of lands into individual possession; as soon as such assembly became impossible, but before the creation of societies and *dominium*, *occupatio* became the only form of legitimate acquisition (*ibid.*, p. 206).
[39] *Ibid.*, p. 189.   [40] *Ibid.*, p. 190.

and was closely associated with the monarchomachic belief that it endowed everyone with rights which they retained into political society. Grotius broadly agreed with this description of the state of nature, but his disagreement with the justification of resistance on these grounds sprang from his view that they were wrong to regard the rights associated with natural liberty as inalienable. Depending on the circumstances under which people agreed to join together in a civil society, translating their property rights into *dominium*, they might even give up their rights over their persons in such a way as to deprive themselves of any justification for resistance against the holder or holders of the sovereign power. Although he believed that a public authority should always act with due regard for 'human frailty', Grotius believed that the argument from natural property rights could only offer a very slender justification for resisting public authority, even when the individual in question was facing death.[41] In that respect, and in comparison with later Lockean theories of appropriation as the basis for enduring political rights, Grotius's theory appears highly conservative. In Karl Olivecrona's view, for example, the central difference between Grotius and Locke is that the former 'allowed appropriation without the consent of others only in the earliest stage of the world and presumably for very limited purposes; it lost its importance with the introduction of *dominium* by way of convention'.[42]

It does seem likely that Grotius saw the idea that individuals have a natural right to acquire property as defunct in the context of the societies he lived in, where ownership was presumably to be understood in terms of *dominium*. But in a different way, Grotius anticipated an element of the more radical theory of appropriation that was later to be at the heart of the Lockean account. Grotius's distinction between *occupatio* and *dominium* rests, as we have seen, on the fact that the associated rights belong to very different situations: the state of nature and civil society. Olivecrona is correct to observe that one way in which Grotius understood this distinction was temporal, in the sense that the state of nature was part of the early history of mankind that preceded the formation of civil societies. At the same time, however, Grotius also took a *geographical* view of the distinction, observing that the natural right to *occupatio* might still be exercised and defended 'if one finds himself in places without inhabitants, as on the sea, in a wilderness, or on vacant islands'.[43] And one would be justified in supposing that the main example he had in mind here was not so much the high seas, where the Dutch were defending their rights to free navigation on the basis of the argument that the seas could never be made

---

[41] *Ibid.*, pp. 149 and 151.   [42] Olivecrona, 'Locke's Theory of Appropriation', 223.
[43] Grotius, *De Jure Belli ac Pacis*, p. 92.

subject to *dominium*, but rather that *locus classicus* of the Lockean theory of appropriation, America, where, according to Grotius, 'the community of property, arising from extreme simplicity' could still be observed even in his era.[44]

The question about the property rights of indigenous peoples in America had already been thoroughly debated when Grotius offered this opinion, and three main positions had previously been worked out. Some medieval canon lawyers, such as Hostiensis, had denied that non-Christians had any rights whatsoever, either public rights of sovereignty or private rights to property, simply on the grounds that they were infidels or heathens. This view was rejected in the context of America, however, by Franciscus de Vitoria, who had countered by insisting that being a non-Christian was not enough by itself to serve as a disqualification from holding property or public office, and that the American Indians could therefore be regarded as rights-holders; Vitoria also argued that there was no evidence to suggest that the Indians were incapable of reason, which was another possible reason for denying them private and public rights.[45] Both the Hostiensian and Vitorian positions were somewhat extreme in their implications. Hostiensis's argument effectively denied any rights whatsoever to non-Christians, and Vitoria was certainly not alone in finding that an uncomfortable and undesirable conclusion; many others, such as the Polish canon lawyer Paulus Vladimiri, had already offered similar rebuttals.[46] Vitoria, however, left Europeans in the situation where they had to show such a degree of respect for other peoples' sovereignty and property that, if taken seriously, it would imply handing back the lands the Spanish had conquered in the Americas and would have put a halt to further colonialism.[47] Because of these problems, the most popular position in the later middle ages and after the Conquest was a more intermediate one, originally associated with Pope Innocent IV, which argued that non-Christians could keep their public and private rights, provided that they properly observed natural law.

[44] *Ibid.*, p. 187. On this theme in Locke's work, see Herman Lebovics, 'The Uses of America in Locke's *Second Treatise on Government*', *Journal of the History of Ideas*, 47 (1986), 567–81, and James Tully, *An Approach to Political Philosophy: Locke in Contexts* (Cambridge University Press, 1993).

[45] Vitoria may well have been worried about the possibility that the denial of rights to Indians on the grounds that they were non-Christians could have led on to a denial of similar rights to sinners, on the grounds that they were not good Christians, a doctrine of John Wycliffe that Vitoria was anxious to refute. See Franciscus de Vitoria, *De Indis et De Jure Belli Reflectiones*, trans. John Pawley Bale (Washington: Carnegie Institution of Washington, 1917), pp. 121–5.

[46] Stanislaus F. Belch, *Paulus Vladimiri and his Doctrine Concerning International Law and Politics*, 2 vols. (London: Mouton, 1965).

[47] See Anthony Pagden, *Lords of all the World: Ideologies of Empire in Spain, Britain and France, 1500–1800* (New Haven: Yale University Press, 1995).

The canonists loved this, because it attached considerable weight to the Pope's authority as the chief interpreter of natural law, but it was also broadly acceptable to both the supporters and the deniers of non-Christians' rights, since it began by granting those rights, while at the same time offering a rationale for removing them if any breaches of natural law occurred.[48]

As Richard Tuck has noted, Grotius's general position on the question of non-Christians' rights was very close to Innocent's doctrine that there was nothing to stop them having rights, but that they were still subject to natural law and could be punished by Christian rulers for breaches of the natural law.[49] But with regard to property, Grotius introduced two further ingenious twists. First of all, his analysis of *occupatio* effectively turned the debate about the legitimate acquisition of property in America from one about the moral or intellectual qualities of the Indians into one about whether or not they actually *had* exercised their natural right of appropriation. It was no longer enough simply that the indigenous peoples of America not be living in a way that breached natural law; they also had to have exhausted all the possibilities for appropriation, and perhaps even formulated their own civil societal institution of *dominium*, if Europeans were to be denied rights to appropriate property in America for themselves. The fact that the American Indians had not done so, but continued to hold large tracts of land in what Grotius took to be a simple state of communal property, was extremely permissive towards colonial settlement.

There is a second, and even more important, strand to Grotius's argument, where he suggested that appropriation could continue even in places where another ruler's jurisdiction had been established and was being properly exercised. Grotius took pains to argue that *occupatio* has a 'twofold' implication (*occupatio duplex*): it is the basis for both the public rights of sovereignty (*imperium*), and the private rights of ownership (*dominium*). In this context, he also distinguished between two different subjects to which sovereignty applies. On the one hand, in its 'primary' sense, sovereignty is jurisdiction over persons; in its other, secondary, sense, it relates to the possession of territory. Usually, Grotius conceded, these two attributes of sovereignty and ownership are acquired together by a single act, but, just as the public rights associated with

---

[48] For an excellent general treatment of medieval thinking on this issue, see James Muldoon, *Popes, Lawyers and Infidels: The Church and the Non-Christian World, 1250–1550* (Philadelphia: University of Pennsylvania Press, 1979); for legal discussions after the Conquest, see L.C. Green and Olive Dickason, *The Law of Nations and the New World* (Edmonton: University of Alberta Press, 1989).

[49] Tuck, *The Rights of War and Peace*, p. 103.

jurisdiction over persons are separable from one another, so the public dimension of jurisdiction always remains distinct from the private rights of ownership.[50] In other words, foreigners may, through appropriate procedures of course, acquire ownership rights to territory in another state, without interfering with the sovereign jurisdiction that a ruler has over his or her subjects. Grotius illustrated his point with a quotation from the classical author Siculus (from a work entitled *On the Condition of the Fields*): 'When the lands assigned to colonies proved to be insufficient, those who were in charge of the allotment and division assigned to future citizens lands which they had taken from neighbouring territories. The jurisdiction over the lands which they assigned nevertheless remained under the control of those from whose territory they were taken.'[51]

This may seem a little arcane at first, but it is essential to realize how significant this thesis about the separability of jurisdiction and ownership is. Although Grotius did not make the point entirely clear, it seems at least plausible to suppose that this might permit ownership rights to be established on territories in other states simply for the reason that they had been never been cultivated or had been vacated for one reason or another; certainly, Grotius said that rights could be transferred 'not only by express agreement, but also by abandonment of ownership and the occupation which follows it or assumes a new force from it'.[52] It might be the case that 'natural equity', which we saw was used in *De Jure Praedae* to justify the Dutch taking a prize that by rights belonged to the king of Johore, would provide sufficient grounds for the unilateral occupation of lands that were in another sovereign's domain. Or even, most permissive of all, the natural right of self-preservation might justify people in crowded countries, whose lands were insufficient for their population, re-locating to less densely populated parts of the world, where they could on their own initiative acquire ownership rights over territories under another ruler's sovereign jurisdiction.

Divisible sovereignty and private property in principle

Let me summarize this analysis of Grotius's account of the law of nations by highlighting the fact that it was organized around a fundamental distinction between public and private wars, and hence between public rights of sovereignty and private rights of property. In a nutshell, the central

[50] Grotius, *De Jure Belli ac Pacis*, pp. 206–7.   [51] *Ibid.*, p. 207.
[52] *Ibid.*, pp. 227–8. This may refer more to the transference of public rights in the context of the gradual usurpation that, as we saw earlier, often attends unequal treaties; but if it could apply to marks of sovereignty, perhaps it could also relate to private property rights.

message of his treatise was that only the holders of marks of sovereignty were permitted to undertake a public war, and he delineated the particular conditions under which they should do so. Although his belief in the divisibility of the sovereign power made this argument less absolutist than it may at first sight appear, it was nevertheless quite a conservative doctrine. It automatically constrained the liberty of anyone who did not possess at least a portion of the sovereign power, since there were no circumstances under which they might undertake a public war; at a stroke, Grotius had ruled out one of the most popular resistance theories of his day, predicated on the notion that 'inferior magistrates' had a right to undertake public wars on behalf of the natural liberties of the people.

The conservative implications of Grotius's theory of public authority in the law of nations were not only moderated by his views on the divisibility of sovereignty, however, but also by his argument that private individuals also possessed rights in the law of nations through their natural rights over their persons and their property. He was careful to ensure that this did not imply an even more general and popular right of resistance by arguing that, with the establishment of civil society, natural rights were replaced by a new institution of private ownership that was subject to the public authority of the sovereign power. But at the same time he identified certain specific circumstances under which individuals or corporations could continue to exercise their natural right to acquire property, and were entitled to defend that right with force if necessary: the key conditions were that lands existed that were still under pre-social communal ownership, and hence available for appropriation; and, for private war, that no recourse to public judicial proceedings was available to correct an injustice. As I have pointed out, it is suspiciously coincidental, to say the least, that this account of public and private rights in the law of nations, despite its broadly conservative orientation, provided justifications for the Dutch 'Revolt' as a public war against the usurpations of Philip II and as a private war with the Portuguese and Spanish in the East and West Indies. I have also speculated that this fact may go some way towards explaining the immediate popularity of *De Jure Belli ac Pacis*, particularly among those governments which were anxious to validate Dutch involvement in the war against the Habsburg powers, but were loath to present their own subjects with a rationale for rebellion.

It is hard to see Grotius's views on divisible sovereignty and individuals' private rights as an account of the emerging Westphalian system, but that should not lead us to reject them out of hand as a nostalgic or idealistic 'domestic analogy'. In fact, they look much more like a remarkably prescient analysis of how Europeans would conduct themselves over the next three centuries in the world beyond Europe, appropriating vast swathes of land and artfully manipulating treaties with indigenous rulers, not even always noticeably 'unequal' ones, so as to give themselves a share in the latter's public authority. Moreover, as we will see in chapter 4, later legal scholars found Grotius's propositions extremely helpful for legitimizing those practices, although they added a number of innovations that reflected both their desire to find some kind of higher moral purpose for the legal order they were describing, and the increasingly indisputable fact that what had become normal for relations between Europeans was distinctly abnormal in relations between Europeans and non-Europeans, and *vice versa*. Before looking at those later theories, though, I first want to turn to the practices of colonialism and imperialism, to see just how close a fit with Grotian ideas they exhibit.

3 Colonialism, imperialism and extra-European international politics

It is hardly surprising that Hugo Grotius's theory of the law of nations gained its colossal popularity. As I have already noted, his account was practically tailor-made for the main Protestant powers in the Thirty Years War, in the sense that it justified their prosecution of the war against Spain and the Habsburgs without endorsing more general theories of resistance that might have proved awkward at home; sufficient reason, no doubt, for Gustavus Adolphus's famous liking for carrying *De Jure Belli ac Pacis* around with him on his campaigns. The more lasting significance of Grotius's work, however, lies in its relevance to people who wanted to justify colonialism on the basis of individuals' rights in the law of nations to appropriate unoccupied or uncultivated lands, and to people who wanted to justify the assertion of public authority by European states in the extra-European world. Both practices were radical extensions of Hugo Grotius's original position, and it is by no means obvious that he would have given an unqualified endorsement to either of them, but it is nevertheless fair to say that over time an especially close relationship developed between the specific propositions of the Grotian theory of the law of nations – his ideas of divisible sovereignty and private property – and the modern practices of colonialism and imperialism. Certainly, there was more of an affinity here than there was between the Grotian theory and the practice of the 'Westphalian' states-system that developed within Europe.

In this chapter I want to turn my attention to these practices, examining how colonial and imperial systems were established and what kinds of international relationships they involved. As I explained in chapter 1, this topic is largely absent from the work of orthodox theorists of order in world politics, who have concentrated overwhelmingly on the evolution of the European states-system and have to all intents and purposes ignored the simultaneous emergence of colonial and imperial systems beyond Europe. My purpose, in brief, is to provide a parallel account of the development of international relations in the extra-European world to that which orthodox theorists have given for the European states-system.

Obviously, it would be impossible to give a comprehensive account of all the dimensions of politics in the entire extra-European world during a period of roughly three and a half centuries. The conventional history of the development of the states-system is a simplification of European politics over a lengthy period, accentuating some aspects of the relations between European states and underplaying others in order to identify a theoretically intelligible pattern. Orthodox theorists pay little attention, for example, to lingering 'anomalies' like the Germanic confederation of states between 1815 and 1870, or the international personality of the papacy, because they believe, with good reason, that these phenomena were departures from the normal pattern of European international relations. Rather than clutter up their accounts with these aberrations, they are more interested in describing how dynastic monarchs consolidated their absolute sovereignty over their territorial possessions during the wars of religion, and how they adopted a practice of recognizing each other's equality and independence. In much the same way, my account of the world beyond Europe is not intended to be anything more than an analysis focused on a few broad and, I believe, significant themes.[1] I recognize that other scholars might identify different and equally significant phenomena in extra-European international relations, and nothing I will say here should be construed as denying that such projects could be carried out.

Even with my self-imposed restriction to looking at the development of this pattern of order, there is still a vast amount of historical material to be considered here, and to make it more digestible I have divided it into two sections. First, I will describe how colonies of European settlers were established in North America, and how the post-revolutionary American states-union colonized the remainder of the continent through its westward expansion. Then, I will explain how Europeans came to acquire their imperial authority over non-European peoples in the East Indies, how they used their authority to transform indigenous property systems and how they defended it through doctrines such as 'paramountcy'. This distinction reflects genuine differences in the kinds of international relations involved in the two instances, but in many respects the division

[1] This, I might add, is how concepts are usually constructed in the social sciences. For a seminal statement, see Max Weber, *The Methodology of the Social Sciences*, trans. E. Shils and H. Finch (New York: Free Press, 1949), and for a worked-out example, see Weber, *The Protestant Ethic and the Spirit of Capitalism*, trans. Talcott Parsons (London: Routledge, 1930). For a good commentary, see Thomas Burger, *Max Weber's Theory of Concept Formation: History, Laws and Ideal Types* (Durham: Duke University Press, 1976). The acid test for a concept constructed on these lines is whether or not it does succeed in highlighting phenomena of significance for its audience, and that can only be assessed once my argument is complete.

I am making here is purely for reasons of clarity, and the key point that I want to stress is that both colonialism and imperialism had very similar dynamics, especially with respect to the degree to which both involved the division of sovereignty and the assertion of individuals' rights to property.

The colonization of North America

The major distinguishing feature of European activity in North America was the establishment of settlements composed of individuals who owned their property on 'free and easy' terms, as the popular description had it. Colonialism, in the British model at least, was also characterized by a highly decentralized system of government, with public authority and jurisdiction divided between the mother country, colonial agencies or proprietors, local settlers and sometimes, albeit rarely, indigenous peoples. Although it underwent a considerable re-structuring after the American Revolution, this framework of property rights and divided sovereignty continued to inform subsequent American practices, and had an especially powerful impact on the tenurial and political arrangements that were made for the subsequent expansion of the United States as it acquired new territories in the West and began to exert its imperial control over states beyond the American continent.

The first question to ask is *why* the practice of colonialism took on these forms. Why did colonial settlers in the New World typically enjoy 'allodial' (i.e. unencumbered) tenures, rather than feudal ones? It is significant, from an international legal point of view, that Thomas Jefferson maintained that this was the result of a 'universal law' that applied to all colonization of unoccupied or uncultivated lands, and his opinion certainly accorded with the widely accepted opinions of theorists like Grotius and Vattel.[2] It is also true that ideas about the 'completeness' of property ownership, and its inherently allodial nature, were well-established themes in both Roman law and pre-Norman English common law, and were central to early modern speculation about natural law. But the details through which colonial land tenures were worked out in practice had a more specific, and somewhat more humble, origin. Most of the first British grants of land in North America, for example, exhibited a strong resemblance to earlier grants that had been made in the context

[2] This theme in Jefferson's thinking is discussed in more detail in chapter 4. Some interesting studies of the influence of Vattel on American revolutionary thought can be found in Daniel Lang, *Foreign Policy in the Early Republic: The Law of Nations and the Balance of Power* (Baton Rouge: Louisiana State University Press, 1985), and Peter Onuf and Nicholas Onuf, *Federal Union, Modern World: The Law of Nations in an Age of Revolutions, 1776–1814* (Madison House, 1993).

of medieval reclamations; in many cases they were modelled on grants that had been made for irrigation and drainage projects in places like the Fens.[3] The parallel should be clear, although it was rather an unfortunate one for the original inhabitants of the Americas, whose rights were yet further denuded by the analogy. During the middle ages, especially in the dramatic expansion of agricultural activity that took place after the tenth century, wildernesses that had never been brought under cultivation before were extensively reclaimed.[4] Established feudal seigneurs generally asserted their political jurisdiction over these areas, but in a sense the activity created entirely new lands and thus opened up the opportunity to establish new forms of tenure. Moreover, the most basic fact about reclamation and colonization in the middle ages was that, even by the normal standards of a medieval peasant, it was exceptionally hard work, and was often conducted in remote places where coercion was hard to apply. To entice people to undertake the work, they needed to be offered some kind of lure, and the usual bait was to grant unusually generous tenures over the land that they reclaimed and then cultivated. By the high middle ages there was a fairly well-established practice, sharply distinguished from other feudal tenures, whereby colonizers of reclaimed 'new' land enjoyed their property with only minimal obligations, and often in a monetized form rather than in terms of requirements to perform military or other services for the seigneur.

The broader significance of this development for the social structure of medieval Europe is questionable because in some cases colonization was undertaken by peoples unable to escape from feudal obligations in the first place, and often when colonizers did win initially permissive tenures they suffered from expansions of feudalization, their liberties giving way under the seigneurial imposition of new encumbrances.[5] Those feudalizing efforts were not always decisive, however. Sometimes, medieval settlements founded through colonization were so ubiquitous that they swamped attempts by seigneurs to reduce peasants to vassalage. The Netherlands are a case in point.[6] Attempts to establish ties of personal dependence

---

[3] Marshall Harris, *Origins of the Land Tenure System in the United States* (Ames: Iowa State College Press, 1953), pp. 15 and 73.

[4] On this topic, see Richard Koebner, 'The Settlement and Colonization of Europe', in M.M. Postan (ed.), *The Agrarian Life of the Middle Ages*, 2nd edn (Cambridge University Press, 1966), pp. 1–91; Bryce Lyon, 'Medieval Real Estate Developments and Freedom', *American Historical Review*, 63 (1957), 47–61; and, for a particularly detailed case study, William H. TeBrake, *Medieval Frontier: Culture and Ecology in Rijnland* (College Station: Texas A&M University Press, 1985).

[5] Koebner, 'The Settlement and Colonization of Europe', p. 5, but for a qualification to this general claim see p. 75.

[6] For two interesting, and somewhat contrasting, discussions, see J.J. Woltjer, 'Dutch Privileges, Real and Imagined', and I. Schöffer, 'The Batavian Myth during the Sixteenth

and vassalage in the Netherlands, especially in the relatively autonomous northern and western regions, were always seriously compromised by the weak material and political resources upon which local elites could draw. Even in the Southern Netherlands, where some feudal ties remained relatively strong, special agreements known as 'copes' were made between the seigneurs and the colonizers that were extremely favourable to the latter: obligations were reduced to the form of a small tax or tithe, in return for which colonists received near-absolute rights over their property, including, for example, the right to dispose of their land as they saw fit.[7] The weakness of the seigneurial system in the Netherlands was exacerbated by the fact that, even in those regions that were relatively well integrated into wider European feudal regimes, the sheer extent of reclamation and colonization assumed such proportions that seigneurial claims to feudal dues were simply outweighed by the practice of free tenure. Here, unusually in comparison with rest of Europe, custom worked against feudalization rather than in its favour, leading to the establishment of what generally came to be known as the 'Dutch' or 'Flemish' right.[8]

Not only did they enjoy these remarkably free tenures, the medieval colonizers in the Netherlands were also granted extensive rights to administer low justice and self-government, normally through a sheriff system. What is more, they were able to retain these political privileges, often because of the practical necessities of maintaining the cultivability of the new settlements. The inhabitants of the newly reclaimed lands in the Netherlands usually had to construct dikes and drainage systems to protect their farms from flooding; this imposed considerable demands on the administrative capacity of the relevant communities, and served to enhance the voice of freeholders in their government, especially in non-cope peat reclamation areas, i.e., those areas in the northern and western Netherlands, where extreme levels of local autonomy were often the original state of affairs.[9] As a consequence of the practicalities of sustaining land productivity after reclamation in these low-lying regions of the Netherlands, colonial settlements did not just develop a surprising degree of individual freedom in the form of allodial property rights; they also

and Seventeenth Centuries', both in J.S. Bromley and E.H. Kossmann (eds.), *Britain and the Netherlands: Volume 5, Some Political Mythologies* (The Hague: Martinus Nijhoff, 1975), pp. 19–35 and 78–101 respectively, and see especially p. 85.

[7] TeBrake, *Medieval Frontier*, p. 50.

[8] G.P. van de Ven, *Man-Made Lowlands: History of Water Management and Land Reclamation in the Netherlands*, 2nd edn (Utrecht: Uitgeverij Matrijs, 1994), p. 61, and George Masselman, *The Cradle of Colonialism* (London: Yale University Press, 1963), p. 10.

[9] Jan de Vries, *The Dutch Rural Economy in the Golden Age, 1500–1700* (London: Yale University Press, 1974), p. 36, and C. Dekker, 'The Representation of the Freeholders in the Drainage Districts of Zeeland West of the Scheldt during the Middle Ages', *Acta Historiae Neerlandicae*, 8 (1975), 1–30.

acquired extensive rights for self-government, although usually within the context of an overarching seigneurial claim to ultimate jurisdiction over the land. One can see, perhaps, whence Grotius's conception of *occupatio*, and especially *occupatio duplex*, might have originated: the transposition of a Roman legal concept onto a familiar Dutch practice.[10]

Attempts to establish colonies in North America faced very similar problems in terms of the exactions involved and the difficulty in maintaining coercive control over settlers, and colonizers dealt with them in very similar ways. It is therefore unsurprising that most settlement agencies and noble proprietors in British North America held their lands under an extremely unencumbered tenure described as of the Manor of East Greenwich, in free and common socage (the exceptions were the grants of Maryland in 1632, Pennsylvania in 1681 and Georgia in 1732). In seventeenth-century England, this particular formula of 'the Manor of East Greenwich' was an increasingly common way of establishing tenurial rights and obligations, the main importance of which was that it represented a way of defusing feudal encumbrances, like the need to render military service, and thus offered the prospect of owning land in as near to an absolute, exclusive form as possible.[11] The principle was employed in colonial land grants for very similar reasons to the grants made in medieval colonization: the offer of free and easy tenures would encourage emigration and colonial settlement, especially given the risks and hardships involved.[12]

Beyond the initial grants to noble proprietors and corporate agencies, the logic of colonization also had an impact on the tenures under which actual settlers held their lands, with individual settlers typically coming to possess relatively absolute and exclusive rights of ownership. To understand how this came about, it is helpful to distinguish between systems adopted in colonies settled under the auspices of corporate settlement agencies, like the Massachusetts Bay Company, and royal colonies or those settled by the efforts of individual proprietors, like William Penn or Lord Baltimore. In New England, the corporate settlement agencies which were granted tracts of land organized settlement

---

[10] There are some fairly extensive discussions of Dutch reclamation practices in Grotius's analysis of the acquisition of property in *De Jure Belli ac Pacis*, although implying, I suspect, that this was more of a local custom than a genuine feature of the law of nations: see Hugo Grotius, *De Jure Belli ac Pacis Libri Tres*, trans. Francis Kelsey (Oxford: Clarendon Press, 1925), pp. 300–5. See also Grotius, *The Jurisprudence of Holland*, trans. R.W. Lee (Oxford: Clarendon Press, 1926), pp. 64–75 and 86–93.

[11] Neil Hamilton, *America Began at Greenwich* (London: Poseidon Press, 1976). It should be admitted that some historians have described this as rather an empty formula, partly because of its growing popularity in England: see Edward Cheyney, 'The Manor of East Greenwich in the County of Kent', *American Historical Review*, 11 (1906), 29–35.

[12] Harris, *Origins of the Land Tenure System*, p. 148.

according to a system of townships. Beyond this official system, however, colonies were also established by squatting (as at Plymouth) and by
unauthorized purchases from the local Indians (as at the Rhode Island
and Providence Plantations). In the townships, and in many of the un-
official settlements, land that had originally been given to the agencies by the king under generous terms, was in turn granted by them
to individual settlers under exceptionally free tenures. In this respect,
colonial practice antedated the general freeing of tenures in England.
Before equivalent developments in England, except for areas where extensive reclamation had already taken place, like the Fens or Kent (where,
in fact, the Manor of East Greenwich was situated),[13] the general tenurial
arrangement of individual land-holding by New England settlers was
allodial in the sense that they owned their property absolutely, with
no associated obligations either to the king or even to the corporate
agencies.[14] Grants were usually small and fairly homogeneous, differing mainly with respect to the size of families, leading to a society composed of townships rather like the Netherlands farming communities of
'free and equal agriculturalists', with allodial and similarly sized land-
holdings.[15] It was, in effect, a system of 'owner-occupiers', with individual
settlers and their families coming into direct and exclusive possession of
land that they could occupy and use: very close to the Grotian theory of
appropriation.

The situation in the proprietorial colonies was slightly different. Here,
a vast tract of land was granted in the first instance to a single individual
(the proprietor), who was then at liberty to establish more or less whatever scheme he desired of granting land to actual settlers. Some large-
scale English proprietors tried to use their original grants to establish
feudal land systems within their domains; this was the case, for example,
in Maryland and the Carolinas (where Locke's main colonial involvement was). However, it was quickly discovered that it was as difficult to
make feudalism work in this new context as it had been in the medieval
Netherlands. This was only partly because settlers were not initially attracted by offers of land bound by feudal obligations to a proprietor, but
also because the availability of free land in the colony and non-feudal land
systems in other colonies made it difficult to sustain feudal tenures in the
face of these rival attractions: settlers, including European 'indentured
labourers', could and did go elsewhere, which goes some of the way towards explaining the attractiveness of importing slave labour from Africa

---

[13] Alan Everitt, *Continuity and Colonization: The Evolution of Kentish Settlement* (Leicester
University Press, 1986).
[14] Harris, *Origins of the Land Tenure System*, p. 116.
[15] Kenneth Lockridge, *Settlement and Unsettlement in Early America: The Crisis of Political
Legitimacy before the Revolution* (Cambridge University Press, 1981), p. 20.

as an option for the colonial planters. Sometimes rival tenurial systems even existed within the same colony, as in the Carolinas where around two-fifths of the land was held as feudal estates and three-fifths owned by settlers under freehold.[16] In general, the proprietorial English colonies illustrate a process by which the land was granted and gradually re-granted to individuals, all the time under free and easy terms. In most cases, ownership rights eventually came to be held by the actual occupier of the land, with hardly any reservations. A broadly similar pattern of colonial settlement unfolded under the auspices of another major colonial state, the Dutch, where *patroons* attempted to create the same kinds of feudal estates, and met with the same problems.[17]

Politically and judicially, the New England townships were again in a rather similar position to farming communities in the reclamation districts of the Netherlands, characterized by weak seigneurial control and a high degree of local self-government with widespread popular participation, often for reasons of distance, and also because of the requirements of maintaining the settlement through crises of various sorts.[18] Of course, this led to considerable confusion about the ultimate location of sovereignty. The formal title of sovereignty was held by the monarch, but the various prerogatives that collectively constituted political authority – the powers to tax, to organize relations between the colony and the Indians or with other foreign powers, to organize the military defence of the colony and to make judicial decisions – were distributed between the Crown, the proprietary agencies and the settlers' local institutions. This situation was exacerbated yet further by the formation of a settlement agency actually based in the colony, the Massachusetts Bay Company, which meant that a local, American-based agency possessed all the municipal rights and legislative authority endowed by its Charter.[19] The formal sovereign title was still held by the Crown; but the crucial legal and political question of who possessed which marks of sovereignty was much more convoluted. This confused situation was put to use in the revolt against Governor Andros: in a well-known 1691 pamphlet, *The Revolution in New England Justified*, the rights in property through occupation and the marks of sovereignty granted under the Charter were

---

[16] Harris, *Origins of the Land Tenure System*, p. 135.
[17] S.G. Nissenson, *The Patroon's Domain* (New York: Columbia University Press, 1937), and Oliver Rink, *Holland on the Hudson: An Economic and Social History of Dutch New York* (Ithaca: Cornell University Press, 1986). Dutch settlement was still relatively small scale because, like the French, they were more interested in developing the fur trade than establishing plantations: see Van Cleaf Bachman, *Peltries or Plantations: The Economic Policies of the Dutch West India Company in New Netherland, 1623–1639* (Baltimore: Johns Hopkins University Press, 1969).
[18] Harris, *Origins of the Land Tenure System*, p. 285.
[19] *Ibid.*, p. 106.

both used to justify resistance, much as they were later used in the more decisive revolution of the eighteenth century.[20]

The proprietary colonies and the estates held by the Dutch *patroons* generally exhibited more feudal, or, perhaps more accurately, 'mock-feudal', political and judicial forms. In these cases, an unusually wide range of sovereign powers were delegated by the Crown to the proprietors, or by the West India Company to the *patroon*. Baltimore, for instance, was 'given all the rights of government' and so, with a few more reservations (including rights of taxation), was Penn.[21] The *patroons* were also, in a manner deliberately reminiscent of feudal institutions, granted full powers of jurisdiction in their colonies.[22] The proprietors and *patroons* were not formally sovereigns; they held their grants as fiefs. But, consistent with that status, they were explicitly granted several marks of sovereignty, and indeed often received far more of those than would have been usual under most normal feudal arrangements on the European continent. In itself, this obviously treated sovereignty as divisible. Furthermore, attempts by proprietors and *patroons* to exercise these sovereign powers to the detriment of the settlers met much the same fate as attempts to settle the land under feudal tenures. It simply led to the loss of tenants to more congenial colonies. The result in the *patroons'* domains of New Netherland, was not so much the construction of local institutions of governance, but a less formal system similar to the fairly participatory systems of the Netherlands.[23]

I raise all these details to illustrate a simple, but very important, point: the settlement of North America is often taken to be one of the principal developments of the modern era; indeed, it is customarily seen as *the* great demarcation between the medieval and modern worlds. But what we see if we look closely at how colonial settlement was actually carried out is an activity that is at odds with the conventional account of the defining characteristics of how the modern form of international order emerged. We do not see international rights and duties being removed from individuals and vested exclusively in the state; states were becoming more important, that should not be denied, but at the same time the private rights of individuals in the law of nations were not simply being maintained, but were actively deepened and extended through the increasingly normal practice of granting tenures under free and easy terms. Moreover,

---

[20] In Peter Force (ed.), *Tracts and Other Papers, Relating Principally to the Origin, Settlement and Progress of the Colonies in North America*, 4 vols. (Washington: Peter Force, 1836–46), vol. IV, especially pp. 15 and 18.

[21] Harris, *Origins of the Land Tenure System*, pp. 120–4.

[22] Nissenson, *Patroon's Domain*, p. 24.

[23] Rink, *Holland on the Hudson*, p. 228, and see also Nissenson, *Patroon's Domain*, pp. 153–65.

we do not witness the consolidation of public authority in the hands of the absolute holders of territorial sovereignty, each possessing his or her own carefully defined zone of domestic jurisdiction. On the contrary, we see the profusion of divided sovereignty, re-cast in the form of decentralized systems of colonial governance. To the extent that we can think of the colonization of North America as an international practice, and one would have to have a peculiarly narrow conception of the 'international' to deny it that status, it is very clear that this reflects a completely different kind of international order from that which was simultaneously developing on the European continent.[24]

The revolution wrought substantial changes in how America was perceived by theorists of international relations. Nineteenth-century international lawyers did talk about the post-revolutionary American Union as an example of the existence of semi-sovereign states in the modern world, but they tended to deny it any real significance because all of the international personality, the 'external' sovereignty, was vested in the Federal government, which was to all intents and purposes an ordinarily equal and independent state like European ones.[25] Complications occasionally intruded into this picture, for example over the question of whether the Confederate States should be internationally recognized during the Civil War, but on the whole America more or less drops off the mainstream picture of international relations after the revolution. What this neglects, however, is one of the most distinctively international activities of the post-revolutionary United States: namely, its continuing tendency towards expansion, especially by purchasing or annexing territories in the West, often after violent conflicts (with Mexico, for example) or prolonged diplomatic engagements with European powers.[26] The Americans also developed a practice of transforming the western territories into new states, i.e., members of the Union, according to a unique procedure that was explicitly designed so as to be different from the imperialism established by Europeans in Asia and Africa, but which nevertheless could be viewed as a particular form of recognition of semi-sovereignty. The post-revolutionary expansion was, however, still governed by certain basic principles that were shared with nineteenth-century European international lawyers and colonial administrators, particularly the belief that the world outside existing European settlements was uncivilized and needed

---

[24] For a good discussion of this point, although one that fails to analyse divisible sovereignty and individuals' property in the colonial context, see Daniel Deudney, 'The Philadelphian System: Sovereignty, Arms Control, and Balance of Power in the American States-Union', *International Organization*, 49 (1995), 191–228.

[25] I will return to this point in chapter 4.

[26] An interesting survey in this respect is David M. Pletcher, *The Diplomacy of Annexation: Texas, Oregon and the Mexican War* (Columbia: University of Missouri Press, 1973).

to be transformed through the establishment of permanent, organized populations; the development of commercial and economic activity; the provision of good government; and the guarantee of the fundamental rights of the individuals living there.[27] Having described the main themes involved in the practice of pre-revolutionary colonial settlement in North America, what I want to do now is to look at their proximity to the subsequent practice of post-revolutionary westward expansion, which involved the conversion of even greater swathes of territory into states.

In part, the expansive tendencies of the American states-union related to the widely held belief that republican virtue would be best safeguarded in the context of a democratic political system by ensuring the dispersal of property ownership throughout the population. In nineteenth-century Britain, they used property ownership to determine who should be given the franchise; in America, they gave everyone the vote, but then decided that everyone ought to own property.[28] One of the foremost spokesmen for this point of view was Thomas Hart Benton, the senator from Missouri, who eloquently summarized the Jeffersonian position on western settlement in the following way:

Tenantry is unfavourable to freedom... The freeholder, on the contrary, is the natural supporter of a free government, and it should be the policy of republics to multiply their freeholders as it is the policy of monarchies to multiply tenants. We are a republic, and we wish to continue so: then multiply the class of freeholders; pass the public lands cheaply and easily into the hands of the People; sell for a reasonable price to those who are able to pay; and give without price to those who are not.[29]

One could hardly wish for a better statement of what differentiated the republican states-union of America from the 'predominant monarchies' in the European states-system, to which (as we saw in chapter 1) A.H.L. Heeren and the English school attached such importance.

Jefferson himself had been closely involved in two key developments with regard to the settlement of the western territories and the spread of American republican civilization. As president, he conducted the Louisiana Purchase in 1803, dramatically expanding the size of the public

[27] This belief is a prominent theme in the classic thesis on American expansion presented in Frederick Jackson Turner, *The Frontier in American History* (Tucson: University of Arizona Press, 1986), but for a more recent, and extremely good, discussion of the concept of civilization in the context of American westward expansion, see Harold Hyman, *American Singularity: The 1787 Northwest Ordinance, the 1862 Homestead and Morrill Acts, and the 1944 G.I. Bill* (Athens: University of Georgia Press, 1986).

[28] For a less facetious interpretation, see Joyce Appelby, *Liberalism and Republicanism in the Historical Imagination* (Cambridge, MA: Harvard University Press, 1992).

[29] Cited in Benjamin Horace Hibbard, *A History of the Public Land Policies* (New York: Peter Smith, 1965), pp. 142–3.

domain of the United States; earlier, he had contributed extensively to the Land Ordinances of 1785 and 1787, which played a vital role in determining the tenurial and political forms of westward expansion, especially the 1787 Northwest Ordinance. The Louisiana Purchase was part of a series of land grants or acquisitions that endowed the United States Congress with an extraordinary range of powers in the nineteenth century. After the revolution, the states' claims to the western territories (which had usually, and often vaguely, been included in colonial land grants to proprietors or agencies) were ceded to the Federal government, creating a 'public domain' which was enlarged by a series of acquisitions: Louisiana from the French, Florida from Spain in 1819 and the Oregon purchase from Britain in 1846.[30] The distinctive feature of this public domain was that the Federal government of the United States did not only hold the political rights granted it by the Constitution; it actually owned the land itself.

Given the financial difficulties of the period after the revolutionary wars, there was a great deal of sympathy for Alexander Hamilton's fiscally prudent point of view that the opportunity to sell off the western territories was too good to miss, especially since it seemed fair to many easterners that the settlers in the West would enjoy the benefits of the revolution and deserved to pay some of its costs. The chief dissenters were Jefferson and his supporters, who believed that the lands should be freely distributed to all settlers. Although they initially lost the battle over the issue of sales, the Jeffersonians were still able to ensure in the 1787 Ordinance that any sales by the government to settlers would be on the least encumbered tenures possible: 'fee-simple', rather than any feudal kind of 'fee-tail'. It is not surprising, given that the revolution had in part been a defence of the allodial nature of Americans' property rights, that this became such a central feature of Jeffersonian republicanism and western settlement. However, it is worth bearing in mind that the Northwest Ordinance was the instrument by which it was effectively guaranteed that feudal tenures would have no place at all in the rest of North America, that individual settlers in the western territories would have complete rights over the land they bought from the government, and that the long-standing colonial principle of appropriation would be extended to the yet un-settled parts of the continent.

Of course, the actual practitioners of frontier settlement hardly corresponded to the Jeffersonian ideal of independent yeoman farmer-citizens: speculation was rife. This problem led to a series of policies designed to improve the position of the 'genuine' settler, the ultimate goal being 'to

[30] Hibbard, *Public Land Policies*, pp. 7–20.

make the public-land system function in a democratic way by assuring the small man the right to acquire a piece of the national domain'.[31] This effort was carried on across three issues: pre-emption, graduation and homesteading. Pre-emption, which meant giving *bona fide* settlers special rights to purchase up to 160 acres of land at a fixed price, began to be introduced from the 1830s, culminating in the 1841 Pre-emption Act. Its main purpose was to ensure the rights of settlers and squatters against speculation, following a rationale set out by the Public Lands Committee in 1828: 'It is right and proper that the first settlers, who have made roads and bridges over the public lands at their own expense and with great labour and toil, should be allowed a privilege greater than other purchasers.'[32] 'Graduation' was more flexible and refers to the graduation of the price of land offered for sale in public auctions depending on its quality, and so forth. Jeffersonians like Benton hoped that graduation would make it easier for settlers to acquire cheaper cultivable land, below the fixed government price at which land sales had hitherto operated.

Homesteading was introduced rather later, in the 1862 Homestead Act. Unlike the other two policies, which merely favourably altered the position of the settlers within the general framework of public auctions for land, homesteading introduced the principle of free land in the West. The act offered up 160 acres of public land free to any who would settle on it and improve it for at least five years, a policy that was subsequently applied beyond the American continent itself, although with less success: for example, in the 1903 Philippine Public Land Law.[33] In very general terms, the development of policy through the nineteenth century revealed a steady movement in the direction of a free land system, with rights increasingly based on the occupation and improvement of land, and with such rights increasingly being codified and institutionalized through the principles of pre-emption and, above all, homesteading. From an international perspective, it is especially significant that the Americans not only sought to apply this principle to the western territories that they had acquired through purchase or annexation, but even to foreign countries such as the Philippines, where they had gained a political role through their defeat of European (Spanish) imperialists. As Stephen Douglas, senator from Illinois, remarked in 1852: Americans had 'a mission to

---

[31] Paul Wallace Gates, *The Jeffersonian Dream: Studies in the History of American Land Policy and Development* (Albuquerque: University of New Mexico Press, 1996), p. 108.
[32] Cited in Hibbard, *Public Land Policies*, p. 151.
[33] Karl Pelzer, *Pioneer Settlement in the Asiatic Tropics: Studies in Land Utilization and Agricultural Colonization in Southeastern Asia* (New York: American Geographical Society, 1945), p. 106.

perform . . . of progress in the arts and sciences – in the science of politics and government – in the development and advancement of human rights throughout the world'.[34]

The political form assumed by American westward expansion is equally interesting from the point of view of the principles I have earlier identified in the context of colonial settlement. The central principle of the Northwest Ordinance in this regard was that 'the goal of all territorial acquisition eventually was to be Statehood'.[35] In essence, this was an egalitarian rejection of the European practice of colonialism: Congress was to assume responsibility for and authority over the territories; not to exploit the territory as a colony but to oversee the process of state-formation, determining the moment at which the territory could be accepted into the Union as an equal state. This plan had three main elements: the establishment of a government in the territories, prior to the latter assuming control over their own affairs; the mechanism for creating new states; and the provisions for internal governance of those new states.

The establishment of territorial government essentially involved the Federal appointment of governors who would have complete responsibility for the territory. The creation of new states was envisaged to follow a very straightforward formula. According to Article 5 of the 1787 Ordinance: 'whenever any of the said States shall have sixty thousand free inhabitants therein, such State shall be admitted, by its delegates, into the Congress of the United States, on an equal footing with the original States, in all respects whatsoever'.[36] Jefferson had intended this to be the culmination of a steady progression of forms of constitutional government, from a first temporary constitution made by an assembly of all settlers, through a permanent constitution devised when the territory's population reached 20,000.[37] One cannot but be struck by the simplicity of this cumulative population requirement, compared with the requirements of sovereign statehood in orthodox legal doctrines on recognition, such as an organized bureaucracy, capacity for control of territory, self-defence and so on. Of course, this was largely because, thanks to the broader division of sovereignty with the Federal government, the new states would not be required to undertake such activities anyway.

---

[34] Robert W. Johannsen, 'The Meaning of Manifest Destiny', in Sam W. Haynes and Christopher Morris (eds.), *Manifest Destiny and Empire: American Antebellum Expansion* (College Station: Texas A&M University Press, 1997), p. 16.

[35] Arnold H. Leibowitz, *Defining Status: A Comprehensive Analysis of United States Territorial Relations* (London: Martinus Nijhoff, 1989), p. 6.

[36] Thomas Donaldson, *The Public Domain: Its History, with Statistics* (New York: Johnson Reprint Corporation, 1970), p. 156.

[37] Thomas Jefferson, *Papers of Thomas Jefferson* (Princeton University Press, 1950), vol. VI, p. 614.

However, although the requirements for qualification as a state were very low by the standards of European positive international law, the Northwest Ordinance was much more intrusive with regard to the internal constitution of the new states than any orthodox international lawyer would have dreamt. In the first place, the right of individual private appropriation of the public lands was guaranteed. In spite of their supposedly equal and independent status, the new states were not allowed to 'interfere with the primary disposal of the soil by the United States in Congress assembled'.[38] In other words, the territories were allowed to devise even a permanent constitution for themselves without being able to make any prescriptions whatsoever concerning the system of tenure on their public lands (which was by far the largest part of their territory). It would be hard to think of a more gross violation of the indivisible and territorial principle of state sovereignty that is conventionally supposed to rest at the heart of modern international political and legal order. In addition, the inhabitants of the new states were at liberty to devise their own Constitution. However, the proviso was added that the inhabitants had to be protected by *habeas corpus*, trial by jury, common law procedure, proportionate political representation, no arbitrary deprivation of liberty or property (all Article 2); that there be no slavery (Article 6); and that their adopted State Constitution be republican (Article 5).[39] In other words, the states formed by the people moving into the western territories were permitted to develop any constitution they liked, provided that it was republican and respected fundamental human rights. Furthermore, the new states founded in the western territories would automatically become equal members of the American states-union, and would consequently have to accept the broader division of sovereignty between the individual states and the Federal government: for example, the new states' relations with foreign powers would be managed by the Federal government of the United States.

The initial assertion of the authority of the Federal government in the western territories aroused considerable ire. In the Northwest Ordinance, Congress at first assumed absolute political authority over the western territories, through appointed governors and judges, as a temporary measure intended to lead to the eventual incorporation of the states as equal members of the Union on satisfying the population requirement. The extensive, even dictatorial, gubernatorial authority permitted by this system of territorial government was the object of much anger among settlers in the west. Far from being grateful for the relatively minor population requirements laid on them before being granted statehood (minor, that

[38] *Ibid.*   [39] Donaldson, *Public Domain*, pp. 155–6.

is, compared with colonies under European domination), the settlers were furious at what they regarded as a patronizing infringement of their already existing rights to self-government.[40] The national electoral success of the Jeffersonian democratic-republicans in 1801 combined with a strong movement in the Northwest Territory for statehood. This aspiration was bound up with republican sentiment, since the governor formed the target of popular criticism, and the territorial government attracted hostility for being, as Michael Baldwin claimed in 1802, 'aristocratic in its principles, and oppressive and partial in its administration'.[41] The movement culminated in the meeting of a Convention in November 1802 to draw up a constitution for the proposed new state of Ohio, which effectively turned things on their heads. The abhorred system of government through federally appointed governors and officials was scaled down, and a properly republican and democratic constitution was established in line with Jeffersonian thinking.[42] Congress accepted Ohio as a state under this constitution in 1803.

For our purposes, it is especially interesting to note the location of sovereignty in this new state: it was neither as clear-cut nor as taken-for-granted a question as one might think. The constitution drawn up by the 1802 Convention had asserted the local sovereignty of the inhabitants of the territory. It was, in this sense, a clear statement of the democratic strand of Jeffersonianism, presented in opposition to the Federalist assertion of the national prerogative. Subsequently, however, this democratic assertion of popular sovereignty was tracked back somewhat, both through a stronger assertion of the role of the judiciary and through an increasing reliance on schemes for internal improvements funded by the Federal government.[43] Gradually, in other words, the more republican side of the Jeffersonians and the nationalist ideas of the Federalists began to re-assert themselves, partly through an increasing division of sovereign powers between institutions within the state, partly through an insistence on the principle of popular sovereignty, but also through a recognition that some functions were best performed by the Federal government, and that these areas of sovereign authority should consequently be alienated to the Federal level. For example, 'the public school and canal movements committed the power of the state government to guiding Ohio and its citizens into responsible roles as parts of a national system. After the 1820s, few could deny for long that the residents of Ohio were independent only

---

[40] See, for example, Nicole Etcheson, *The Emerging Midwest: Upland Southerners and the Political Culture of the Old Northwest* (Bloomington: Indiana University Press, 1992), p. 20.
[41] Cited in Andrew Cayton, *The Frontier Republic: Ideology and Politics in the Ohio Country, 1780–1825* (Kent State University Press, 1986), p. 69.
[42] *Ibid.*, pp. 77–8.   [43] See *ibid.*, chs. 7 and 9.

to the extent that their interdependence with the rest of the American and European worlds allowed them to be.'[44]

In its early stages, then, the establishment of states in the western territories illustrates the classic constitutional features that seem to characterize the logic of colonial settlement more generally, in the sense that the marks of sovereignty came to be divided between different institutions at different levels. In the specific case of Ohio, the division was both *de jure* and *de facto*. The state Constitution located sovereignty in the people and their elected representatives; however, through the US Constitution foreign relations were all conducted through the US Congress, and the recognition of the territories as states still required an act of the Federal government.[45] *De facto*, things were even messier, as the need for orderly administration and for Federal assistance in certain areas (notably education and 'internal improvements') made further qualifications to local popular sovereignty inevitable. Sovereignty, as in the pre-revolutionary colonial system, remained divided; now, however, that division provided a powerful rationale for the American practice of offering prompt and equal recognition to the territories that came under the control, unlike the European imperial powers in the East Indies, who denied that recognition to their dominions for as long as possible.

European imperialism in the East Indies

Compared with what they were doing in North America, European activities in the East Indies focused relatively less on colonial settlement and relatively more on the imperial administration of indigenous peoples. The principal reasons for this difference do not lie in the different domestic politics of the European states themselves so much as in the situations they encountered: there were fewer 'vacant' lands available for the planting of colonies and, in any case, Europeans believed that they could make more profits by inserting themselves into already existing systems of trade and taxation. Despite this important difference, however, in very general terms there were some striking similarities in the way that international relationships evolved in the East Indies compared with North America. The division of sovereignty was again integral to the development of European public authority in the region, although the practice typically involved the gradual acquisition of prerogatives from indigenous rulers rather than the decentralized system of colonial administration that I described in the previous section; nevertheless, with that proviso in mind, the structures of governance that developed were

[44] *Ibid.*, p. 150.   [45] *Ibid.*, p. 80.

remarkably alike. In the East Indies, also, the establishment of individuals' property rights was a prominent feature of European activity, with considerable efforts made to endow indigenous peoples with the kinds of property rights that Europeans felt they ought to have, on a similar model to the way in which colonial settlers had been granted their property rights in North America.

It is easy to overlook these aspects of European imperialism in the East Indies because the conventional picture tends to highlight the overwhelming military and commercial dominance of European powers, their superior attitude towards the indigenous peoples under their rule, and the economic exploitation that was one of the central purposes of imperial administration. Certainly, one should not down-play these dimensions of modern imperialism, but it is nevertheless important to take seriously the normative and legal environment within which imperial forms of governance were constructed and maintained in the East Indies. It is significant, for example, that even at the apogee of British imperialism in India roughly two-fifths of the territory and two-ninths of the population of present-day India were not directly under British rule, but were organized into over 600 'Princely' or 'Native States'.[46] The official line was that these states were 'semi-sovereign', a concept borrowed from classical theories of the law of nations that was explicitly intended to reflect the principle of divisible sovereignty. Indeed, legal experts with an interest in British imperialism like Henry Sumner Maine frankly argued that '[s]overeignty is a term which, in international law, indicates a well-ascertained assemblage of separate powers or privileges ... there is not, nor has there ever been, anything in international law to prevent some of those rights being lodged with one possessor and some with another. Sovereignty has always been regarded as divisible.'[47]

My main purpose in this section is to describe how this practice of dividing sovereignty between European governments, imperial administrators and indigenous rulers developed; in the course of that discussion, I will also explain some of the ways in which Europeans used their public authority to reorganize local property systems. I will begin in the early seventeenth century, when the Dutch were struggling with the Portuguese for control over the spice trade. We have already touched on some aspects of this conflict when we looked at Hugo Grotius's defence of the capture

---

[46] S.R. Ashton, *British Policy Towards the Princely States, 1905–1939* (London: Curzon Press, 1982).

[47] Henry Sumner Maine, Minute from 22 March, 1864, printed as Document 65 in Adrian Sever, *Documents and Speeches on the Indian Princely States*, 2 vols. (Delhi: B.R. Publishing Corporation, 1985), p. 251, and see also pp. 25–7.

of a Portuguese ship in *De Jure Praedae*, but now I want to look more broadly at how the Dutch regarded the sovereignty of indigenous rulers, and ask precisely how they manipulated treaty agreements and contracts in order to establish control over strategically important territories and to create trading monopolies. The French revolutionary wars considerably disrupted these arrangements, and although the Dutch eventually recovered many of their possessions, notably Indonesia, they did so thanks to the British, who now established themselves as the leading military power in India and the East Indies in general. I will conclude this section, then, by asking how the Dutch and British consolidated their imperial administrations in Indonesia and India, paying particular attention to their treatment of indigenous rulers. The latter were usually permitted to retain some prerogatives of sovereignty, but were now made subject to doctrines like the one that the British eventually formalized, with deliberate vagueness, under the heading of 'paramountcy'.

A crucial point to notice here is that the goals of imperial administration in the period after 1815 were no longer defined simply in terms of maximizing the power and profits of the mother country by monopolizing trade. Although that goal was never far from the minds of imperial administrators, it was increasingly advanced in conjunction with the belief that Europeans had a responsibility to promote 'civilization' and 'good government' in the countries under their imperial authority. The division of sovereignty was now no longer just part of the attempt to acquire prerogatives that were necessary to exert control over trade, as it had been in the seventeenth century. It began to be employed also in accordance with the principle that indigenous rulers should hold only those prerogatives which they were competent to exercise. This led imperial administrators to intervene more frequently in the domestic affairs of rulers who had demonstrated themselves incompetent or corrupt in European eyes, occasionally even annexing territories where no suitable alternative could be found, or where Europeans saw a distinct strategic or commercial advantage for themselves. It also helped to further the conversion of customary local systems of property use into legally codified and judicially administered systems of property rights and ownership; as with the division of sovereignty, these reforms were intended to suit both the material goal of maximizing revenues and the more ideological purpose of promoting 'civilization'. Thus, by the end of this discussion, we will be able to reflect on the normative, legal and institutional structure of relations between European and non-European peoples in the East Indies, observing some important similarities both with the pattern of order that developed in North America and with the Grotian theory of the law of nations that I outlined in chapter 2.

To begin with, though, it should be noted that it is somewhat mislead-ing to use the idea of 'European dominance' to understand international politics in the East Indies during the seventeenth century. For most of this early period in their relations together, Europeans confronted in-digenous rulers on terms of parity, or even, on occasion, inferiority. The idea of European dominance is also misleading because it suggests that Europeans presented a united front in their efforts to subjugate non-European peoples; nothing could be further from the truth. An ingenious local ruler could often play one European power off against another, since they were all competing for the same thing: control of trade in goods which were, in most cases, produced under the local ruler's authority. Europeans typically needed to make alliances with indigenous rulers to acquire the resources with which to defeat their competitors, and, just as importantly, they needed to make agreements with those same rulers in order to have access to the goods that they wanted to sell to European markets. The more successful European powers in this context, by which I principally mean the Dutch and the British, fully appreciated this fea-ture of East Indian international politics, and accordingly they showed considerable respect for the political authority of indigenous rulers in this early period, treating them as potential allies rather than savages or hea-thens, and often accepting classifications of sovereignty and status that the local rulers used.[48]

It would be a mistake, however, to take this apparent benevolence at face value. Once European competitors had been seen off, the strate-gic value of these alliances rapidly declined. Moreover, once European trading corporations had gained access to the goods they wanted, they tried to reduce the prices they paid as much as possible, and sought to gain sovereign prerogatives for themselves that would allow them to cut these potentially awkward local rulers out of the commercial picture altogether. The result was that, from the later seventeenth century on, numerous indigenous rulers found their authority coming under increas-ing pressure. An example of this tendency can be seen in the changing relationship between the Dutch East India Company (the VOC) and the kings of Kandy, in present-day Sri Lanka. The Dutch had a chance to insinuate their presence here because of the naval weakness of the ruler, Raja Sinha II, and his resulting need for allies against the Portuguese. The Dutch offered their services and, after securing a victory over the Portuguese at the battle of Gannoruwa, concluded a treaty with Raja Sinha in May 1638. The treaty did not, at first glance, offer many obvious

---

[48] See especially Charles Alexandrowicz, *An Introduction to the History of the Law of Nations in the East Indies* (Oxford: Clarendon Press, 1967).

advantages to the Dutch – a disingenuous attempt to interpret it as giving the Dutch a right to garrison forts without Raja Sinha's permission was quickly exposed by the Kandyans – but the VOC did find a convenient article that dealt with Raja Sinha's repayment of the debts he had incurred during the war: a fine illustration of the uses to which Grotius's 'natural equity' argument could be put. The VOC controlled the statements of the king's level of debt, which offered numerous opportunities for creative accounting. They also refused to be paid off in cash, and instead insisted on payment in cinnamon, for which they offered a lower and lower price. Thus, 'the Dutch could not only get the cinnamon . . . for a mere song, but they could also keep the king in their debt as long as they wanted to'.[49]

This was an effective strategy, but the VOC needed more of Raja Sinha's cinnamon than it could get through these means alone, and retained an interest in establishing control over as much of the producing regions as possible. They sought to achieve this through an independent expedition against the Portuguese in 1644, in the course of which they gained command of the land around the key strategic fort of Galle, whereupon they promptly agreed a truce with the Portuguese, in which the latter recognized the company's control over Galle. With good reason, Raja Sinha regarded the truce as an act of betrayal, and responded by withdrawing his people from the lands, resettling them in the interior. This posed a serious problem for the Dutch, since, in the absence of the indigenous farmers, no cinnamon could be obtained at all. They tried to establish a colony of Dutch settlers to make up the difference, offering them exactly the kinds of free and easy terms that we have already seen were such an important feature of settlement in the American colonies, but this time the lure proved insufficient to persuade sufficient numbers of Dutch people or company workers to 'become free', as the expression had it. The main problem was that the VOC was unwilling to extend the really lucrative commercial privileges for 'private trade' to the settlers, for fear of undermining their monopoly, and when they did so out of desperation it was in far too grudging and haphazard a way to make the colony a going concern.[50]

As their colonial ambitions for Ceylon receded into the distance, the Dutch now declared war on Raja Sinha. The ensuing conflict resulted in serious military reversals for the Dutch, and they were forced to agree

---

[49] K.W. Goonewardena, *The Foundation of Dutch Power in Ceylon, 1638–1658* (Amsterdam: Djambatan, 1958), p. 45, and see also pp. 18ff.

[50] See Sinnappah Arasratnam, *Dutch Power in Ceylon, 1658–1687* (Amsterdam: Djambatan, 1958), pp. 203–12, and K.W. Goonewardena, 'A New Netherland in Ceylon: Dutch Attempts to Found a Colony During the First Quarter-Century of their Power in Ceylon', *Ceylon Journal of Historical and Social Studies*, 2 (1959), 203–44.

terms with Raja Sinha on a revision of the 1638 treaty in the latter's favour, which resulted in a real erosion of the Dutch cinnamon monopoly. On the pretext that Raja Sinha still had outstanding debts to the VOC, however, some of the cinnamon-producing territory around Galle was retained by the Dutch. This left the VOC with a tricky legal problem. Throughout all of their colonizing activities, the Dutch had continued to observe Raja Sinha's sovereignty over the whole of Ceylon, which was, on their legal understanding, perfectly consistent with the occupation of territories he had 'voluntarily' vacated. However, they still needed to acquire as strong a legal title as possible to the lands that were now under their control, against both European competitors and the Kandyans themselves. Unfortunately, all they had in that regard was a right of conquest from the Portuguese (of dubious validity, since the lands had never been under Portuguese sovereignty at all), and the argument that the lands they held were in trust from Raja Sinha, the sovereign ruler, until such time as the VOC's expenses had been fully paid.[51]

Increasing pressure on the cinnamon trade from other European powers, notably the English and the French, forced the Dutch to introduce other arguments, such as length of occupation, to justify their control. They also began to assert their claims in an increasingly exclusive manner, denying Raja Sinha any rights at all in the coastal regions, which were, of course, vital not just for cinnamon production but also for the continuation of trade and for conducting foreign relations with other states, both European and Asian. Nevertheless, although the new Dutch arguments were much more far-reaching than had hitherto been the case, they were still careful to stop short of declaring Dutch sovereignty. That reticence continued well into the eighteenth century. Baron van Imhoff, governor-general in Ceylon from 1736 to 1740, was still arguing then that:

The great number of years during which we have been in exclusive possession gives us the right to maintain our right, if necessary even by force. Our rights have been legalised by the undisputed exercise of them by the Company's possession of West and East, and this will serve also as proof of proprietorship, of other parts, so far as it concerns a third party, although the King is and remains the sovereign.[52]

But even while recognizing the sovereignty of the Kandyan kings, by virtue of their control of these important territories the Dutch could exercise a stranglehold over communications between the kingdom and the outside world. Gradually the indigenous rulers became increasingly cut

---

[51] Arasaratnam, *Dutch Power in Ceylon*, pp. 5–6.
[52] Cited in Sinnappah Arasaratnam, 'Dutch Sovereignty in Ceylon: A Historical Study of its Problems', *Ceylon Journal of Historical and Social Studies*, 1 (1958), 105–6.

off as all foreign communication and commerce was channelled through the Dutch. The kingdom of Kandy, one time ally and partner of the Dutch, became, as Sinnappah Arasaratnam puts it, 'a sovereign entity, but deprived of the right of foreign control'.[53]

If we recall Grotius's analysis of divided sovereignty, unequal treaties and usurpation, it is easy to see how closely this practice accords with his theory of the law of nations. An initial treaty was made – in this case, especially after the revisions to 1638 treaty, by no means an obviously 'unequal' one – the provisions of which were manipulated so as to endow the now-stronger party with more and more of the rights of the weaker one; if, as Grotius had argued, this usurpation was not resisted, after a period of time the rights became genuine. Overall, the Dutch approach was to accede to the formal sovereignty of the Kandyans, but to chip away at the marks of sovereignty contained therein, until they were in a position to begin to claim something approaching complete sovereignty for themselves; eventually, after a further war with the Kandyans, the Dutch managed to gain a treaty (1766) that formally recognized their sovereignty over the coastal lands. This practice clearly constitutes an important qualification to the idea that Europeans recognized the equality of sovereign rights granted to East Indian rulers under the law of nations. While they may have initially been treated as equals with European sovereigns, that recognition still left them vulnerable (as was also the case for European rulers) to the *division* of their prerogatives and the acquisition of some of their rights, particularly those which were commercially important, by the European powers. It is, I think, also interesting to note that in this early period these transfers were made through treaties, albeit with considerable manipulation on the part of the Dutch. Appeals to natural law were not really a feature of the insinuation of Dutch power in this regard. They were, at least on the surface, simply involved in a free exchange of legal rights from the king of Kandy to the Dutch East India Company, a classically Grotian rationale.

The gradual acquisition of the Kandyan kings' sovereignty by the Dutch is, of course, just one example within a number of different practices that were going on at the same time in other parts of the East Indies. The reason I have chosen this example is that it presents a particularly clear-cut illustration of what was involved in the acquisition of public authority, the legal environment that underpinned and rationalized it, and the lengths to which European powers would go in order to obtain the territorial controls that were vital to the construction of trading monopolies. Most

---

[53] Sinnappah Arasaratnam, 'The Kingdom of Kandy: Aspects of its External Relations and Commerce', *Ceylon Journal of Historical and Social Studies*, 3 (1960), 114.

European states were engaged in roughly similar activities elsewhere, the main difference being that in some cases, most obviously the British in India, they encountered already existing structures of imperial suzerainty, into which they usually inserted themselves at quite a humble level, at least in the first instance. The acquisition of further sovereign prerogatives was comparatively easier in this context, when many indigenous rulers were already used to relationships of suzerainty with regard to an imperial power, although not all welcomed the intrusion of Europeans in that role.

After the French revolutionary wars, European states began to go beyond simply establishing a commercial foothold in the East. Increasingly, they began to use their sovereign prerogatives to bring about social change, particularly with an evolving concept of civilization in mind. European activities were now determined by two main considerations, which occasionally were in conflict with one another. First, they still wanted to make a profit from their imperial possessions, partly through trade, but also, as they acquired more and more rights of political authority, through taxation as well; simply put, they wanted to maximize imperial revenues while ensuring the lowest-cost and most efficient administrative system possible. Secondly, especially from the middle of the nineteenth century on, they wanted to civilize the peoples under their imperial rule, encouraging economic and technological progress and giving them the best possible government, at the expense of the authority of indigenous rulers if necessary.

With regard to the reform of indigenous property systems, there were two main issues involved: how to extract a satisfactory revenue from the Indies, to cover the administrative costs involved and still provide opportunities for profit; and how to use the land tenure system to promote social reforms, and hence civilization. The Dutch framed the two leading options here in terms of a choice between a 'system of trade' and a 'system of taxation'.[54] The system of trade was not dissimilar to the way in which the East India Companies had tried to make a profit from the region in the past: inserting themselves into indigenous structures of production and tribute, and manipulating monopoly advantages, especially in the export of cash-crops to Europe. From the point of view of the colonial power, the main advantage of this system was its practicality and low cost: it made use of already existing systems of exploitation, and required little administrative effort other than that which had traditionally been involved in trade with the Indies. The system of taxation, on the other

[54] Clive Day, *The Policy and Administration of the Dutch in Java*, revised edition (Kuala Lumpur: Oxford University Press, 1966).

hand, generally required much higher administrative costs and burdens, but had the advantage of being more systematic, and was seen by liberals as both ethically and economically superior.

The British were especially enthusiastic about the system of taxation. In India, they introduced the 'Permanent Settlement' of 1793, which took away the administrative prerogatives of the old landed elite in Bengal, the *zamindars*, but 'turned their loose landholding rights into strict private property, dependent however on their capacity to pay the fixed amount of revenue for their land and tenants'.[55] This agreement clearly reflected prevailing British ideas about the social, economic and political importance of a stable landed gentry, owning their land in an absolute and exclusive manner, and dedicated to improving their property; the whole system, as Bernard Cohn observes, was intended 'to encourage improvement of the land...to protect property rights and make property secure'.[56] The British did not stop with the 'Permanent Settlement', of course. The nineteenth century also saw the extension of private property rights to other parts of India, often by Indians with British encouragement or assistance.[57] Similar policies were also adopted outside India. Following their invasion of Java in 1811, for example, the British under Lieutenant Governor Sir Thomas Stamford Raffles tried to introduce the same kind of land-rent system to Indonesia.

After the Charter of the Dutch East India Company (VOC) expired in 1799, some Dutch liberals had already begun to press for the establishment of a system of secure private property, and Raffles took these visions further, ambitiously planning to gain revenue through, as in India, the introduction of a systematic land tax. He began from the convenient proposition that in Java the indigenous ruler had always been the owner of the soil, and that the Europeans had taken over this right: effectively all the land on the island was in the public domain.[58] This allowed the government freely to dispose of the uncultivated waste lands, whether to Javanese or Europeans. Thus, while claiming that the government enjoyed the sole right of property, Raffles also established a commercial relationship directly with the individual settlers, ignoring intermediaries in the

---

[55] Maarten Kuitenbrouwer, 'Aristocracies under Colonial Rule: North India and Java', in C.A. Bayly and D.H.A. Kolff (eds.), *Two Colonial Empires: Comparative Essays on the History of India and Indonesia* (Lancaster: Martinus Nijhoff, 1986), p. 80. For a good analysis of the impact of this and other reforms on India, see Rajat Kanta Ray, 'Indian Society and the Establishment of British Supremacy', in Marshall (ed.), *Oxford History of the British Empire*, vol. II, especially p. 521.

[56] Bernard Cohn, 'From Indian Status to British Contract', *Journal of Economic History*, 21 (1961), 613.

[57] C.A. Bayly, 'Creating a Colonial Peasantry: India and Java, c. 1820–1880', *Itinerario*, 11 (1987), 94–6.

[58] Day, *Dutch in Java*, p. 176.

form of local village chiefs and the indigenous elites, christened *regenten* by the Dutch. This policy of dealing directly with individual farmers was primarily instigated to answer political concerns about the arbitrary rule of native elites. As Raffles put it,

The agency of intermediate renters is considered as quite unnecessary to be adopted in the future. It is deemed that such a plan of settlement will leave the bulk of the people entirely at the mercy of a numerous set of chiefs, who, however well they may have hitherto conducted themselves, would certainly, in such case, possess an ability of injury and oppression, against which the ruling [European] power would have left itself no adequate means of prevention or redress, and which cannot therefore be permitted consistently with the principles of good government.[59]

The British solution, in short, was to grant extensive property rights to individual farmers, which would, it was believed, provide a useful bulwark against the dangers of misgovernment. It was, in effect, a precise institutional demarcation of the separation between a private sphere of liberty, and a public sphere where dangers of misgovernment still had to be carefully monitored.

Raffles's ideas about the beneficial civilizing effects of property owner-ship, broadly similar to those held by the advocates of American westward expansion, always had to be juxtaposed against the other crucial element of imperial policy: the need for revenue and, ideally, profit. Indonesia was returned to the Dutch following the Treaty of London of 1814, and, despite the intentions of the commissioners from the Netherlands to persevere with a reformed version of the land-rent system (which in-volved increasing the colonial administrative personnel considerably), they 'failed to make Java profitable to the Dutch treasury . . . in the short term, because the Javanese peasant did not have any inclination to cul-tivate export crops like coffee or sugar voluntarily'.[60] Consequently, in an attempt to improve the colonial finances, the heads of the local colo-nial administration, especially the new Governor General Baron van der Capellen and his successor van den Bosch, drifted back towards the fa-miliar old 'system of trade', which had earlier been adopted by the VOC as a way of increasing revenue. What was introduced, from the late 1830s on, was an infamous system of the forced cultivation of designated crops. They wanted to ensure the maximization of the production of cash-crops that could then be sold by the Netherlands Trading Company on be-half of the treasury. Essentially, under the cultivation system the Javanese peasants were required to produce the crops the Dutch needed in lieu

---

[59] Cited in *ibid.*, pp. 178–9.
[60] Cornelis Fasseur, *The Politics of Colonial Exploitation: Java, the Dutch and the Cultivation System*, trans. R.E. Elson and Ary Kraal (Ithaca: Cornell University Press, 1992), p. 23.

of payment of Raffles's land-rent; the peasant-farmers would also receive cash payments for their crops, although not large ones, which they could use to improve their land or (more likely) pay off their outstanding debts from the old land-rent system.[61]

Although it undoubtedly fulfilled its primary goal of gaining revenue for the Dutch treasury, the cultivation system increasingly came under attack from liberals in the Dutch parliament, especially after crop failures in 1844 resulted in severe famines that persisted into 1845 and 1846; famine struck again in 1849. While it is unclear whether these famines can be directly attributed to the burdens on the peasants imposed by the cultivation system,[62] it certainly presented the Dutch with an uncomfortable paradox. As one of the leading spokesmen for the liberals, W. R. van Hoevell, succinctly put it: 'we have in Java the strange phenomenon that this island annually produces almost 40 million guilders in profit, but that the people of this same island are unable to provide for their own needs'.[63] Administrative changes in the Netherlands in 1848 also contributed to the liberal backlash against the cultivation system. Prior to 1848, in the Constitutions of 1806 and 1815, control over colonial policy had been vested exclusively in the monarch; after 1848, the States-General was given a role in colonial policy, especially in terms of supervision of the budget. The new role for the Dutch legislative body simultaneously increased the liberals' awareness of the acuteness of the problems associated with the cultivation system, and also gave them the means to do something about them. However, the liberals faced a dilemma posed by the fiscal success of the cultivation system: how could a more liberal system of property rights be introduced without losing the colossal revenue that the Dutch treasury was receiving from its colonial possessions?[64] Dutch colonial policy only gradually began to move in a liberal direction, painfully slowly and with considerable qualification, since new ways of raising revenue had to be found to replace those secured by the cultivation system.

There were two main strands to the liberal plan. On the one hand, they believed that the customary Javanese *adat* land use practices should be respected, and this concern was built into the new Colonial Constitution (*Regeerings Reglement*) of 1854. While it permitted the continuation of the cultivation system, it insisted in Article 56 that 'so far as the cultures occupy land cleared by the native population for its own use, this land be disposed of with justice and with respect for existing rights and customs'.[65] On the other hand, the liberals believed that the revenues of

[61] As well as *ibid.*, see Day, *Dutch in Java*, and R.E. Elson, *Village Java under the Cultivation System, 1830–1870* (Sydney: Allen and Unwin, 1994).
[62] See Elson, *Village Java*, pp. 114–18.   [63] Cited in *ibid.*, p. 102.
[64] For an excellent summary, see Fasseur, *Politics of Colonial Exploitation*, p. 160.
[65] Cited in Day, *Dutch in Java*, p. 328.

the cultivation system could be preserved, and more satisfactorily raised, if the forced government cultivations were to be replaced by cultivations managed by private enterprise and worked by 'free labour'. This policy was included in Article 62 of the Colonial Constitution, stating that '[t]he Governor General can let land according to rules which are to be established by general ordinance'.[66] However, two principal restrictions were placed on this governmental right to dispose of waste lands: only letting was permitted, outright sale of the lands was not (for fear of creating the kind of quasi-feudal private estates that the *patroons* had tried to build in America); and, as noted above, the *adat* rights of the Javanese were supposed to be respected. A Royal Decree of 1856 extended these restrictions on hiring out waste land to private enterprise, capping the leases at 20 years, imposing restrictions on the goods that could be produced and mandating the planters not to interfere with indigenous village administration.[67]

The main problem with the liberal plan was that its two components were in direct contradiction with each other, which considerably restricted the capacity of the government to establish 'free' cultivations on a liberal market-oriented model. This problem sprang from an uncertainty among Dutch legal experts, reflected in the difference between two very different views of the content of indigenous *adat* law. One, associated with lawyers at Leiden University, assumed an extensive village right of disposal over the waste-lands, in which Raffles's notion of a distinct sovereign title over the land was absent: 'The state and its ruler are fitted into the total and conflictuous *adat* order of rights.'[68] On the other hand, lawyers at Utrecht tended to assume the existence of a 'domain right' of government, meaning that the government as sovereign was owner of the land. Raffles's land-rent system, the cultivation system and the liberal plan of 'free cultivations' managed by private enterprise had all depended on the 'domain right' theory.[69] If the Leiden scholars, most notably the defiantly Grotian international lawyer Cornelis van Vollenhoven, were correct in their assessment of *adat* law, and there was an increasing belief that they were, then the whole property right structure of the cultivation and liberal system would be unworkable as a system of revenue raising.[70] The result of this uncertainty over land rights was that, few 'waste' lands

---

[66] Cited in A.D.A. de Kat Angelino, *Colonial Policy*, trans. G. Renier, 2 vols. (The Hague: Martinus Nijhoff, 1931), vol. II, p. 438.

[67] Fasseur, *Politics of Colonial Exploitation*, pp. 165–7.

[68] J.C. Heesterman, 'State and Adat', in Bayly and Kolff (eds.), *Two Colonial Empires*, p. 193.

[69] Fasseur, *Politics of Colonial Exploitation*, pp. 30–1.

[70] See Herman Slaats, 'The Imposition and Radiation of Dutch Law in Indonesia', in Jap de Moor and Dietmar Rothermund (eds.), *Our Laws, Their Lands: Land Laws and Land Use in Modern Colonial Societies* (Münster: Lit, 1994), pp. 105–9.

were brought under private cultivation, and the late nineteenth-century liberal policy led to a steady budget deficit with regard to the Indies from the mid-1880s on.[71]

For our purposes it is interesting to note that, despite van Vollenhoven's recognition of the unique and non-Western character of land 'rights' under *adat* 'law', there was a gradual development towards trying to codify the basic principles of *adat* law as a single system, especially among lawyers in Batavia itself.[72] This drift exacerbated a tendency to treat *adat* rights to land as if they were communal rights on a more Western formulation, which had initially arisen as 'a rather desperate response of the *adat* to the pressure of the cultivation system'.[73] The key point here is that the system in effect acknowledged the property rights of the indigenous occupants of the land, not unlike the British Permanent Settlement, even at the expense of projects of direct imperial exploitation or of liberal private enterprise. What emerged, in short, was a reworked version of *adat* law, which broadly harmonized with the colonizing tendency to treat individual property according to the established legal principle of *occupatio*. As in the process of American westward expansion, there was thus a gradual drift towards a policy in which individual settlers (in this case meaning the indigenous population rather than western settlers) would have allodial rights to the land, independent of the sovereign authority of the government, although in this case moderated by a tax to offset the costs of colonial administration.

I have already noted that the 1848 Dutch Constitution opened up a role for the States General in Dutch colonial policy, and provided a channel for the increasingly important liberal attitude to colonial affairs. In particular, this was reflected in the emergence of an 'ethical policy' that was particularly important to the Netherlands, because their international status almost entirely depended on their 'splendid empire of fifty millions of inhabitants'.[74] The weak state of the colonial economy and the administration's finances risked leaving the colonial authorities powerless in the event of either an uprising in the East Indies or a foreign takeover: as L. W. C. Keuchenius put it, 'if the Netherlands proves itself to be no longer worthy of its East Indian possessions...we might

---

[71] Fasseur, *Politics of Colonial Exploitation*, p. 167, and see also Anne Booth, 'The Evolution of Fiscal Policy and the Role of Government in the Colonial Economy', in Booth, W.J. O'Malley and Anna Weidemann (eds.), *Indonesian Economic History in the Dutch Colonial Era* (New Haven: Yale University Southeast Asia Studies, 1990), p. 239.

[72] Slaats, 'Imposition and Radiation', p. 107.

[73] Heesterman, 'State and Adat', pp. 196–7.

[74] C. van Vollenhoven, 'Holland's International Policy', *Political Science Quarterly*, 34 (1919), 194, and see also Eduard Schmutzer, *Dutch Colonial Policy and the Search for Identity in Indonesia, 1920–1931* (Leiden: E.J. Brill, 1977).

lose our colonies altogether, either through the recalcitrance of their people or an attack by foreign enemies'.[75] Initially, the 'ethical policy' was aimed at economic and cultural development, but increasingly it came to include political reforms, and especially the development of institutions for colonial self-government in certain spheres. This was intended to build on the Dutch constitutional and legal reforms of 1848 and the subsequent legislation in the 1860s that had helped to establish parliamentary control over colonial policy-making and new tenurial policies. The two centre-pieces of the constitutional reforms associated with the ethical policy were the idea of an equal 'association' between the motherland and the colony, which has some echoes with developments in the United States but was not substantially pursued, and the principle of 'decentralization' within the colonial administration, which was more fully developed. The latter policy was articulated through the 1903 Decentralization Law, which transferred authority from the centre of colonial government in Batavia to the lower agencies, and also expressed a role for local self-government.[76] This culminated in 1916 in the formation of the *Volksraad* as a popular representative body. The *Volksraad* only had advisory powers, with a mandatory consultative role on the budget. It had thirty-nine members, with a Chair appointed by the Crown and nineteen appointed by each of the governor-general and a mechanism of indirect suffrage. The composition was changed in the 1927 Revised East India Government Act, to allow for sixty-one members: twenty-five Indonesian, thirty Dutch and five other members.[77]

The process of decentralization was carried further in the 1922 revision of the Netherlands Constitution, which made a series of important changes to the articles governing colonial affairs. Initially, governmental control had largely been vested in the Netherlands, in the Crown until 1854 and subsequently in Parliament (formally acting on behalf of the Crown). In the 1922 revision,

A large amount of legislative authority was granted to the Indies. To governmental organs established in the Indies was delegated the power to regulate East Indian internal affairs, while to the Crown was reserved the right to regulate only such subjects and on such occasions as the law might specify. However, the Crown received the right to suspend all ordinances passed by East Indian organs when judged in conflict with the Constitution, the law, or the general interest, while the right of vetoing East Indian ordinances on the same grounds was left to the States

---

[75] Cited in Maarten Kuitenbrouwer, *The Netherlands and the Rise of Modern Imperialism: Colonies and Foreign Policy, 1870–1902* (New York: Berg, 1991), p. 160.
[76] Amry Vandenbosch, *The Dutch East Indies: Its Government, Problems and Politics*, 3rd edn (Berkeley: University of California Press, 1944), p. 68.
[77] *Ibid.*, pp. 111–14.

General, And, finally, though Parliament retained the right to legislate on colonial subjects, it must first consult the representative body of the territory concerned.[78]

Where, then, did 'sovereignty' over the Netherlands Indies lie? Formally, particularly in so far as other European powers were concerned, sovereign authority lay with the main legislative and executive institutions in the Netherlands; but in practice, the authority to decide policy on specific issues was increasingly being delegated to colonial institutions, both in the Batavian administration and in more locally representative bodies.

An interesting further complication to this already bewildering constitutional picture concerns the position of the 'Outer Territories': i.e., the other islands in the Indonesian archipelago. Here, the Dutch claimed sovereignty over the various islands, but acknowledged the quasi-independent status of the three governments of the islands (Sumatra, Borneo and the Great East), and also for those states in areas not under established colonial administrative control, which constituted around half of the area of the Outer Territories.[79] The decentralization produced by the 'ethical policy' in the main territories of the Dutch East Indies was accompanied by the spread of Dutch authority into the Outer Territories, through the 'Short Declarations', by which the rights of the local peoples to self-government were granted in exchange for a formal recognition of overall Dutch sovereignty. This allowed the Dutch a justification for considerable direct intervention in the affairs of the native states, but that was quickly halted in order to strengthen the indigenous rulers in their native states so as to stabilize the fabric of imperial administration.[80] In the 1919 Native States Regulations, the independence of the self-governing territories was shored up, with three restrictions being formally imposed: the self-governing native states had no control over foreign affairs, and some internal issues were delegated to the Dutch colonial administration; the native rulers had to accept Dutch administrative guidance; and extra-territoriality was introduced for Europeans and Indonesians from areas under more completely established Dutch administration.[81]

This particular problem was perhaps even more acute for the British in India, who faced a situation in the nineteenth century where roughly 600 'Native States' remained in existence, and occupied an extremely unclear legal position with respect to both the British government and the government of British India. The East India Company had concluded treaties with most of the larger or more important of these states, and increasingly relations with the rest were framed against a broad doctrine, based

[78] *Ibid.*, pp. 76–7.   [79] *Ibid.*, pp. 139–40 and 147.
[80] *Ibid.*, p. 150, and see also V.J.H. Houben, 'Native States in India and Indonesia: The Nineteenth Century', *Itinerario*, 11 (1987), 112.
[81] Vandenbsoch, *Dutch East Indies*, pp. 152–3.

in part on customary ideas about Mughal suzerainty and in part on the force of British arms demonstrated in the Mutiny, that the British called 'paramountcy'. Although the treaty-based relationships were a more secure footing to which indigenous rulers could appeal, paramountcy was taken to mean that all foreign relations and military decisions of the Native States were in the hands of the British. Rather interestingly, the position of the Native States with respect to the Empire 'was held to be analogous to the States of the United States of America, which had also surrendered certain external powers (e.g. defence and foreign affairs) to a central government, but which nevertheless retained residual sovereign powers'.[82]

Paramountcy was obviously flexible and, ominously for the rulers of the Native States, could be defined and redefined by the British more or less at will. An activist governor-general or viceroy, like Dalhousie or Curzon, could interpret it as a permission to be extremely interventionist with regard to the domestic affairs of the Native States, or even to conduct a policy of annexation. If it is possible to generalize about paramountcy, however, we might say that there was a profound disagreement between liberals and conservatives about its use. Many liberals were extremely concerned about allowing the rulers of Native States to retain what often amounted to quite full rights of internal sovereignty: 'Convinced that western civilisation was superior and inspired by the belief that Britain had a moral obligation to reform Indian society, the reformers were appalled to learn that British policy encouraged princely mismanagement. Despite their anti-imperialist sentiments, they thus advocated the termination of princely rule and became committed to a policy of annexing the states.'[83] Conservatives, on the other hand, were obviously less inclined to castigate the rulers of the Native States merely on the grounds that they represented an archaic and illiberal feudalism. Moreover, in a point of view that gained some reinforcement after the Indian Mutiny, they believed that respecting the (limited) sovereignty of the Native States would allow them to act as 'safety valves in order to provide for the security of British rule'.[84]

There are two interesting points about the official doctrine of paramountcy. First, it was legally eclectic. It derived partly from custom and treaty, but it also depended on natural legal principles: 'the paramount power took upon itself the task of suppressing inhuman practices . . . there existed a universal prohibition throughout the sub-continent against *suti*, slavery and infanticide'.[85] Perhaps more explicitly than when dealing with an independent sovereign over whom they did not claim

[82] Sever, *Indian Princely States*, vol. I, p. 26.
[83] Ashton, *British Policy towards the Princely States*, pp. 12–13.
[84] *Ibid.*, p. 14.   [85] Sever, *Indian Princely States*, vol. I, p. 24.

paramountcy, the British were prepared to assert the natural and universal character of their values, and vigorously imposed them. Secondly, irrespective of the political disagreement between liberals and conservatives about the application of paramountcy, the doctrine itself had profound implications for conceptualizing sovereignty. The Native States were not independent, but nevertheless, they retained their sovereignty in some sense. The core of the position can be seen in the British viceroy's comment in 1857, on the controversy surrounding the deposition of the indigenous ruler of Baroda, the Gaekwar:

> He has been acknowledged as sovereign of Baroda, and he is responsible for exercising his sovereign powers with proper regard to his duties and obligations alike to the British government and to his subjects. If these obligations are not fulfilled, if gross misgovernment be permitted, if substantial justice be not done to the subjects of the Baroda state, if life and property be not protected, or if the general welfare of the country and people be persistently neglected, the British Government will assuredly intervene in the manner which in its judgement may be best calculated to remove these evils and to secure good government.[86]

This was the context that Maine, who combined (not insignificantly) the dual roles of being an expert on international law and on Anglo-Indian relations, used to illustrate his point about the divisibility of sovereignty in international law that I mentioned in the Introduction. Maine's work in fact provides a nice concluding point for this discussion of British and Dutch colonial administrations during the nineteenth century. As well as defending the idea of divisible sovereignty, he also advanced the point of view, consistently with the idea of *occupatio* and natural rights thinking in general, that the main feature of 'progressive societies' is a move 'from status to contract', especially with respect to the issue of land tenure.[87] These two principles offer perhaps the best way of thinking about the enduring legacy of Grotian thinking in international law in the nineteenth century and, because of the progressiveness that Maine attached to the move towards contractual relations, an insight into the intimate relationship between the division of sovereignty, the assertion of individuals' property rights and the promotion of 'civilisation'.[88]

---

[86] Cited in D.B. Somervell, 'The Indian States', *British Year Book of International Law*, 11 (1930), 59.

[87] See Henry Sumner Maine, *Ancient Law* (London: John Murray, 1861), and *Village Communities in the East and West* (London: John Murray, 1871), as well as Maine, *International Law: The Whewell Lectures of 1887*, 2nd edn (London: John Murray, 1915).

[88] For another important nineteenth-century line of argument in this regard, see John Stuart Mill, 'A Constitutional View of the India Question' and 'Maine on Village Communities', both in *Collected Works, Volume 30: Writings on India* (London: Routledge, 1990), pp. 175–8 and 215–28 respectively.

Divisible sovereignty and private property in practice

The political structures of modern colonial and imperial systems were founded on that supposedly 'medieval' notion: divisible sovereignty. In North America, sovereignty was always treated as divisible in the pre-revolutionary colonial system, not least because it was impractical for a single ruler or parliament to assert its undivided sovereignty over both Britain and the American colonies; attempts to assert such a right usually only ended in revolution. And, even after the revolution, the American political system continued to be founded on the practice of dividing sovereignty between the states that composed the Union, as well as among the new states that were eventually created in the western territories. The division of sovereignty within a confederal or federal system was extremely flexible, and allowed the statehood of settlements in the west to be recognized on equal terms with the other members of the Union fairly easily. An important reason for this relatively permissive American attitude towards recognition may well have been that the new states in this context were mainly founded by white, European settlers, and did not pose the dilemmas for theories of racial hierarchies in the world that non-white and non-European political communities presented; certainly, the white-settler Dominions in the British Empire gained rights of self-government in a relatively accelerated manner, compared with colonies such as India.

Divisible sovereignty also characterized the imperial systems that the Dutch and British created in the East, although here the emphasis was more on the suzerainty or paramountcy of the imperial power and less on the collaborative decision-making of the American republic. In part, this difference arose because the Europeans were plugging themselves into existing imperial hierarchies, where the principle of suzerainty was already established, but it also arose from the manipulation of treaty provisions, so as to gain control over commerce and place once-independent rulers in a position of subordination. Nevertheless, despite their assertions of paramountcy it would be quite wrong to suppose that either the Dutch or the British ever attempted to impose direct rule, or anything even approaching absolute, unitary or undivided sovereignty over their imperial possessions. 'Indirect rule' and 'double government' were generally believed to be more cost-effective, more practical and, especially after the Indian Mutiny, more secure in the long run. One of the signatures of paramountcy and indirect rule, however, was that the independence of indigenous 'semi-sovereign' rulers was constrained by imperial and moral considerations. Their sovereignty was acknowledged, but they were placed under an obligation to obey the paramount power in matters of strategic and military security concern. They were also vulnerable to interventions by the imperial power in order to check the dangers of mis-government that, in European eyes, arose from placing political authority in the hands of uncivilized rulers. As politicians and colonial administrators made clear time and again, they would not hesitate to interfere with a ruler of a Native State if they believed that it was necessary to do so in order to secure 'good government' for his or her subjects.

A second interesting point is that in both American colonialism and European imperialism a considerable degree of importance was attached to the rights of individuals. This is obvious for North America, where colonial settlers enjoyed allodial property rights, and where the conception of property ownership in identical terms was one of the key elements of the legal arrangements made for westward expansion in the Northwest Ordinance. But broadly similar attempts to assert the rights of individuals, especially to their persons and property, can be seen at work in the imperial administrations. Nor was this effort solely directed at the extra-territorial rights of Europeans; certain groups of indigenous peoples had their rights of property ownership confirmed, for example through the Permanent Settlement, and all peoples were supposedly protected from misgovernment and 'barbarous' practices by the paramount power. For all the high-handed and unilateral ways in which imperialists sought to promote these ideas, it should nevertheless not be ignored that they had little respect for the 'conspiracy of silence' that orthodox theorists believe to have characterized official attitudes towards the rights of individuals in modern world politics. The conspiracy may have held between European states, but it was repeatedly breached in the world beyond Europe. It is therefore quite inaccurate to say that participants in modern international affairs had no conception of human rights, and thought and acted entirely in statist terms. For many, the idea that individuals had, or should have, rights was so obvious, so axiomatic, that it was unnecessary to make a formal statement of the point; nevertheless, one of the central themes of international politics in the extra-European world over a period of 300 years was the vigorous assertion of the rights that individuals possessed in the law of nations.

Leaving aside for the moment the explicit colonial context of *De Jure Praedae*, Grotius himself made very little explicit reference to these practices in *De Jure Belli ac Pacis*. As I noted in chapter 2, there is a suggestive observation on the natural simplicity of the American Indians, and there are a few direct references to Greek colonialism and Roman imperialism in his discussions of unequal treaties and appropriation; but there is little on which to base either the claim that Grotius himself was an imperialist, or that modern imperialism was a distinctively 'Grotian' kind of international activity. Nor would it be entirely plausible to suggest that colonizers and empire-builders were really concerned about the legal environment in which they conducted themselves. It is surely reasonable to suppose that many times they did what they wanted to do, whether appropriating land or acquiring public rights to control trade, and then looked around for an *ex post* legal justification, finding an especially convenient one in Grotius. Much the same could be said, though, for the way in which the European states-system developed around the Bodinian conception of absolute sovereignty, and the equality and mutual independence of its members. European rulers did not originally set out to build an international society conceived in those terms; it evolved through their actions, as certain normative principles began to become more or less regularly codified and observed thanks to a convenient conjunction of theory and practice, and especially as lawyers began to discern a higher moral purpose in the institutions that had grown up around the self-interested behaviour of absolutist, dynastic monarchs. To the extent that it makes sense to talk of Bodinian or Hobbesian sovereignty as an animating principle of order in the European political system, it makes equal sense to describe the structure of relationships in the colonial and imperial systems beyond Europe in terms of the Grotian idea of divisible sovereignty.

It has always been hard for orthodox theorists to appreciate the international dimensions of these relationships in the extra-European world, largely because they make the misguided assumption that their unitary conception of sovereignty has always defined the discipline of international politics and international law. They argue that international relations are relations between mutually independent states, because that is the only conception they possess as a way of thinking about the modern world; they lack the more flexible conceptual vocabulary of Grotius, and thus are at a loss to know how to describe, say, relations between the British paramount power and the 'semi-sovereign' Native States of India. What they typically do, then, is simply ignore this way of organizing international relations, perhaps giving it a breezy acknowledgement but hastily moving on to the familiar business of international politics in the European states-system. The inadequacy of their conceptual apparatus and the narrowness of their historical vision are faults of the orthodox theory that continually reinforce one another. To grasp the importance of the alternative elements of modern international politics that I have described here may require a certain degree of imagination, but it is hardly asking for a leap of faith.

In this chapter I have taken on the ambitious task of trying to do in a few thousand words what orthodox theorists have had two hundred years and literally hundreds of books to do: namely, to give an historical account of the origins, evolution and dynamics of a particular pattern of modern international relations. I do not presume to think that the account I have given here is as pared down, as easily understood, or as immediately familiar and plausible, as the orthodox account of the emergence of the Westphalian system and the European society of states. But I think it is, at the very least, a start; after all, the only alternative is to pretend that extra-European international politics do not exist. In chapter 4, I want to try to pull together the historical arguments I have presented, and offer a more analytical discussion of the specific nature of the pattern of political and legal order that developed in the world beyond Europe, comparing and contrasting it with the order that evolved in the context of the European states-system.

4   Two patterns of order in modern world politics: toleration and civilization

I have contested the orthodox view that order in modern world politics rests on the conjunction between the Grotian legal concept of international society and the historical concept of a states-system. In the first place, it is misleading to interpret Hugo Grotius's work as an anticipation of what legal order might look like in the emerging society of territorially sovereign states, since two of its central themes reflected the quite different propositions that sovereignty is divisible and that individuals as well as sovereigns have rights in the law of nations. I have also tried to fill in one of the crucial gaps that arises from orthodox theorists' decision to concentrate on the development of European public order in virtual isolation from the rest of the world. At the same time that the 'Westphalian system' of equal and mutually independent territorially sovereign states was taking shape, quite different colonial and imperial systems were being established beyond Europe, predicated above all on the division of sovereign prerogatives across territorial boundaries and the assertion of the rights of individuals, especially to property. We therefore ought to reject the view of Hedley Bull, to take just one recent example, that '[t]he idea of international society which Grotius propounded was given concrete expression in the Peace of Westphalia'.[1] It is the colonial and imperial systems beyond Europe that have the closest affinity with Grotian ideas about the law of nations and, if we are to talk about a 'Grotian conception of international society' at all, we should rather be concerned with the distinctly non-Westphalian structure of political and legal order in the extra-European world.

My analysis of Grotian theory and the practices of colonialism and imperialism has already indicated some important ways in which this pattern of political and legal order differed from the one that developed within the European states-system. The fundamental normative principle of the Westphalian system was that each state should recognize the

---

[1] Hedley Bull, 'The Importance of Grotius in the Study of International Relations', in Bull, Benedict Kingsbury and Adam Roberts (eds.), *Hugo Grotius and International Relations* (Oxford: Clarendon Press, 1992), p. 75.

territorial sovereignty of the others, and therefore that states should respect each other's equality and independence. The logic of this norm implied that the institutions that maintained order in the society of states had to be extremely decentralized and voluntaristic, both of which criteria were fulfilled by the balance of power, diplomacy and positive international law. The fundamental normative principle of the colonial and imperial systems beyond Europe, by contrast, was that sovereignty should be divided across national and territorial borders as required to develop commerce and to promote what Europeans and Americans saw as good government. One might say that instead of *cuius regio eius religio*, it operated according to the principle of *cuius regio meas religio*. This arrangement was inevitably more centralized and more hierarchical than the Westphalian system, and its institutions differed accordingly: paramountcy (in the British Empire), federal union (in the United States) and the assertion of a universally applicable code of natural law substantially replaced the balance of power, diplomacy and legal positivism.

Although I have criticized Bull for his misinterpretation of Grotius and his acceptance of an oversimplified historical perspective on modern world politics, I broadly agree with his general understanding of the concept of social order, particularly his view that the concept does not just speak to any and every regularity in international affairs but more specifically to 'a pattern that leads to a particular result, an arrangement of social life such that it promotes certain goals or values'.[2] Consequently, it is important to set the divergences that I have identified between the norms and institutions of the European and extra-European systems into the context of the different goals or values that each pattern of order pursued, and that is my main purpose in this chapter. Within Europe, the leading purpose of international order was to promote peaceful coexistence in a multicultural world through the *toleration* of other political systems, cultures and ways of life. Its basic principle of respecting dynastic rulers' rights to govern their domestic possessions in their own way, which gradually changed into the principle that each nation had a right to self-determination, was rooted in the beliefs that different cultures were equally valuable and should be given space to flourish; and that the best way to ensure peace in the society of states was to encourage its members to eschew violence for religious, cultural or ideological reasons.

Beyond Europe, however, international order was dedicated to a quite different purpose: the promotion of *civilization*. Simply put, Europeans and Americans believed that they knew how other governments should be organized, and actively worked to restructure societies that they regarded

---

[2] Hedley Bull, *The Anarchical Society: A Study of Order in World Politics* (London: Macmillan, 1977), p. 4.

as uncivilized so as to encourage economic progress and stamp out the barbarism, corruption, despotism and incompetence that they believed to be characteristic of most indigenous regimes. Especially in North America, this was also connected with the idea that the whole continent was an uncultivated wilderness, which needed to be civilized through the establishment of properly organized settlements and through the provision of republican constitutions for the new states created thereby. In both cases, and again in contrast to the Westphalian system, statesmen, diplomats and international lawyers were quite prepared to entertain the possibility that violent actions and other interventions might have to be made in order to civilize savage peoples, or to prevent them from retarding the civilization of the wildernesses that they insisted on treating as their homelands.

Obviously, the order of toleration in the European states-system has received a great deal of attention from orthodox theorists, and it is unnecessary for me to supply anything more than the briefest of outlines here, merely for purposes of comparison. For the reasons I discussed in chapter 1, however, the colonial and imperial systems outside Europe and the order of civilization have received much less attention from students of international politics and international law. Indeed, many orthodox theorists appear to believe that the extra-European world did not contain a pattern of *international* order at all, since it was not based on relations between equal and independent, territorially sovereign states. I should acknowledge that this is a long-standing point, as old as the orthodox theory of order in world politics itself. Many nineteenth-century international lawyers, for example, insisted that international law only applied to the 'family of civilized nations', and that the uncivilized world was simply beyond the scope of international law properly conceived, not so much because it was unregulated by legal rules, but because it belonged to the sphere of the *constitutional* law of whichever state was recognized by its civilized counterparts as holding the decisive measure of international personality.[3] Nevertheless, the issue was by no means a settled one. Serious questions about whether relations between the British government and the Indian Native States, or even between the members of the

---

[3] See John Westlake, *Chapters on the Principles of International Law* (Cambridge University Press, 1894), ch. 10, and for a more blunt statement of the orthodox position, apart from the extreme Austinian positivism, see T.J. Lawrence, *The Principles of International Law*, 3rd edn (Boston: D.C. Heath, 1905). Lawrence did attract criticism for his un-nuanced interpretation of classical Grotian thinking about international law from scholars with a better grasp of the complexities of the issue: see Philip Baker, 'The Doctrine of Legal Equality of States', *British Year Book of International Law*, 4 (1923–4), 7, 8–9. It is worth adding that this debate is revealingly similar to the current dispute among students of the European Union about whether their subject is best understood through the theoretical apparatuses of international relations or comparative politics.

American States-Union, to take just two examples, should be considered as topics of international law were still raised by nineteenth-century scholars, notably Henry Sumner Maine. And, although seldom appreciated today, many eighteenth, nineteenth and even twentieth-century lawyers and political theorists continued to operate with the classical Grotian concepts of divisible sovereignty and property, applying them above all to international politics in the world beyond Europe.

I will begin my discussion of the extra-European order of civilization by offering some evidence of this persistence of the core Grotian ideas of divisible sovereignty and individuals' rights in the later legal literature, with a view to correcting the widespread misapprehension that modern theorists were exclusively concerned with analysing relations between equal and independent territorially sovereign states in the Westphalian system. Then, I will look more specifically at the concept of civilization, asking how it was construed by various British and American thinkers, what role it played in modern international law and how the various institutional arrangements that I outlined in chapter 3 were dedicated to its pursuit. In terms of how I will develop my argument in chapter 5, my most important contention here is that modern international lawyers were only able to maintain the coherence of order in world politics as a whole by adopting a discriminatory attitude towards the relative status of European and non-European peoples in terms of the degree of civilization each had attained. Although this proposition was logically distinct from theories of racial inequality and social evolution, and the two were kept separate by some thinkers, ideas about peoples' advancement towards civilization and their innate racial characteristics nevertheless became closely interwoven with one another during the later nineteenth century.

Thus, although the two patterns of modern international order had contrasting purposes and very different normative and institutional arrangements, the potential for this to become a serious contradiction in international legal thought and diplomacy was defused by restricting each to its own particular geographical and racial sphere. The key assumption was that Europeans and whites in general were already civilized, and that while they should tolerate one another's idiosyncrasies, they had a responsibility to correct those of backward non-European or coloured peoples. This way of demarcating the boundaries of the two patterns of international order was never perfect, and I will show that even in the nineteenth century there were some important, and awkward, overlaps between them. In chapter 5, however, I will examine how the discriminatory distinction between the civilized and uncivilized worlds broke down completely during the first half of the twentieth century, leading to the construction of a global political and legal order, but one with a fundamental duality of purpose since it attempts to pursue both of the goals of toleration and civilization at the same time.

Property and divisible sovereignty in the post-Grotian law of nations

By about a hundred years after his death, Grotius was widely regarded as old-fashioned and out of date. Many lawyers continued to pay him lip-service as the father of their 'science', but often that was little more than politeness; they were well aware that enquiries into the law of nations had changed dramatically since Grotius's day. The *philosophes*, on the other hand, could seldom even be bothered to be polite. We saw in chapter 2 that Voltaire, who admittedly was slow with a compliment for anyone, had no time for Grotius, arguing that his works substituted classical allusion for independent thought and 'didn't deserve the respect that the forces of ignorance paid to them'.[4] It was certainly true that the style, method and philosophy of treatises on the law of nations had become very different from those of Grotius's time, but what I want to do here is explore some ways in which Grotius's substantive propositions about the content of the law of nations persisted even through this methodological and philosophical shift. Scholars continued to offer remarkably similar views on the public and private rights contained within the law of nations, albeit on the terms of their own, vastly different, intellectual environment. What evolved, as I will go on to discuss in due course, was a theory of the law of nations that echoed Grotius's substantive opinions on divisible sovereignty and individuals' rights, but increasingly expounded within the context of a new idea of 'civilization', and especially a distinction between the civilized world of the society of states and the uncivilized world beyond.

As a starting point, let us begin with what is probably the most obvious similarity between Grotius's account of the law of nations and later, more obviously modern, treatises: his theory of how individuals acquire private property rights through the appropriation of communal property in the state of nature. Several scholars have remarked on the affinities between Grotius's thinking here and the subsequent arguments of Locke and other liberal political theorists, noting especially Grotius's use of the American Indians to illustrate a contemporary people that still lived in the simplistic, natural manner of communal property, and therefore where the natural right of *occupatio* might still be exercised by colonial

---

[4] Voltaire, *Political Writings*, trans. David Williams (Cambridge University Press, 1994), p. 89.

settlers in his own time.[5] We have seen that, in his account of the law of nations, Grotius had significantly amended the earlier canonical theories of Innocent IV with respect to the private and public rights of non-Christian peoples. He broadly upheld the earlier line that these peoples had rights, and that there was nothing to prevent them from holding both public authority and private property, but he extended the scope for colonial settlement in the extra-European world by developing the idea of what individuals had to do to acquire property rights through the notion of *occupatio*, and he worked out a theory of the separability of ownership and jurisdiction that permitted the colonial settlement of 'vacant' lands even if they were under another, European or non-European, ruler's jurisdiction.

Nevertheless, from a colonizer's point of view, the Roman law concept of *occupatio* that Grotius used was flawed because it was vulnerable to different, and more restrictive, interpretations. As Richard Tuck has recently demonstrated, scholars who were less favourably inclined to colonialism, such as Christian Wolff, argued that the American Indians *had* exercised their natural rights simply by inhabiting the lands in question, rather than actively using them at any given time, which inevitably circumscribed the opportunities for European appropriation.[6] Those who wanted to endorse the practice of planting settlements in the New World, like John Locke or Emerich de Vattel, therefore had to extend Grotius's argument yet further, building the idea of *occupatio* into a theory of appropriation that stressed the importance of making 'improvements' to the land as a necessary condition for ownership. In Vattel's account of the law of nations, for example, cultivation became a duty imposed by natural law on all nations, and one that was explicitly held up as a justification for the settlement of North America. Thus, as Tuck remarks, in Vattel's theory, 'we have a more or less faithful version of the Grotian arguments, as developed by Locke, and we can see how [these] themes . . . were still vividly alive in the middle of the eighteenth century'.[7]

Nor were they solely of use to the colonizing powers in Europe: as the American revolutionaries were to demonstrate in the late eighteenth century, the rights that individuals had obtained through colonial settlement could also be used as a justification for resistance against the mother country. An illuminating example of this use of the concept of appropriation in the context of revolutionary American thought can be

---

[5] Barbara Arneil, *John Locke and America: The Defence of English Colonialism* (Oxford: Clarendon Press, 1996), pp. 46–54, and Richard Tuck, *Rights of War and Peace: Political Thought and the International Order from Grotius to Kant* (Oxford University Press, 1999), pp. 102–8.
[6] See Tuck, *Rights of War and Peace*, pp. 190–1.   [7] *Ibid.*, p. 195.

found in Thomas Jefferson's famous 1774 pamphlet, 'A Summary View of the Rights of British America', the argument of which is closely related to previous European notions of ownership through occupation.[8] Jefferson sought to justify resistance against the British on a number of grounds, one of the foremost of which was the nature of land ownership in the colonies. He explained the nature of the American tenurial system by comparing it with the Saxon colonization of Britain, which was then, so he claimed, in a similar condition in the sense of being less populated. In establishing settlements, the Saxons established a land system under which they 'held their lands, as they did their personal property, in absolute dominion, disencumbered with any superior, answering nearly to the nature of those possessions which the Feudalists term Allodial'.[9] Jefferson went further than this purely historical account, to claim the right of appropriation as a right given to men by nature, 'of departing from the country in which chance, not choice has placed them, of going in quest of new habitations, and of there establishing new societies'; indeed, the Saxons had colonized Britain, so Jefferson claims, 'under this universal law', of which the American settlers had since availed themselves.[10] Thus, Jefferson could offer a theory of the private rights of American colonists in the law of nations that validated their rejection of British attempts to attach new taxes and encumbrances to their allodial tenures: a kind of private war that Grotius would probably not have endorsed, but which was nonetheless broadly consistent with his position. Of course, this thesis was not only handy for attacking the British. It continued to provide a convenient rationale for the mistreatment of the American Indians that persisted through the nineteenth century.[11]

The importance of individuals' property rights within the modern law of nations has seldom been appreciated because of the widespread assumption that a cardinal feature of modern international law is that international personality is restricted exclusively to states. The whole question of whether or not individuals have rights and duties in international law is thus supposed to have been suppressed by a grand 'conspiracy of silence' between states.[12] In terms of the full range of what are now called 'human rights', there is some truth to that claim, but with respect to their *property* individuals were always much better off in the modern law of nations,

---

[8] In Thomas Jefferson, *Papers of Thomas Jefferson* (Princeton University Press, 1950), vol. I, pp. 121–37. For a good commentary, see Eugene C. Hargrove, 'Anglo-American Land Use Attitudes', *Environmental Ethics*, 2 (1980), 121–48.

[9] Jefferson, *Papers*, vol. I, p. 132.   [10] *Ibid.*, p. 122.

[11] For an exemplary statement of the nineteenth-century conventional wisdom on Indians' property rights, see *Johnson* v. *McIntosh*, in *United States Reports*, Wheaton 8 (New York: Donaldson, 1823), especially pp. 573–4, 588ff. and 603.

[12] Bull, *The Anarchical Society*, p. 83.

to the delight of colonial settlers and, for the most part, the chagrin of indigenous peoples. Even here, though, there is a tendency to treat individuals' property rights as if they did not exist in modern international law, because there were no hard-and-fast treaties or agreements among states to render it as such. The definition and protection of individuals' property rights, it is often assumed, was simply a matter for municipal law, which only became an issue in the international realm under the rubric of the private international law doctrine on 'conflict of laws'.[13] And it is taken to be symptomatic of Grotius's medieval archaism that he did not grasp the distinctions between municipal and international, natural and positive, or public and private, that are so central to modern international society, but believed that individuals' natural rights to property were as much part of the law of nations as were the sovereign rights of public authorities.

The point, however, is that his belief in the importance of individuals' property rights has always been there in modern international law. It was explicitly made part of the law of nations in the works of Grotius, Locke and Vattel, who could treat it in that way because they were all comfortable with the notion that natural law constituted at least a part of the working law of nations of their time. As the invocation of natural law became less fashionable in the nineteenth century, so these explicit discussions of private property largely disappeared from textbooks on international public law. But we should not leap to the conclusion that because lawyers largely stopped talking about the subject, their silence amounted to a denial of individuals' rights. On the contrary, by the time of the first Hague Conference of 1899 the principle that individuals' private property rights should be respected was regarded as so self-evident that there was no need to work out a formal convention to that effect: as Konstantin Katzarov puts it, the recognition and protection of individuals' private property rights, their inviolable nature and their distinctness from state territorial jurisdiction was seen as one of the 'firmly established norms of public international law', at least until it began be undermined around the time of the first world war when the victorious powers' demand for reparations led them to engage in the seizure and sale of the property of citizens from the defeated states.[14] Moreover, within private international law the basic principle of the inviolability of individuals' rights to property was not merely accepted but was treated as an axiom of how relations between European states should be conducted. Private international lawyers believed that it constituted, to all intents and purposes a 'common law' for

[13] Konstantin Katzarov, *The Theory of Nationalisation* (The Hague: Martinus Nijhoff, 1964), pp. 284ff.
[14] *Ibid.*, p. 287.

the civilized world, where similar municipal codes governing property had been consistently developed.[15]

The relevance for the modern law of nations of Grotius's views on private rights to property is fairly easy to see. His conception of divisible sovereignty, however, might well seem to be much more archaic. It recalls the complex hierarchies of overlapping jurisdictions that, from the conventional point of view, were symptomatic of medieval Christendom, and precisely the opposite of the modern world where political authority is believed to come in neat territorial packages labelled 'sovereignty'. Once again, though, orthodox theorists wear blinkers with respect to an array of theoretical writings that continued to treat sovereignty as divisible. For a start, plenty of seventeenth-century scholars agreed with Grotius, and disagreed with Bodin, on the question of the divisibility of sovereignty. The imperial constitution, the territorial sovereignty of the states and the reserved rights of the emperor made it hard for lawyers to ignore the fact that, whatever the attractions of the Bodinian theory in principle, sovereignty was divided in practice.[16] And not all of them took seriously Bodin's (and Hobbes's) warnings of the dire peril that this meant for the commonwealth. As Leibniz rather bluntly pointed out, 'I . . . know that no people in civilized Europe is ruled by the laws that [Hobbes] has proposed', and, while he admitted that dissensions might arise from a division in the sovereign power, he did not think the risks were too great: 'experience has shown that men usually hold to some middle road, so as not to commit everything to hazard by their obstinacy'.[17]

It is no exaggeration to say that in the seventeenth century it was the more speculatively metaphysical system-builders who believed in the principle of the indivisibility of sovereignty, while the more pragmatic and constitutionally minded experts on the law of nations were the ones who upheld the empirically verifiable doctrine that sovereignty was divisible. In the eighteenth century, especially with growing demands for a rationalization of society precisely in accordance with philosophical

---

[15] A.V. Dicey, *A Digest of the Law of England with Reference to the Conflict of Laws* (London: Stevens, 1896), pp. 15, 24 and 29. See also L. von Bar, *The Theory and Practice of Private International Law*, 2nd edn, trans. G.R. Gillespie (Edinburgh: William Green, 1892), pp. 5–6, and, as I mentioned in the introduction, Alexander Fachiri, 'Expropriation and International Law', *British Year Book of International Law*, 6 (1925), 159–71. An excellent recent discussion, especially on the later development of this theory, is L.C. Green, 'The Common Law and Native Systems of Law', in Robert Wilson (ed.), *International and Comparative Law of the Commonwealth* (Durham: Duke University Press, 1968), pp. 81–107.

[16] Julian Franklin, 'Sovereignty and the Mixed Constitution: Jean Bodin and his Critics', in J.H. Burns (ed.), *The Cambridge History of Political Thought, 1450–1700* (Cambridge University Press, 1991), pp. 298–328.

[17] Gottfried Wilhelm Leibniz, *The Political Writings of Leibniz*, ed. and trans. Patrick Riley (Cambridge University Press, 1972), pp. 118–19.

visions of natural law, the theory of divisible sovereignty was inevitably pushed slightly to the margins. But, like the concept of property, it never went away completely. There could be few more rationalist philosophers than the American revolutionaries, for example, but even they made extensive use of the idea of divided sovereignty to justify their actions. They pointed out that the long-established colonial system of government had widely distributed public authority rights across an extremely decentralized system of proprietors, chartered settlement agencies and partially self-governing local townships, rendering British attempts at consolidation unjust usurpations of colonial liberties.[18] Indeed, in its combination of a theory of individual property rights based on appropriation with a theory of divided sovereignty, the political theory of the American revolution could almost be seen as a practical demonstration of the enduring force of Grotian principles in the modern world, albeit wrapped up in the more radical philosophical climate of the mid-eighteenth century. And, to the extent that there is a link in that respect, it is hardly surprising that conventional histories and theories of modernity have always found it difficult to place America in their conceptual schemes.

The theory of divisible sovereignty survived well beyond the eighteenth century, and not just in America. Soon after the French Revolutionary wars, indeed, a new term was coined to describe similar arrangements in Europe: 'if one state depends on another state in the exercise of one or more of the various rights that essentially inhere in sovereignty, but is free with respect to the others, it is called dependent or semi-sovereign (*mi-souverain*)'.[19] In fact, the majority of nineteenth-century textbooks on international law follow a nearly identical pattern to Grotius's own argument, beginning with a general assertion of the indivisibility of sovereignty, to which is added the resulting doctrine of the equality and independence of sovereign states, but then offering a host of examples to illustrate the continuing importance of the practice of dividing sovereignty in the modern world. Here, in fact, the nineteenth-century lawyers were often explicitly critical of those earlier theorists, such as Vattel, whom they criticized

---

[18] Although the most celebrated documents (like the Declaration of Independence) make great play of monarchical tyranny and the usurpation, really the revolutionaries were much more anxious to contest the Whiggish doctrine of absolute (British) parliamentary supremacy, by pointing to the traditionally decentralized nature of authority in the empire and colonial system of government. See Bernard Bailyn, *The Ideological Origins of the American Revolution* (Cambridge, MA: Belknap Press, 1967), especially pp. 202–16, and James Muldoon, *Empire and Order: The Concept of Empire, 800–1800* (London: Routledge, 2000).

[19] Jean Loius Klüber, *Droit des Gens Modernes de L'Europe*, 2 vols. (Stuttgart: Cotta, 1819), vol. I, p. 46. Klüber also noted some earlier expressions referring to '*quasi-regna*' and 'second-order states'.

for making too strong an assertion of the indivisibility of sovereignty, and made instead a clear distinction between sovereignty and nationality that suggested the two terms were not at all synonymous.[20] Practical instances of divided sovereignty were usually discussed under two main headings. First, lawyers dealt with unions of sovereign states, ranging from the loose German confederation, where the individual states were deemed to have retained a measure of international personality, to the more centralized structure of the American States-Union, where most lawyers believed that all international personality had been vested in the federal government. Secondly, they discussed the status of dependencies and protectorates: independent states that had, through whatever means, accepted an inferior relationship towards another state, such that the latter acted as the former's guardian in international affairs, and often exercised considerable control over the protectorate's capacity for independent relations with third parties. The classic examples of this kind of polity, within the European political system at least, were Poland and the Ionian Islands.[21]

In short, to persist in the belief that modern international lawyers were all committed to a Bodinian or Hobbesian conception of indivisible sovereignty is to ignore the evidence of what they actually wrote. Admittedly, the Bodinian and Hobbesian thesis about the singularity of sovereignty was given a powerful and influential restatement in the middle of the nineteenth century through John Austin's famous 'positive' theory of law. Austin loathed the idea of divisible sovereignty, although even the venom he poured on to it does indicate the continuing popularity of the concept, and he insisted that the whole doctrine of divisibility, with its cognate ideas of semi- or demi-sovereign entities, was 'absurd', 'nominal' and 'illusive'.[22] But Austin did not have everything his own way. In response to his rather abstract approach, later nineteenth-century scholars like Henry Sumner Maine developed an equally, or even more, popular theory of 'historical jurisprudence', effectively replaying the same debates that had been carried on between Bodin, Hobbes and

---

[20] Travers Twiss, *The Law of Nations Considered as Independent Political Communities: On the Rights and Duties of Nations in Time of Peace* (Oxford University Press, 1861), p. 23.

[21] For fairly representative examples, see Henry Wheaton, *Elements of International Law*, 6th edn, revised by William Beach Lawrence (London: Sampson Low, 1857), pp. 45ff.; Robert Phillimore, *Commentaries upon International Law*, 2nd edn, 2 vols. (London: Butterworths, 1871), vol. I, pp. 93ff.; William Edward Hall, *A Treatise on International Law*, 2nd edn (Oxford: Clarendon Press, 1884), pp. 27ff.; and George B. Davis, *The Elements of International Law with an Account of its Origins, Sources and Historical Development*, 2nd edn (New York and London: Harper and Brothers, 1900), pp. 34ff.

[22] John Austin, *Lectures on Jurisprudence, or The Philosophy of Positive Law*, 4th edn (London: John Murray, 1879), pp. 257 and 260.

the constitutionalist historians of the seventeenth century.[23] Maine, like Bodin's critics a couple of hundred years earlier, weighed in with the obvious practical objection to Austin: the division of sovereignty might not work in your theoretical scheme, but it seems to work perfectly well in practice.

It is necessary to the Austinian theory that the all-powerful portion of the community which makes laws should not be divisible, that it should not share its power with anybody else, and Austin himself speaks with some contempt of the semi-sovereign or demi-sovereign states which are recognized by the classical writers on international law. But this indivisibility of sovereignty, though it belongs to Austin's system, does not belong to international law. The powers of sovereigns are a bundle or collection of powers, and they may be separated one from another. Thus a ruler may administer civil and criminal justice, may make laws for his subject and for his territory, may exercise power over life and death, and may levy taxes and dues, but nevertheless he may be debarred from making war and peace, and from having foreign relations with any authority outside his territory.[24]

That, he added, was the precise position in which the Indian Native States now found themselves.

Nor was Maine alone in this view. John Westlake agreed that 'sovereignty is partible', and took the idea of 'semi-sovereignty' to be a useful and valid concept, although he was more reticent than Maine about the international status of the Indian Native States.[25] Arthur Berriedale Keith, yet another prominent British international lawyer of the period, began his analysis of the circumstances of the British Dominions with the observation 'that sovereignty can be divided, and that in any country both internal and external sovereignty may be shared by various authorities'.[26] Even as late as 1940, Hersch Lauterpacht was still arguing that: 'from the point of view of international law, sovereignty is a delegated bundle of rights. It is a power which is derived from a higher source [the normative framework of the international legal order itself] and therefore divisible, modifiable and elastic. This is so although international law has suffered for a long time from the theory of the indivisibility of sovereignty.'[27] In fact, the only puzzle in Lauterpacht's statement is his apparent belief that the

---

[23] For an analysis of Maine's approach, see Paul Vinogradoff, *Outlines of Historical Jurisprudence*, 2 vols. (London: Oxford University Press, 1920).

[24] Henry Sumner Maine, *International Law: The Whewell Lectures of 1887*, 2nd edn (London: John Murray, 1915), p. 58.

[25] Westlake, *Chapters on the Principles of International Law*, p. 87.

[26] Arthur Berriedale Keith, *The Sovereignty of the British Dominions* (London: Macmillan, 1929), p. 1.

[27] Hersch Lauterpacht, 'Sovereignty and Federation in International Law', in Lauterpacht, *International Law: The Collected Papers of Hersch Lauterpacht*, ed. E. Lauterpacht, 4 vols. (Cambridge University Press, 1970), vol. III, p. 8, and for another discussion, see vol. I, pp. 370–7.

theory of the indivisibility of sovereignty had previously dominated inter-national law. This may well be one of the first examples of the widespread underestimation that later twentieth-century international legal scholars have consistently made of the flexibility and complexity of seventeenth, eighteenth and nineteenth-century thinking about sovereignty and semi-sovereignty.

The concept of civilization and modern international legal order

International lawyers, in short, continued to use the classical Grotian concepts of property and divisible sovereignty right through into at least the early twentieth century. Nevertheless, it would be vastly overstating the continuity between Grotius's position and those held by eighteenth or nineteenth-century scholars to treat these arguments as evidence for a sustained Grotian tradition. Although similar concepts were still being used, they were located in a wider intellectual context that was quite different from that which animated Grotius's theory of the law of nations. The philosophical orientation and practical context of international law had changed radically from Grotius's day, and this development goes right to the heart of how the difference between the European and extra-European patterns of order was understood. To understand it, we need to appreciate how the vast majority of international lawyers came to hold the belief that a distinction needed to be made between the pursuit of toleration and civilization in modern world politics.

The idea that order in modern world politics possessed two distinct purposes, and consequently was divided between two different norma-tive and institutional systems, was not a major feature of Grotius's work on the law of nations, if it could even be said to have figured in his ar-gument at all. In the first place, as I noted in chapter 2, Grotius did not really think about international relations in purposive terms at all. He was interested in the rights and duties that actors did hold, rather than those which ought to be vested in them in order to realize the best possi-ble political or legal system. His attitude was that legal rights should be respected, but he did not try to define a particular distribution of rights that ought to be established in order to create a more tolerant or a more civilized world. Secondly, for the most part Grotius did not make any radical distinctions between order within and beyond Europe, or even Christendom. Apart from his description of the American Indians as liv-ing in a condition that was still characterized by natural simplicity and community of property, he tended to regard the rights and duties of extra-European and non-Christian peoples in much the same way. In principle, there was nothing to prevent the American Indians from setting up an institution of *dominium* among themselves, in which case they would have exactly the same rights over their property as Europeans enjoyed, while the division of sovereignty applied just as much to European rulers, exemplified by Philip II's relationship to the Dutch, as it did to non-European rulers like the king of Johore. There are very few references in Grotius's work to the idea that Christendom might have had systematically different legal arrangements from the non-Christian world, and often they relate to issues like postliminium that have little relevance to the subsequent development of colonialism and imperialism beyond Europe.[28]

Most eighteenth-century international lawyers and political theorists parted company with Grotius in these respects. They increasingly believed that enquiries into the law of nations ought not only to say what that law was, but also to discern some moral purpose that either validated the existing order or provided an ideal that indicated how it should be reformed.[29] For example, the struggle between the French revolutionaries and the defenders of the old regime revolved around this issue, and the counter-revolutionary perspective on European public order which ultimately won out was based on the thesis that the principle of 'internal freedom' was desirable because of its ability to sustain the purposes of peace and tolerance in international affairs. Moreover, although Grotius had seen the law of nations as an all-embracing code, eighteenth-century lawyers could not avoid the increasingly obvious fact that international relations were beginning to operate in systematically different ways in the European and extra-European worlds. As Robert Plumer Ward argued, for example, it was impossible to ignore that 'what is commonly called the Law of Nations falls very far short of *universality* . . . the Law is not the Law of *all* nations, but only of particular classes of them . . . there may be a *different* Law of Nations for *different* parts of the globe'.[30]

There were two main ways of dealing with the problem that Ward had identified. The first response was simply to ignore what was happening in the extra-European world. Even though there were plenty of treaties between European and non-European rulers, for the most part the new legal

---

[28] Even as Martin Wight proposed that Grotius held a 'dualistic' or 'concentric conception of international society', he qualified his claim by making precisely this observation: *Systems of States* (Leicester University Press, 1977), p. 128.

[29] An excellent study of this feature of modern international legal discourse is Martti Koskenniemi, *From Apology to Utopia: The Structure of International Legal Argument* (Helsinki: Finnish Lawyers' Publishing Co., 1989), especially pp. 106–17, and see also David Kennedy, 'Primitive Legal Scholarship', *Harvard International Law Journal*, 27 (1986), 1–98.

[30] Robert Plumer Ward, *An Enquiry into the Foundation and History of the Law of Nations in Europe*, 2 vols. (London: Butterworth, 1795), vol. I, p. xiii, emphases in original.

historians chose not to include them in their treatises, and gradually developed an account of the law of nations that was entirely derived from the treaties agreed within the European states-system.[31] The beauty of this strategy was that it effectively wiped the slate clean, liberating European rulers from treaties they had made that had often been signed under conditions of parity or even inferiority with non-European rulers. It thus left them free to enjoy to the full the benefits of their growing military and commercial domination over non-Europeans.[32] The second response was to posit some kind of qualitative difference between European and non-European peoples or geographical conditions to explain the divergence in international relations. Montesquieu, for example, produced an extended series of reflections on the effects of climate and other natural phenomena to the social development of peoples.[33] Much the same line of thinking can be discerned in Thomas Jefferson's famous remark that America's 'geographical peculiarities may call for a different code of natural law to govern relations with other nations from that which the conditions of Europe have given rise to there'.[34]

Generally speaking, in both of these approaches, lawyers and political theorists tended to think about order in world politics in terms of a radical distinction between civilized and uncivilized societies. At the risk of some oversimplification, they developed an approach that treated the principles of appropriation and divisible sovereignty as especially closely related to the particular legal code that governed relations between civilized and uncivilized peoples, fulfilling a morally desirable purpose by enabling the former to bring civilization to those parts of the world that did not yet enjoy its benefits. I have already touched on the importance of the idea of civilization, and its cognate notions such as 'manifest destiny', to extra-European international politics, and I have also pointed to the pivotal role that these ideas played in the further development of Grotian ideas about divisible sovereignty and individuals' rights by theorists who wanted to view the international legal order in more purposive terms than Grotius himself had done. What I want to do now is offer a more detailed analysis of precisely how this concept operated and what its content was: what

---

[31] See Charles Alexandrowicz, 'Empirical and Doctrinal Positivism in International Law', *British Year Book of International Law*, 47 (1974–5), 286–9.

[32] See Charles Alexandrowicz, *An Introduction to the History of the Law of Nations in the East Indies* (Oxford: Clarendon Press, 1967). I have to admit that I feel Alexandrowicz overstated the case for this point, and that on the whole Europeans were better at manipulating the early treaties than he believed.

[33] Baron de Montesquieu, *The Spirit of the Laws*, trans. Thomas Nugent (New York: Harper, 1966).

[34] Cited in Albert K. Weinberg, *Manifest Destiny: A Study of Nationalist Expansionism in American History* (Baltimore: Johns Hopkins University Press, 1935), p. 29.

exactly did people mean when they talked about bringing 'civilization' to the world beyond Europe?

A good starting point for answering this question can be found in the work of John Stuart Mill, an individual who neatly combined both roles of a colonial administrator and an expert commentator on international law. Mill identified four main characteristics that defined a civilized people, as opposed to a savage or barbaric one. Civilization implied, he said, 'a dense population . . . dwelling in fixed habitations, and largely collected together in towns and villages'; a highly developed level of agriculture, commerce and manufacturing industry; 'human beings acting together for common purposes in large bodies, and enjoying the pleasures of social intercourse'; and a state of affairs 'where the arrangements of society, for protecting the persons and property of its members, are sufficiently perfect to maintain peace among them'.[35] These were all attributes that savage peoples lacked, to greater or lesser degrees. This conception of civilization has two main dimensions: it speaks to material development, in the sense of economic and technological progress; and it has a moral dimension, in the sense that a civilized society would be based on an educated and refined population, and good government based on fair and effective political, administrative and judicial systems.[36] Although the concept of civilization was so ubiquitous in nineteenth-century scholarship that it is difficult to make a general survey about how its meaning was understood, Mill's point of view was clearly widely shared. American ideas about 'manifest destiny', for example, had almost identical connotations, being concerned with, in Robert Johannsen's summary, 'the movement of Americans to new and permanent homes in the far reaches of the

[35] John Stuart Mill, 'Civilization', in Mill, *Collected Works, Volume 18: Essays on Politics and Society* (London: Routledge, 1977), p. 120. It is worth noting that Mill did not necessarily understand this concept in unambiguously positive terms. For a start, he tried to define it in a technical way, not to distinguish between good and bad societies, but to identify what made a 'wealthy and powerful nation' different from 'savages and barbarians' (*ibid.*, p. 119). He recognized that the term was popularly used to denote general moral goodness, a position with which he had some sympathy, but he was careful to observe that one might easily see civilization as incapable of providing, or even hindering, the attainment of other socially desirable goals; he thought that it led, for example, to the rise of mass influence in politics and culture, 'and the weight and importance of an individual, as compared with the mass, sink into greater and greater insignificance' (*ibid.*, p. 126).

[36] The point about the dual, material and moral aspects of the concept of civilization is nicely captured by Fernand Braudel, *A History of Civilizations*, trans. Richard Mayne (London: Penguin, 1994), p. 5, although Braudel's point about the mid-eighteenth-century origins of the concept in France could clearly be taken further back, especially for the English-speaking world: see, for example, Thomas Patterson, *Inventing Western Civilization* (New York: Monthly Review Press, 1997), and Jane H. Ohlmeyer, ' "Civilizinge of those Rude Parts": Colonization within Britain and Ireland, 1580s to 1640s', in Nicholas Canny (ed.), *The Oxford History of the British Empire, Volume 1: The Origins of Empire* (Oxford University Press, 1998), pp. 124–47.

continent, the advances in the economic and political environment that seemed to add up to progress, the humanitarian reform efforts to sweep away the obstacles to perfection', alongside more uniquely American interests in religious salvation and the growing republic's status *vis-à-vis* the longer-established European powers.[37]

In both its material and moral senses the idea of civilization had a very close association with the practices of dividing sovereignty and asserting individuals' property rights that characterized the extra-European colonial and imperial systems. The reformation of indigenous property systems in the East Indies and American practices like homesteading were both directly associated with the spread of civilization. Not only were these intended to stimulate the improvement of uncultivated or poorly cultivated land, and hence promote economic growth, but they were also intended to act as a check on arbitrary and despotic government, as Thomas Stamford Raffles's comments on 'intermediate renters' indicate. As with many aspects of the language of civilization, this was most overt in America, where, as John Dix, a New York senator, made clear in 1848, the logic of westward expansion meant that 'aboriginal races, which occupy and overrun a portion of California and New Mexico must there, as everywhere else, give way before the advancing wave of civilization, either to be overwhelmed by it, or be driven upon perpetually contracting areas'.[38] The division of sovereignty was also integral. The basic point of paramountcy in India, as well as maintaining the security of the empire itself, was to provide a rationale under which Europeans could intervene in the domestic affairs of the Native States to ensure the provision of good government and to promote commerce as the basis for economic and technological progress. In America, even though the division of sovereignty within the federal Union was less hierarchical, its explicit purpose was to provide the necessary coordination involved in projects like the building of canals and railroads that were generally regarded as crucial elements of the project of civilization.[39] The concept also validated American practices beyond the colonization of the West that more closely resembled European imperialist assertions of paramountcy. As one commentator put it, 'interference in the affairs of populations not wholly barbaric, which have made some progress in state organization, but which manifest incapacity to solve the problem of political civilization with any degree of completeness, is a justifiable policy. No one can

---

[37] Robert Johannsen, 'The Meaning of Manifest Destiny', in Sam W. Haynes and Christopher Morris (eds.), *Manifest Destiny and Empire: American Antebellum Expansion* (College Station: Texas A&M University Press, 1997), p. 15.

[38] Cited in Thomas R. Hietala, ' "This Splendid Juggernaut": Westward a Nation and its People', in Haynes and Morris (eds.), *Manifest Destiny*, p. 53.

[39] See *ibid.*, p. 62.

question that it is in the interest of the world's civilization that law and order and the true liberty consistent therewith shall reign everywhere upon the globe.'[40]

As well as its dual application between material and moral phenomena, another crucial feature of political and legal thinking about civilization was the distinction between it as an *event*, especially as a state of affairs already achieved, and civilization as an ongoing *process* towards a target that, in many accounts, was seen as an ideal never to be fully realized.[41] In practical terms, for the most part (although not entirely, as we will see in a moment) this translated into the idea that civilization had already been attained by European states and by the American States-Union. A consistent theme in textbooks on international law from the middle of the nineteenth century on was the distinction between the family of civilized nations, which was seen as roughly synonymous with the society of states who had achieved recognition as fully independent sovereigns, and the uncivilized world beyond, of territories and peoples that had not yet achieved such recognition. The orthodox principles of international law, especially the principle of national self-determination and the doctrine of the equality and independence of states, applied only to those peoples that were already recognized as civilized; with respect to other peoples, civilized states had a responsibility, in so far as they could discharge it without damaging their own prosperity and domestic liberty, to facilitate the former's advancement. As the international lawyer James Lorimer put it:

The moment that the power to help a retrograde race forward towards the goal of human life consciously exists in a civilised nation, that civilised nation is bound to exert its power; and in the exercise of its power, it is entitled to assume an attitude of guardianship, and to put wholly aside the proximate will of the retrograde race. Its own civilisation having resulted from the exercise of a will which it regards as rational, real, and ultimate, at least when contrasted with the irrational, phenomenal, and proximate will of the inferior race, it is entitled to assume that it vindicates the ultimate will of the inferior race – the will, that is to say, at which the inferior race must arrive when it reaches the stage of civilisation to which the higher race has attained.[42]

It is worth noting that the boundaries of the civilized world were never precisely defined, and were not exactly the same as the society of states. On the one hand, it kept on shifting over the course of the

---

[40] Cited in Weinberg, *Manifest Destiny*, p. 429.

[41] A classic statement of this distinction is Arthur de Gobineau, *The Inequality of Human Races*, trans. Adrian Collins (New York: Howard Fertig, 1967), p. 77, and see also Patterson, *Inventing Western Civilization*, p. 42.

[42] James Lorimer, *The Institutes of the Law of Nations: A Treatise of the Jural Relations of Separate Political Communities*, 2 vols. (Aalen: Scientia Verlag Aalen, 1980; reprint of the 1883 Edinburgh edition), vol. I, pp. 227–8.

nineteenth and early twentieth centuries as new states, such as Turkey, China, Japan, Persia and Siam, gradually acquired recognition as members of the family of civilized nations.[43] Another odd anomaly was that not all civilized peoples were fully sovereign because some of them, such as the members of the German confederation, still laboured under the stigma of semi-sovereignty. One legal textbook from 1900, for example, treated only Russia, England, France, China, Japan and the United States as fully sovereign states, but no-one would have treated that as a complete description of the membership of the civilized world.[44] The picture was further complicated by the fact that private international lawyers had a significantly different view of the extent to which civilization had reached. Because they were more interested in the spread of common law, especially English common law, they were quite prepared to treat parts of the world that had not yet come close to sovereign recognition as civilized on the grounds that they possessed appropriate legal and judicial systems thanks to the activities of imperial powers. On this view, Mexico and British India were civilized, whereas Turkey and China, members of the family of civilized nations by most public lawyers' reckoning, were not.[45]

Although some international lawyers, like Lorimer, explicitly used racially discriminatory theories, most of them debated these different views of the extent of civilization in terms of doctrines about recognition and the spread of the common law. Among experts on international politics, however, racial discrimination was a much more widely used approach to thinking about civilization. This line of argument became enormously popular in the mid-nineteenth century, when it became hooked up first with theories of race and then with theories of evolution, to produce scientific, or pseudo-scientific, justifications for the existence of two different patterns of order in the world.[46] American ideas about their 'manifest destiny' made this kind of argument absolutely explicit.

[43] See William Edward Hall, *A Treatise on International Law*, 2nd edn (Oxford: Clarendon Press, 1884), p. 40; Lassa Oppenheim, *International Law: A Treatise*, 2nd edn, 2 vols. (London: Longmans, Green and Co., 1912), vol. I, pp. 32–3; and for a more recent and more detailed analysis, Gerrit Gong, *The Standard of Civilization in International Society* (Oxford: Clarendon Press, 1984).

[44] George Davis, *The Elements of International Law with an Account of its Origins, Sources and Historical Development*, 2nd edn (New York and London: Harper and Brothers, 1900), p. 35.

[45] A.V. Dicey, *A Digest of the Law of England with Reference to the Conflict of Laws* (London: Stevens, 1896), p. 29.

[46] For one of the leading examples of this social evolutionist position, see Benjamin Kidd, *The Control of the Tropics* (London: Macmillan, 1898), and *Principles of Western Civilization* (New York: Macmillan, 1902). One of the earliest political theories based on race, Gobineau's *Inequality of Human Races*, adopted the idea of multiple civilizations, each of which had its own specific racially defined orientation. Amongst Anglo-American theorists, the superiority of both the white race and its civilization was much more generally agreed.

Congressional and journalistic debates are littered with confident assertions that their expansion was the work of a 'superior race, with superior
ideas and a better civilization' and of the 'excellent white race... whose
power and privilege it is, wherever they may go, and wherever they may
be, to Christianize and to civilize, to command to be obeyed, to conquer
and to reign'.[47]

I should admit that not all Europeans were enamoured with this thesis
about the desirability of civilization, or about the tendency to limit the
process to non-European peoples alone. Assertions of both the moral
and material value of civilization were largely restricted to the English-
speaking world, and particularly among German scholars, civilization was
seen as largely material, and was negatively counterposed to the moral
value of *Kultur*.[48] Moreover, even among British and American thinkers
there was a significant constituency that regarded civilization as something that was still applicable to European peoples as well. Many of these
arguments took the form of early theses about increasing interdependence
that anticipate current analyses of globalization in the degree to which
they recognize that the further development of economic and technological progress might involve closer integration to the detriment of the
independent territorial sovereignty of states.[49] Even Lorimer, that vigorous advocate of the civilization of non-European peoples believed that
'it is obvious that, at the stage which intercommunication has reached,
Europe is no more independent of the other continents of the globe than
the separate States of Europe are independent of each other. Europe has
burst her bounds in all directions, and in becoming the centre of cosmopolitan life, she has ceased to be self-sufficing.'[50] And Kidd, one of
the principal international relations theorists to expound racial theories of
social evolution and their relevance to the civilizing mission of European
powers outside Europe, realized that the further advance of civilization
would have massive consequences for the West as well, leading to the

[47] Cited in Johannsen, 'The Meaning of Manifest Destiny', p. 15, and John Belohlavek,
'Race, Progress and Destiny: Caleb Cushing and the Quest for American Empire', in
Haynes and Morris (eds.), *Manifest Destiny*, p. 25.

[48] For a classic analysis, see Norbert Elias, *The Civilizing Process: Sociogenetic and Psychogenetic Investigations*, trans. Edmund Jephcott, revised edn (Oxford: Blackwell, 2000),
ch. 1, and for a fascinating recent discussion of the evolution of the German critique of
Zivilisation, see Arthur Herman, *The Idea of Decline in Western History* (New York: Free
Press, 1997), especially chs. 3, 7 and pp. 194–8.

[49] This might seem odd, but the concept of interdependence is as old as the idea of the
states-system itself. So far as I am aware, the first statement of the idea that interdependence will lead to closer cooperation among states, and hence more peaceful international relations, can be found in John Campbell, *The Present State of Europe, Explaining
the Interests, Connections, Political and Commercial Views of its Several Powers*, 3rd edn
(London: Longman, 1752), p. 24.

[50] Lorimer, *Institutes of the Law of Nations*, vol. II, p. 288.

'dissolution of all the absolutes in which the hitherto ascendant present had strangled the future'.[51]

I will return to some of these fault-lines in the distinction between the family of civilized nations and the rest of the world in chapter 5. For now, though, the main point that I want to highlight is that the persistence of Grotian ideas about the divisibility of sovereignty and the rights of individuals was closely bound up with the concept of civilization, which was such a prominent feature of nineteenth-century international legal and political thought. It would be quite wrong to conclude that the extra-European order, with its institutions of federal government and paramountcy, was originally designed with this goal in mind; as I explained in chapter 3, the development of colonial and imperial systems was most heavily influenced by the trading interests of European states and corporations. But just as the European states-system eventually came to be viewed in terms of the principle of toleration and national self-determination, so the extra-European systems were gradually re-conceived in terms of the increasingly popular ideas of civilization and white racial supremacy. To have an adequate conception of order in modern world politics, we have to go beyond the orthodox theory of toleration, reciprocal recognition and territorial sovereignty in the European states-system, and we need to appreciate the importance of the idea of civilization not merely as a standard for regulating the entry of new states in international society, but also for validating an entirely different set of legal rules and political institutions in its own right.

An overview of order in modern world politics

I have concentrated on the concept of civilization and its importance to modern international politics and international law because students of international relations will already be familiar with the structure of the international order that developed in the context of the European states-system. As implied by one of its foundational principles, *cuius regio eius religio*, its ultimate purpose was to promote toleration in a world of different religions, nations, cultures and political systems. It therefore operated in accordance with the normative principle that each member of international society should respect the sovereign independence of other states in their domestic jurisdictions, whether defined in territorial or national terms. To describe the emergence of this pattern of international political and legal order, orthodox theorists concentrate on the rise of dynastic monarchs, and the developing logic of their relations with one another.

---

[51] Kidd, *Principles of Western Civilization*, p. 349. Compare with the later functionalist theories developed in the interwar period by, *inter alios*, David Mitrany.

These monarchs consolidated their absolute sovereignty over their territorial possessions during the wars of religion; they then adopted a practice of recognizing their mutual independence partly to reduce conflicts among themselves over religious questions, but also so as to affirm each other's authority and reduce the status of other kinds of international actors. The emergence of a states-system and a society of states depended, in short, on a certain conjunction of power and interests, through which developed the norms of acceptable or appropriate conduct and the international legal rules and institutions of what has come to be known, accurately or not, as the 'Westphalian system'. Although the system's beginnings lay in the self-interested activities of absolutist monarchs, gradually scholars, statesmen and diplomats developed an account of the moral purposes of this kind of international order, arguing that its great virtue lay in its ability to handle the political and cultural pluralism of modern Europe, allowing states to live together in moderately peaceful coexistence through the toleration of their different ways of life.

Something else unfolded in the world beyond Europe, with different actors; different conjunctions of power and interest; different norms, rules and institutions of international relations; and, ultimately, a different purpose for international order. The range of actors was more diverse, including the absolutist monarchs from the orthodox narrative, but also chartered corporations engaged in trade and colonization, noble proprietors, individual settlers, colonial administrators, and, of course, indigenous rulers and peoples. And instead of monarchs trying to consolidate their absolute authority, the principal thrust of European activity in the world beyond Europe was the acquisition of wealth through the *control* of trade; not simply trade itself, but the manipulation and monopolization of trade with East and West. There were two main ways to establish control over trade: through the establishment of colonies of settlers from the mother country, or by inserting the European power into indigenous networks of political authority and commerce. Depending on the circumstances at hand, different approaches met with differing degrees of success. The British, who managed to establish themselves as the European colonial power *par excellence*, were adept at both.

Over time, as with the Westphalian systems, these originally haphazard activities began to take on a regular pattern, and it becomes possible to identify certain norms, rules and institutions in the conduct of international relations in the extra-European world, which shaped expectations of appropriate or legitimate behaviour and actively worked to sustain this particular pattern of order. From the beginning, the most consistent features of European colonialism and imperialism were the division of sovereignty across territorial boundaries, and the assertion that individuals had certain rights over themselves and their property that commanded respect from public authorities. Just as the assertions of supremacy by absolutist monarchs in Europe did not go unchallenged, so it took time for these norms to establish their validity. In America, it took a successful revolution to assert the rights of the individuals and the colonial authorities themselves; beyond Europe, it took a number of wars, no less vicious for the fact that they seldom appear in textbooks on international relations, in the course of which Europeans' increasing dominance in naval power, finance, the use of gunpowder and battlefield tactics eventually proved decisive. Eventually, both in North America and the East Indies, a pattern of relationships evolved where the division of sovereignty and the rights of individuals were accepted facts of international and interstate relations.

Because of its particular normative foundation, the institutional and legal structures of international order beyond Europe were quite different from those which evolved within Europe. The European society of states possessed institutions, like the balance of power or positive international law, that were well adapted to the highly decentralized and voluntaristic nature of the states-system upon which it rested. International order beyond Europe was, by contrast, more centralized and hierarchical: its institutions differed accordingly. In North America, the central institution was confederalism; in the East Indies, imperial paramountcy. The legal framework for this system of international relations already existed; it had been provided by Grotius in his account of the law of nations, and, with relatively few alterations, was carried forward by later international lawyers interested in questions of colonial and imperial politics. The great novelty of eighteenth and nineteenth-century international legal thought was to explain the increasingly obvious systematic divergence between European and non-European politics in terms of a highly discriminatory concept of civilization. That distinction, which really only became central to mainstream textbooks on international law around the middle of the nineteenth century, has not survived into the later twentieth century. In chapter 5, then, I want to look at the subsequent career of discrimination in international politics and international law, and its eventual eclipse by the construction of a global political and legal order.

5   Order in contemporary world politics, global but divided

By the late nineteenth century, international lawyers and diplomats considered it perfectly reasonable that there should be one kind of political and legal order for the 'family of civilized nations' and another for the uncivilized world beyond. No such distinction is made by diplomats and lawyers today, at least not in public; it is generally assumed that a single, global pattern of political and legal order exists, which should be indiscriminately applied to all peoples. Of course, that is not to say that there are no controversies about the fundamental principles on which this global order is based, or about how it operates in practice. There is a profound tension, for example, between state sovereignty and human rights, since the assertion of individuals' rights in international law and the protection of those rights by international organizations can be seen as compromising the principle that each state possesses an inviolable domestic jurisdiction by virtue of its sovereignty. That, moreover, is but one of several ways in which the sovereign independence of states is perceived to be threatened by the increasingly centralized, even supranational, authority of international organizations at both the global and regional levels. In this chapter, I want to explain how this global order was constructed, and why it suffers from such serious dilemmas about the relationship between state sovereignty and other aspects of the political and legal structure of international relations today.

The crucial step towards the construction of a single political and legal order for the entire world was the abandonment of the discriminatory way in which the concept of civilization had previously been employed. We have already seen that, in its nineteenth-century version, the concept was bound up with various theories explaining the relative backwardness of non-European peoples, especially a form of natural scientific argument about the impact of factors like geography or race on social and political evolution. European states, and the white race more generally, were therefore presumed to have a special responsibility to civilize those backward peoples who had come under their administration during the previous 200 years. During the first half of the twentieth century, that position became untenable, albeit very gradually and perhaps only ever at the formal, official level of diplomacy and international law. The most important reason for this development was that the concept of civilization increasingly began to separate Europeans from each other, and came to be seen in terms of an ideological divide rather than a racial one. The main problem of international order between 1914 and 1945, as civilized nations saw it, was not so much the backwardness of non-European peoples but rather the rise of barbarous ideologies in European states, such as Prussian militarism, communism and, most importantly of all, Nazism. The struggle on behalf of civilization against Nazism represented the crowning moment of this intellectual transformation, since now the concept was explicitly being deployed *against* the scientific theories of race that previously had given it much of its legitimacy as a way of articulating the rationale behind the bifurcated nature of order in world politics. Once that move had been made there was no going back to the old theoretical apparatus of nineteenth-century international law, and the 'reconstruction' of international order after 1945 was in that respect a genuinely original project.

But the terms in which that project was conceived were not always so original. The use of the idea of civilization to discriminate between the European and non-European worlds had become impossible to sustain, but that did not constitute a rejection of the idea of civilization as a goal for the new global political and legal order. On the contrary, in the struggle against Nazism the Allies had been fighting *for* civilization, and they were hardly about to abandon that belief in their moment of triumph. The elements of the old concept of civilization – economic and technological progress, the provision of good government and respect for the rights of individuals – remained largely intact, and were retained as fundamental goals that the new order was intended to deliver. Indeed, if anything, the scope of these goals was now wider than ever, because one consequence of the movement away from racial discrimination was that it could no longer simply be assumed that, by contrast with non-Europeans, Europeans themselves were already civilized and had no further need of its benefits. As a goal of international order, civilization was increasingly seen as applicable to relations between European states as well as to those between non-European ones, and the former were now encouraged to give up some of their sovereignty in order to attain a more civilized way of life, especially with regard to facilitating post-war reconstruction and the pursuit of rapid economic growth. There is a certain irony in the nationalistic protests that have since been raised against this transfer of sovereignty, since it hardly differs from what Europeans had been doing for generations to the peoples under their imperial control.

That last comment indicates one way in which the logic of this development has left the post-1945 global order with deep internal contradictions. In the nineteenth century, there were two very different patterns of political and legal order in the world, but there was also a popular belief in the validity of discrimination that prevented this dichotomy from posing any serious difficulties for international lawyers and statesmen: each order was confined to the peoples and parts of the world where it was deemed appropriate, and the two seldom came into conflict with one another. Once discrimination became unacceptable, however, it became impossible to maintain the easy separation between the two patterns of modern international order. We now live in a world where we have a singular political and legal framework that is schizophrenically trying to realize two different purposes at the same time. The legacy of the European society of states, with its emphasis on respect for the sovereign independence of states, still exercises an important influence on the contemporary order, but the core elements of the modern extra-European international order, with its emphasis on the division of sovereignty across territorial borders and respect for individuals' rights, also plays a crucial role in determining the content of international law and the structure of international organization today. The result is a superficially unified global pattern of political and legal order for the whole of humankind that is actually pointing in two directions at once, simultaneously promoting both toleration *and* civilization. The ensuing confusion, or worse, is clearly apparent in areas such as the tension between state sovereignty and human rights, or the dilemma about intergovernmentalism and supranationalism in organizations intended to promote economic growth.

The orthodox perspective on the construction of the global order

Before getting into the details of the argument, I ought to acknowledge that my account of the development of this global order in contemporary world politics differs substantially from the way in which that process is usually understood by international relations theorists. As I have already explained, orthodox theories of order in world politics begin from the assumption that the modern world was organized as a society of states that was originally confined only to European members. It is therefore inevitable that they think of the construction of a global political and legal order solely in terms of the expansion of the European society of states, concentrating, in particular, on the entry of non-European peoples into that society upon the recognition of their sovereignty. Of course, it would be quite unfair to suggest that that approach is simply mistaken, since the spread of the practice of recognition of sovereignty was a crucial factor in the emergence of the contemporary world order. Furthermore, a lot of insightful work has been done on this issue by orthodox scholars, particularly those who have argued that in its early stages the expansion of international society operated according to a 'standard of civilization' in the sense that, before being recognized as sovereign, non-European peoples were required to accept certain basic diplomatic and legal principles of the society of states (such as reciprocity), and to acquire the technological and political apparatuses of a civilized state.[1]

That line of argument at least acknowledges the importance of the idea of civilization in modern international law, but orthodox scholars have otherwise shown little awareness of the deep roots that the concept had in the pre-existing international political and legal order that had already been constructed in the extra-European world through colonialism. By concentrating on the entry of 'new states' into international society, orthodox approaches tend to overlook the long-standing centrality of ideas about civilization to, for example, the organization of relations between the British and the Indian princely states, and they fail to elucidate the crucial importance of the practice of dividing sovereignty to the pattern of order that was established on that basis. That makes it harder to understand the relationship between the principle of civilization and various phenomena in the contemporary global order, since it obscures, among other things, the proximity of the division of sovereignty in the old extra-European order to similar institutional arrangements in contemporary world politics. Even more importantly, orthodox scholars have looked only at the outward movement of the European international society, and have ignored the fact that, while the principle of toleration was gaining ground beyond Europe, the principle of civilization was making significant inroads into the European society of states itself. The construction of a global political and legal order was really a two-way process, as much about the increased effort by the British, French and Americans to civilize other Europeans (especially the Germans) as to tolerate non-Europeans. To focus only on the entry of non-European peoples into the 'family of civilized nations' misses a crucial part of the story: the entry of some civilized states – notably Germany, Russia and Japan – into the uncivilized world.[2]

---

[1] Gerrit Gong, *The Standard of Civilization in International Society* (Oxford: Clarendon Press, 1984).

[2] It is perhaps interesting to reflect on the viewpoint of one anonymous German shortly after the rise of Hitler: 'The frontier of Europe and of civilization has been shifted from the Vistula to the Rhine.' Cited in Ludwig Lewisohn, 'The Revolt against Civilization', in Pierre van Paassen and James Wise (eds.), *Nazism: An Assault on Civilization* (New York:

A second point where my approach differs from current scholarship on the contemporary world order is that it is popularly supposed that the construction of the new order after 1945 was an effort to realize idealistic principles that previously had only had a theoretical existence in the minds of philosophers, and no practical relevance to modern international politics or law. It is a commonplace, for example, for books on the development of the great twentieth-century international organizations, the League of Nations and the United Nations, to begin not by looking at two of the largest and most sophisticated organs of international and interstate governance that the nineteenth-century world possessed, the British Empire and the United States of America, but rather at the projects for a perpetual and universal peace advanced, *inter alios*, by the Abbé Saint-Pierre and Immanuel Kant.[3] One is presumably supposed to conclude that the international organizations we have today are attempts to realize those utopian visions, albeit with a more pragmatic recognition of the difficulties of translating such blueprints into reality (and, in the case of the League, not always even with that). The possibility that nineteenth-century structures of imperial and confederal governance might have a relevance to the growth of international organization in the twentieth century is seldom considered.[4]

Most scholarship on international human rights law has been similarly unforthcoming on the historical roots of the international practice of asserting and protecting the rights of individuals as human beings. It seldom does anything more than gesture in this direction with a cursory reference to the abolition of the slave trade, and often shows no regard at all for the importance that colonial administrators attached to codifying and protecting the property rights of individual settlers and indigenous peoples, or their frequent interventions to correct the mistreatment of individuals by local rulers. It is usually asserted instead that 'human rights were not an accepted subject of international relations prior to World War Two'; that during the eighteenth, nineteenth and early twentieth centuries international society 'gave punctilious respect to the sovereign prerogative of each state to treat its own citizens as it saw fit'; and that it is only since 1945 that states have 'taken on a revolutionary purpose, adding

Harrison Smith, 1934), p. 143. Civilization, the Europeans learnt in 1933 (as in 1914 and 1917), was not an irreversible process.

[3] For an early example of this line of argument, see S.P. Duggan, *The League of Nations* (Boston, 1919), pp. 27–32. This is in spite of the fact that the Americans and members of the British Empire, including South Africans, Australians and Canadians, played exceptionally important roles in the formation of both the League and the United Nations.

[4] For an exception that proves the rule, see Frederick K. Lister, *The European Union, the United Nations and the Revival of Confederal Governance* (Westport: Greenwood Press, 1996).

the needs and interests of individuals . . . to their traditional preoccupation with peace and security among themselves'.[5] The idea that individuals have rights, we are led to believe, was nurtured behind the protective shell of state sovereignty, in the work of natural lawyers and liberal political theorists whose teachings fell on deaf ears, internationally at least, until they were picked up in 1945 and, almost overnight so it seems, became a central and universally accepted part of the established international legal order.

A common theme across these approaches to international organization and human rights is that they make very little effort to relate the new twentieth-century forms of international political and legal order to the late nineteenth and early twentieth-century forms that immediately preceded them; it is almost as if the experiences of the first and second world wars were so shocking that everyone suddenly came down with collective amnesia and could only think in terms of seventeenth and eighteenth-century political philosophy. I admit that there are excellent reasons to suppose that, for example, Woodrow Wilson knew and admired Kant's vision for a perpetual peace guaranteed by a federation of free republics, but in most respects he and the other architects of the League system were operating with a world-view that was broadly similar to that which had defined pre-1914 ideas about international order. For all the novelty and apparent idealism of his proposals for preserving international peace, even Wilson shared some fundamental beliefs with earlier forms of international legal thought. As John Coogan has observed, for example, the Wilsonian administration adopted a hierarchical and discriminatory world view: 'Europe was more important than Latin America, which was more important than East Asia, which was more important than Africa; Anglo-Saxons were superior to other white races, which were superior to yellow, which were superior to brown, which were superior to black.'[6] Although increasingly serious doubts were being expressed about these beliefs, by 1919 they had definitely not been superseded, even by the most prominent critic of European colonialism at the Peace Conference. I will look at that issue more closely in just a moment, but for now the main point that I want to make is that it is unhelpful to place the work of statesmen like Wilson into the intellectual context of Kantian idealism. We need to compare what they were doing with the pre-war theory and practice of international order: it is only by doing that that we can see

---

[5] The first two quotes are from Jack Donnelly, *International Human Rights*, 2nd edn (Boulder: Westview Press, 1998), pp. 4 and 27; the last is from R.J. Vincent, *Human Rights and International Relations* (Cambridge University Press, 1986), p. 93.
[6] John W. Coogan, 'Wilsonian Diplomacy in War and Peace', in Gordon Martel (ed.), *American Foreign Relations Reconsidered* (London: Routledge, 1994), pp. 74–5.

what genuinely new ideas they were introducing, and in what respects they were preserving old assumptions.

The internationalization of civilization

I have said that the construction of a global political and legal order was really a two-way process: the principle of toleration was gradually extended to non-European peoples through their recognition as independent sovereign states; the principle of civilization was creeping into the European political system, dividing the 'family of civilized nations' from one another and effectively leading to the eviction (if only temporarily) of some of its members. Unfortunately, while we have plenty of good accounts of the expansion of the society of states,[7] we have very little in the way of a general analysis of how the principle of civilization was internationalized, and eventually globalized, beyond its extra-European context to become a central goal of political and legal order in the world as a whole. Here, I want to chart the initial stages in that long process by examining how the use of the idea of civilization was changing during the first world war and the debates about the League of Nations. I will start off by making the point that the concept's orientation was beginning to change under the pressure of the war, but then show that by the end of the first world war most of the diplomats and lawyers who were involved in the reconstruction of the post-war international order retained many of the pre-war assumptions about the uncivilized nature of non-European peoples. Doubts had been raised about the security of civilization in the European world, but this had not yet in any significant way affected the treatment of non-Europeans. To show how this rather unpromising beginning developed further during the interwar period, I will then look more closely at the system of 'mandates' that was created for the administration of the former German and Turkish colonies. This made a crucial change to the structure of international political and legal order by introducing a new form of global regulation to govern the practice of colonialism, essentially making the promotion of civilization a concern of international society as a whole, rather than exclusively the responsibility of the relevant imperial power. Even at this early stage in the process of constructing a global international order, this brought a series of dilemmas about the nature of sovereignty, especially regarding

---

[7] As well as Gong, *Standard of Civilization*, see Hedley Bull and Adam Watson (eds.), *The Expansion of International Society* (Oxford: Clarendon Press, 1984); Robert Jackson, *Quasi-States: Sovereignty, International Relations and the Third World* (Cambridge University Press, 1990); and James Mayall, *Nationalism and International Society* (Cambridge University Press, 1990).

the possibility of its divisibility, right to the foreground of mainstream international legal scholarship.

A serious problem for the legal belief that relations between European states operated in the context of a 'family of civilized nations' arose as the European system became divided over the 'German question'. Of course, and with good reason, this crisis is usually interpreted as resulting from a destabilisation of the balance of power, brought on either by German aggression, the inflexibility of the alliance system, or the destructive consequences of the principle of national self-determination. The last of these may have been especially pivotal, since it provided an irresistible rationale for the unification of Germany and thus removed one of the classic pillars of the European balance established in the 'Westphalian system': the existence of a mass of small, inert and essentially neutralized states in west-central Europe that made it difficult for any potentially hegemonic state to establish its preponderance. But although the causes of the confrontation with Germany may have lain in the growing instability of the balance of power, as the intensity of the conflict developed it increasingly began to be expressed in terms of a struggle for and against civilization, an issue, as I noted in chapter 4, that had already been brewing in the minds of German critics of *Zivilisation* well before it found an outlet in violent conflict.

As the first world war became a war of attrition involving unprecedented sacrifices, so the wartime leaders in all countries did everything they could to ratchet up the stakes that they were fighting for. One result was that the defence of civilization was to become one of the principal rallying cries through which the British sought to justify their involvement in the war and shore up domestic support. As one, admittedly rather jaded, British author reflected a decade after the first world war:

We wanted not merely to be fighting against things; something we wanted to be fighting for. For what? Belgium seemed too small, too grubby, Christianity indiscreet, the balance of power old-fashioned, ourselves improbable. We longed for a resonant, elevating and yet familiar objective; something which Christians and Agnostics, Liberals, Conservatives and Socialists, those who had always liked war and those who on principle detested it . . . could all feel proud and pleased to make other people die for. And then . . . came the fine and final revelation that what we were fighting for was Civilization.[8]

The British were already well used to fighting for civilization in other parts of the world, and it made for excellent rhetoric even in this novel and unusual context. Some of their opponents also shared this sense of

---

[8] Clive Bell, *Civilization and Old Friends* (University of Chicago Press, 1973), pp. 15–16. (First published in 1928.)

what was at stake, although naturally with a different attitude towards the values involved. The rather tortured wartime reflections of the German novelist Thomas Mann, for example, show that from his perspective at least the war was an attempt to defend the specifically German conception of *Kultur* against 'that intellectual tendency that has the democratic civilization-society of "mankind" as its goal; *la république sociale, démocratique et universelle*; the empire of human civilization'.[9] And Mann well understood the main source of this tendency: 'Who could remain indifferent to a threat that before the war had already taken on the form of an impudently calm statement: "The world is rapidly becoming English!" '[10]

It would be something of an understatement to say that, in terms of how the concept of civilization was used in the latter stages of the war and immediately afterwards, matters were complicated by the Russian Revolution. Although that Revolution had a host of implications for international law over the next several decades, the immediate reaction of many Western legal experts was to forget, for the moment at least, the barbarism of Prussian militarism, and focus instead on the dangers of socialist internationalism. Robert Lansing, the US secretary of state, was unequivocal about the nature of the problem: it represented a struggle between two rival conceptions of world order, one founded on individuals and nations; the other on classes and what he labelled 'mundanism' (i.e., a theory of the world-state). Unsurprisingly, it was his favoured position of individual and national self-determination that was 'the very lifeblood of modern civilization'.[11] Increasingly habituated to thinking of their struggles as battles on behalf of civilization, politicians and international lawyers were increasingly ready to turn the concept against whoever or whatever seemed like the most immediately serious problem. The whole question of who was in the uncivilized world, and why, was becoming increasingly difficult to answer, because the concept was now being asked to do much more work than it ever had before, particularly in an international legal context. As barbarism came to be associated with militaristic or communist ideologies, so civilization began to be understood in broader terms as built upon an order of peace-loving and self-determining nations, not exclusively white or European ones.

But there was still one point on which there was fairly widespread agreement: no matter that the status of Germany and Russia as members of the 'family of civilized nations' was now in doubt, the vast majority of the

---

[9] Thomas Mann, *Reflections of a Nonpolitical Man*, trans. Walter Morris (New York: Frederick Ungar, 1983), p. 23. (First published in 1918.)

[10] *Ibid.*, p. 325.

[11] Robert Lansing, 'Some Legal Questions of the Peace Conference', *American Journal of International Law*, 13 (1919), 649.

non-European peoples of Asia and Africa were still to be excluded.[12] As I have already mentioned, even Wilson's administration, while very hostile to the exploitative aspects of European imperialism, nevertheless did not believe in anything approaching racial equality, and certainly would not have regarded those non-European peoples under imperial domination as ready for entry into the family of civilized nations themselves. This was not remarkable: essentially similar views had been widely held among earlier American advocates of some kind of international 'League' for the preservation of peace worldwide, not all of whom were the Kantian idealists one hears so much about. Hard-headed old Theodore Roosevelt was one of the most prominent exponents of the League idea in the early twentieth century, and had won a Nobel Prize for his advocacy of an international system of arbitration after the 1905 Russo-Japanese war. He recognized that this system, to be effective, would require the formation of a 'League of Peace' to administer it, but the first step would be to construct a system of arbitration treaties, and here we see the old prejudices creeping in: 'all really civilized communities should have effective arbitration treaties among themselves', Roosevelt insisted, but there were 'states so backward that a civilized community ought not to enter into an arbitration treaty with them'.[13] He repeated his proposal with more urgency in 1915, but again insisted that a lasting peace could only be preserved if '[t]he great civilized nations of the world which do possess force, actual or immediately potential, should combine by solemn agreement in a great world league'.[14]

Although Roosevelt called this a 'world league', it is clear that to all intents and purposes its membership would be restricted to the 'great civilized nations' only, and many participants at the Versailles peace conference after the first world war were equally clear on the importance of that point. British Prime Minister David Lloyd-George insisted that 'uncivilized nations' should be excluded from any post-war League, while

---

[12] The principal exceptions, apart from colonies of white settlement, were China and Japan. Both of these states had already passed the 'standard of civilization', and, in any case, had always been regarded by Europeans differently from other peoples who had been more comprehensively under their imperial control. For good discussions of the Chinese and Japanese entry into the society of states, see Gong, *Standard of Civilization*, and Hidemi Suganami, 'Japan's Entry into International Society', in Bull and Watson (eds.), *Expansion of International Society*, pp. 185–99. The Japanese, of course, were evicted from the family again after the invasion of Manchuria, causing much regret to Americans who had previously admired them for 'their rapid assimilation of western culture': E.T. Williams, 'The Conflict between Autocracy and Democracy', *American Journal of International Law*, 32 (1938), 678.

[13] Theodore Roosevelt, 'Mr. Roosevelt's Nobel Address on International Peace', *American Journal of International Law*, 4 (1910), 701.

[14] Cited in D.F. Fleming, *The United States and the League of Nations, 1918–1920* (New York: Russell and Russell, 1932), p. 5.

South African General Jan Smuts, whose influence on the evolution of
the Mandates System was profound, regarded many of the non-European
peoples as 'barbarians who cannot possibly govern themselves'.[15] There
was no question of granting proper self-government to the former German
colonies in Africa; all that 'self-determination' meant for those peoples
was to have some say in which European power should be their colonial
ruler (and a great deal of manipulation was employed to ensure that they
would come up with the right answer).[16]

Critics of the League idea often held broadly similar views, objecting
to the possibility that by being involved in a relatively inclusive international organization they might find themselves being obliged to pay more
heed to the wishes of uncivilized peoples. In America, for example, while
there were certainly grave misgivings about the risks of the new collective
security regime for embroiling the United States in distant conflicts in
which it had no national interest, that was not the only concern. One of
Wilson's strongest opponents in the Senate, Henry Lodge, raised another
possibility that might follow from the creation of the League:

> Suppose the Asiatic powers demand the free admission of their labour to the
> United States, and we resist, and the decision of the League goes against us,
> are we going to accept it? Is it possible that anyone who wishes to preserve our
> standards of life and labour can be drawn into a scheme...which would take
> from us our sovereign right to decide alone and for ourselves the vital question
> of the exclusion of Mongolian and Asiatic labour? These are not fanciful cases
> drawn from the region of the imagination. They are actual, living questions of
> the utmost vitality and peril today. In them is involved that deepest of human
> instincts which seeks not only to prevent an impossible competition of labour but
> to maintain the purity of the race.[17]

I am certainly not suggesting that the fear of 'Mongolian and Asiatic'
immigration was *the* reason why the United States declined to join the

---

[15] Both cited in Michael D. Callahan, *Mandates and Empire: The League of Nations and Africa, 1914–1931* (Brighton: Sussex Academic Press, 1999), pp. 16 and 25. Another interesting discussion of the issue, although better for later periods, is Michla Pomerance, *Self-Determination in Law and Practice* (London: Martinus Nijhoff, 1982).

[16] Callahan, *Mandates and Empire*, p. 20. Later in the League period, 1937, the then British under-secretary of state for foreign affairs, Lord Plymouth, offered the following remark which underlines the discriminatory thrust of thinking on this issue: 'It would greatly confuse the minds of these simple peoples [i.e., the mandated peoples] to superimpose on, or indeed to substitute for this loyalty [to the British crown] an alternative loyalty to a body in Geneva of which they would necessarily have very little knowledge or un-derstanding.' See 'Speech by Lord Plymouth', Doc. 153 in Kenneth Bourne, Cameron Watt and Michael Partridge (eds.), *British Documents on Foreign Affairs*, part 2, series J, vol. X: Mandates etc. (University Publications of America, 1995), p. 311. And of course, if they would be confused by a change in their administrators, how on earth could these simple peoples be expected to govern themselves?

[17] Cited in Fleming, *United States and the League of Nations*, pp. 16–17. (The lines are taken from the US *Congressional Record*, vol. V, 1 Feb. 1917.)

League, but the nature of the concern and the terms in which Lodge articulated it do reveal the resilience of pre-war attitudes towards post-war international organization.

The use of the concept of civilization in the war with Germany, and then to stigmatize Bolshevik Russia, had to some extent undermined the self-assurance that diplomats and lawyers used to feel about the conjunction between the European society of states and the 'family of civilized nations', but it is clear that these growing doubts had not yet been translated into the abandonment of the concept as a discriminatory vehicle for contemplating the differences between that family and the world beyond. Nevertheless, the widespread nature of participation in the 'Great War for Civilization' was a major reason why the diplomats went further than Roosevelt's insistence that the League should just be composed of the great civilized nations. The contribution of the British Dominions (the former colonies of white settlement) to the Allied war effort, for example, had already ensured that along with the significant degree of self-government they already enjoyed, they would be treated as signatories to the peace treaty and would enjoy their own representation in the League; but they were still not regarded as possessing full sovereign statehood. The Dominions were relatively easy to include, because they posed less of a threat in the racial terms in which the distinction between the civilized and uncivilized worlds was largely perceived. However, their inclusion in the League while still nominally under the sovereignty of the British crown posed real difficulties for those legal scholars who liked to think about sovereignty in an absolute and unitary way. The best, perhaps only, answer that could be given to the new dilemma was the same as the one that had long been used to deal with the essentially identical problems that had arisen within the old British Empire: that it was 'but one result of the fact that "sovereignty" is infinitely divisible'.[18]

The question about the status of the British Dominions was deeply unsettling to mainstream international lawyers, but an even more significant challenge arose from the fact that the war had clouded the status of those territories and peoples that had been part of the imperial Dominions of the defeated powers. Rather than simply permit the annexation of these territories by the victorious powers, as many British and French proposed, Wilson insisted that their administration should be subject to regulation by the League itself. The compromise solution was the mandates system: the victorious powers would take over the administration of the German colonies, but only under the League's authorization and ultimately responsible to the League for their administration. The fact that

---

[18] Philip Noel Baker, *The Present Juridical Status of the British Dominions in International Law* (London: Longmans, 1929), p. 371.

the compromise became fixed on the idea of mandates was in large part due to Smuts's influence: he derived the concept itself from Roman law (still prominent in South Africa), and added to it his general understanding of how the British colonial system had always worked, along with his 'special knowledge of the needs of backward peoples' to the fore.[19]

In practice, the actual distribution of the mandates was a carve-up between the old imperial powers, without regard for the other members of the League, and with, as I have noted, a somewhat hypocritical concern for the expressed wishes of the peoples concerned. Formally, though, the League Covenant maintained the old idea that there was a 'sacred trust of civilization' to promote the 'well-being and development' of those peoples in the former colonies of the defeated powers who were 'not yet able to stand by themselves under the strenuous conditions of the modern world'.[20] The 'tutelage' of these peoples was placed in the hands of whichever 'advanced nation' was best placed in terms of resources, experience or geography to provide it as 'Mandatories on behalf of the League'. The terms of each mandate were based on 'the stage of the development of the people, the geographical situation of the territory, its economic conditions and other similar circumstances'. Some former colonies

---

[19] Mark Carter Mills, 'The Mandatory System', *American Journal of International Law*, 17 (1923), 52.

[20] This and the subsequent references to the mandates system are all taken from Article 22 of the League Covenant. The concept of civilization also appeared in Article 9 of the Statute of the Permanent Court of International Justice, in an interestingly open formula, requesting that in making appointments to the Court it should be borne in mind that 'in the body as a whole the representation of the main forms of civilization and of the principal legal systems of the world should be assured'. (The same wording was retained in Article 9 of the Statute of the International Court of Justice.) Of course, because of the restricted nature of the League, the 'main forms of civilization' do not appear to have been understood very broadly. The judges and deputy judges of the first Court of 1922 comprised one judge from the United States, two Latin Americans (Brazil and Cuba), a Japanese, and no fewer than seven Europeans (Britain, Denmark, France, Italy, the Netherlands, Spain and Switzerland). The first Chinese and Eastern European judges only appeared on the Court in 1931, along with a Salvadoran, a Colombian and a German; although several of the British Dominions (including India) were League members, I believe I am correct in saying that none of their nationals became a judge on the PCIJ. Nowadays, the ICJ is elected on a similar regional formula to the Security Council. For an interesting note on Article 9 presented by the delegations of Islamic states to the San Francisco conference, see UNCIO, *Documents of the United Nations Conference on International Organization at San Francisco*, 22 vols. (London: UN Information Organization, 1945), vol. XIV, pp. 375–9, where the autonomy, originality, venerability and level of intellectual and ethical development of Islamic law are employed to demonstrate that the Arabic civilization and the legal system of Islam constitute 'one of the main forms of civilization'. It is also interesting that attempts to reduce the size of the Court were rejected at San Francisco on the grounds that the ICJ should consist of fifteen judges in order to fulfil the demand of Article 9 to represent all the main forms of civilization and principal legal systems of the world (*ibid.*, p. 276). Quite why fifteen should be the magic number in this respect is not made clear.

(A Mandates), notably those in the Turkish Empire, were deemed to 'have reached a stage of development where their existence as independent nations can be provisionally recognized'. Others, in Central Africa (Class B) and Southwest Africa and the Pacific Islands (Class C) were placed under more restrictive conditions. The latter were to be governed effectively as parts of the mandatory state itself because, 'owing to the sparseness of their population, or their small size, or their remoteness from the centres of civilization, or their geographical contiguity to the territory of the Mandatory, and other circumstances, [they] can be best administered under the laws of the Mandatory as integral portions of its territory'. In the former German colonies of Central Africa (B Mandates), the mandatory power was expected to perform its function of 'tutelage' for a lengthy period, but nevertheless with certain restrictions that were to be checked on by the League: guarantees for freedom of conscience; the prevention of slavery, arms trading and liquor trafficking; the restriction of native military training; and the provision of equal commercial opportunities in the territory to other League members. Some more general points about international order were also asserted in Article 23, which stated that *all* powers, not just ones exercising a League mandate, were required to ensure, among other things, 'just treatment of the native inhabitants under their control' and the freedom of commerce, transit and communications for all states in their imperial domain.

Although most commentators on the League as an international organization have concentrated on its collective security system as its most important element, in some ways the mandates system had an even more lasting impact on the structure of international order, especially in legal terms. The most important general point about the system is that it represents a further step towards the internationalization of the principle of civilization. Prior to the formation of the League, the promotion of civilization in the non-European world was regarded as the responsibility of whichever European state happened to be the colonial power in the region. Some distinctions were made between different European countries in that regard, but there was no general forum within which concerns about European maladministration could be publicised and corrected. To all intents and purposes, each individual European state was permitted to go about the task of civilization in its own way, and was not answerable to anyone for the consequences: effective criticisms of imperial exploitation typically needed to be made within the home country's government (as we saw, for example, with Dutch critics of the culture system). In this regard, the mandates system represented a new international environment within which colonial administration was to be conducted. The basic features of colonial governance, the division of sovereignty, the

establishment of individuals' property rights, and so forth, remained essentially the same, but, as Michael Callahan has observed, 'the mandates
system had fully internationalized and institutionalized the principle of
trusteeship'; even though this did not formally interfere with the operation of older imperial systems outside the League's mandatory regime, it
did transform the outlook of colonial administrators.[21] The promotion
of civilization was increasingly the concern of international organizations
rather than imperial powers, and that was a vital step in the direction of
making civilization a central goal in a political and legal order conceived
in more global terms.

Another important consequence of the mandates system was that, by
establishing the principle that the 'sacred trust of civilization' was shared
by the entire international community as a whole, it made it much harder
even for the most orthodox modern international lawyers to ignore the
specific practices that had long been involved in colonial administration,
especially the division of sovereignty, and which (as we have seen) were
well known to those lawyers with experience of the operation of such
systems. For many mainstream international lawyers, this was a major
shock to the system. Among the several questions that Lansing raised
about the outcome of the Versailles Conference, for example, this was
one of the most vexatious, and one can perhaps detect a note of hysteria,
or at least querulousness, in his treatment of the subject:

In the case of territory subject to a mandatory, the question therefore arises as
to who possesses the sovereignty of such territory. Certainly not the mandatory which derives its authority solely from an agreement conferring upon it a
limited exercise of sovereign rights. Is it then the League of Nations which possesses the full sovereignty, the exercise of which is delivered in part only to an
agent or trustee? That would seem to be the logical answer, and yet consider the
questions which that answer raises. Does the League of Nations possess the attributes of an independent state so that it can function as a possessor of sovereignty
over territory? Is the League then a supernational world state clothed with world
sovereignty? If the League possesses the sovereignty, can it avoid responsibility
for the misconduct of its agent, the mandatory? If the League is not capable of
possessing sovereignty, then who does possess it, who is responsible for the acts
of the mandatory; and upon what ultimate authority does the League base the
issuance of a mandate?[22]

These questions were insoluble for those legal experts, like Lansing, who
thought that the key question to ask about the mandates system was

[21] Callahan, *Mandates and Empire*, p. 103.
[22] Lansing, 'Some Legal Questions', 640, and see also Fred Northedge, *The League of
Nations: Its Life and Times, 1920–1946* (Leicester University Press, 1986), pp. 197–8.
Personally, I enjoy Lansing's rather understated conclusion that, if the system were not
thoroughly thought out, there would be a danger that it might 'lead to some confusion'.

who possessed *the* sovereignty. The trouble with that approach was that the operating structure of the system was shaped by people who had a close familiarity with the operation of the British colonial system, and its legal framework reflected the pattern of order they had grown up with, especially the well-established principle that sovereignty was divisible.[23] The status of the mandates posed far less of a difficulty for international lawyers who understood the nature of colonial administration and had always been comfortable with the notion of divisible sovereignty.

The crucial point, however, is that now no international lawyer could ignore this dimension of the concept of sovereignty, even though many found it unpleasant. Not only had the promotion of civilization become a concern of an international organization, but also as international lawyers tried to make sense of the new apparatus they were forced to come to terms with the particular political and legal arrangements that had long been associated with the promotion of civilization in the context of colonialism. While this internationalization of the principle of civilization was hardly complete it was, I submit, at least as significant a feature of the League system as the further extension of the principle of toleration to non-European peoples through the recognition of their sovereign equality and independence, which was achieved only to a very limited extent.

The construction of a global political and legal order

I have described the formation of the League system in terms of the 'internationalization' of civilization because in 1919 there were still insurmountable obstacles in the way of the construction of a truly *global* political and legal order. Although ideological concerns were beginning to become more important in defining the boundaries of the civilized world, racial discrimination was still a major element in deciding which peoples were entitled to membership in the new organization and thus to have their sovereign status recognized. I therefore think it would be wrong to describe the League system as a global order, but we can see it in terms of the gradual interpenetration of the two patterns of order that characterized the modern world. This merger, if you like, was brought to completion with the establishment of the United Nations. In terms of international political and legal order, the most far-reaching

---

[23] Lansing's confusion points, I think, to the penetration of orthodox international legal theories into the United States. It is highly surprising, in my view, that he did not make the obvious connection between the situation of the mandates and the earlier treatment of the western territories in North America. Perhaps this did occur to him, and in a later piece he displayed a much more penetrating understanding of the possibilities for a 'Federal World State': see Lansing, 'Notes on World Sovereignty', *American Journal of International Law*, 15 (1921), 19.

change that took place as the League gave way to the United Nations was not the refinements that were introduced to the collective security system, but rather the virtual abandonment of the distinction between the 'family of civilized nations' and the rest of the world. In the United Nations, this way of demarcating between different peoples was largely avoided; in that respect, it did represent an attempt to build a genuinely global order, where all peoples would be governed by an identical code of legal rules, and would all be able to participate on equal terms in the same organization. Simply put: the United Nations was envisioned as, or quite rapidly became, an organization *of* all the world's peoples, with universal participation in the projects of preserving peace and developing global civilization; whereas the League had, above all, been an organization of civilized nations, working collectively *for* all the world's people. What I want to try to do now is to explain how that change took place, and identify some of its major political and legal consequences.

Let me begin with three observations about how the concept of civilization was developing during the interwar years. First, a new challenge arose to confront the defenders of civilization, based on a transformed version of German *Kultur* that drew from a hybrid range of sources but, in particular, made into an instrument of national policy the racial science that had previously been a central pillar in the discriminatory international political and legal thought of the late nineteenth century. As one commentator remarked in 1934, the core of the National Socialist argument was the contention that 'Germans are, in quite the sense of the old-fashioned British colonizer, the only really "white men".'[24] For the first time, other Europeans experienced the uncomfortable sensation of being on the receiving end of racial discrimination from another 'master race' and did not enjoy it.[25] But it was awkward, to say the least, to affirm the supremacy of the white race over African or Asiatic races, while simultaneously denying the validity of Nazi attempts to demonstrate Aryan supremacy. By projecting civilization against Nazism, its defenders were inevitably calling old assumptions about the racial boundaries of the civilized world into question.[26]

Secondly, within the victorious powers of the first world war, and especially Britain, a rejection of the old values that had animated the imperialist project was beginning to take hold, reflecting some sympathy with

---

[24] Lewisohn, 'Revolt against Civilization', p. 150.
[25] For an interesting example, see Gilbert Murray, *From the League to UN* (Westport: Greenwood Press, 1988), pp. 103–5.
[26] Although some still tried to dispute the Nazi theory of racial supremacy while simultaneously upholding racial discrimination: see Frank Hankins, *The Racial Basis of Civilization: A Critique of the Nordic Doctrine* (New York: Knopf, 1926).

the German historical writings on *Kultur* and the decadent character of Western civilization, a recognition of the force of the increasingly vociferous criticisms of the exploitative dimensions of imperial rule, and a growing sense of disillusionment with Victorian morality more generally. This new attitude, centred on the Bloomsbury intellectuals, combined a liberal political outlook with a new conception of the role of Europe and its civilization in the world. Arthur Herman summarises it thus:

> Tolerance, compassion, humanitarian concern, and reasonable compromise would define this new Western civilization; its chief virtue would have a spiritual rather than a material basis. The British Empire, and by extension Europe and the West, would accept their political eclipse, as non-Western nations with their teeming millions rose up from the horizon. However, this kinder, gentler West would establish in effect a new universal empire of peace and harmony, with its humane civilized values serving as the basis for a world government and unity among peoples everywhere.[27]

The vision, in other words, was of a non-imperial civilization, reflecting the best moral and spiritual elements of Western values, and presented as the template for a pattern of global order in which everyone would participate as free, self-governing and mutually tolerating peoples. The idea that the promotion of civilization should necessarily involve the rule of non-European peoples by European administrators was increasingly losing its once prominent place in liberal political thought.

These two developments combined with a third: the inability of the civilized nations to combat the autocratic barbarians by themselves. And in their assessment of the threat it was clear that the civilized world would need to find allies in unlikely places if it was to survive. The seriousness with which the Americans regarded Nazism, for example, can be detected in the assessment of one international lawyer, L. H. Woolsey, that 'Hitler has proved...that there is a danger to civilization greater than communism.'[28] And, as Woolsey pointed out, it was through the 'forced cooperation' among this disparate group of peoples that 'the rudiments of a world organization' were being created.[29] The growing strength of the Soviet Union and its pivotal role in the alliance of United Nations against Hitler and the contribution of non-European forces to the struggle against the Japanese (like the Germans, once regarded as civilized, but no longer) combined to radically transform ideas about the scope of

---

[27] Arthur Herman, *The Idea of Decline in Western History* (New York: Free Press, 1997), pp. 257–8. Although ideas about the desirability of economic and technological progress remained central to the vision of what a civilized world would look like.

[28] L.H. Woolsey, 'Editorial Comment: A Pattern of World Order', *American Journal of International Law*, 36 (1942), 621.

[29] *Ibid.*

this world organization as it was gradually taking shape in the minds of statesmen and intellectuals. In all of these respects, the second 'great war for civilization' was significantly different from the first. The headline, if you like, was the same; but the substance of what people were fighting for, what they were fighting against, and who was doing the bulk of the actual fighting, had all changed. Civilization was now being defended against a philosophy of autocratic government based on the principle of racial discrimination; the civilization that was being defended was increasingly regarded as separable from the imperialistic rule and tutelage of non-European peoples; and some of its most important defenders were states that, until recently, had been well beyond the pale of the 'family of civilized nations', the Soviet Union being the most obvious example. The result was that when diplomats began to turn their attention to the question of how international order should be reconstructed after the war, their frame of reference was quite different from before.

That is not to say that everyone was thinking in exactly the same way. Some contributions to the debate on the new world organization, particularly from the British, had very strong echoes of earlier international legal and political thought. A group of British lawyers in the 'Grotius Society', for example, produced a series of suggestions on the 'future of international law' that clearly recognized the novelty of contemporary conditions, but still clung to some of the older legal assumptions: 'To ensure universal peace and order, international law must be universal. Its operation, however, requires the existence of some minimum level of civilization and moral values among the nations subject to it. While therefore the aim must be a universal law, the development of a new international law from a nucleus of States must be envisaged as a possibility.'[30] Although not quite so explicit, or undiplomatic, the British government's proposals to the wartime conferences on the treatment of self-governing territories and the trusteeship system also reflected the earlier language of the League directly, using phrases like the 'sacred trust of civilization' and the notion that certain peoples were unable to 'stand by themselves under the strenuous conditions of the modern world'.[31] What had been acceptable in the days of the League, however, was no longer so, and the British proposal received remarkably short shrift from the other delegates at the San Francisco Conference. For a start, other proposals did not adopt the same language at all: neither the French

[30] Grotius Society, 'The Future of International Law', *Transactions of the Grotius Society*, 28 (1941), 291. For a broadly similar concern from another international lawyer, see Philip Marshall Brown, 'Reserved International Rights', *American Journal of International Law*, 38 (1944), 282–3.
[31] UNCIO, *Documents*, vol. III, p. 609.

nor the American drafts included the phrases. Moreover, in the subsequent committee discussions it was argued that the British reference to people unable to 'stand by themselves' was 'outmoded', because in a military sense 'very few countries if any were now able to stand alone in protecting themselves', and, more generally, 'very few countries were economically self-sufficient'. Signifying the radical change in tone of the proceedings, it was also argued that the British government's preferred choice of wording might be 'objectionable to certain peoples', especially because it did not account for the fact that 'among dependent peoples there were ... peoples with a long heritage of civilization'.[32]

In other respects as well, the UN system reflected a much less discriminatory attitude to non-European peoples, and a much broader and more flexible concept of civilization. Membership was opened to all 'peace-loving states', not least because the Nazis – the new barbarians – were guilty not just of genocide, but also of the crime of aggressive militarism. Precisely what characteristics would define a 'peace-loving' state were never made exactly clear, but one notable state to be excluded, even though it had remained neutral during the war, was Francoist Spain: Fascist authoritarianism was seen as incompatible with being 'peace-loving', but not much else was. Of course, several states were still excluded from the United Nations, at least until 1955, but that had a lot more to do with Cold War rivalry than with the imposition of a new standard of civilization. Since 1955, the UN system has become even more committed to the principle of non-discrimination both with respect to its membership and in the conduct of international affairs more generally, through landmark statements such as the 1960 Declaration on the Granting of Independence to Colonial Countries and Peoples, and the 1970 Declaration on Principles of International Law concerning Friendly Relations and Co-operation among States.

Although the construction and subsequent development of the UN system reflected a much more inclusive attitude towards non-European peoples, in keeping with the recognition that they were no less civilized than their European counterparts, the idea that the new global order should pursue the traditional goal of promoting civilization had by no means been rejected. The Preamble to the Charter makes explicit that among its various goals the United Nations is dedicated to affirming 'fundamental human rights', reflecting 'the dignity and worth of the

---

[32] *Ibid.*, vol. X, pp. 497–8. For a good overview, see Leland M. Goodrich, Edvard Hambro and Anne Patricia Simons, *Charter of the United Nations: Commentary and Documents*, 3rd edn (New York: Columbia University Press, 1969), pp. 450–1. Although, for a somewhat contrary point, see *Public Papers of the Secretaries-General of the United Nations, Volume 1: Trygve Lie, 1946–1953* (New York: Columbia University Press, 1969), p. 32.

human person' and 'the equal rights of men and women', and that it is also committed to the promotion of 'social progress and better standards of life'. In Article 55, these goals are stated at greater length:

the UN shall promote: (a) higher standards of living, full employment, and conditions of economic and social progress and development; (b) solutions of international economic, social, health and related problems; and international cultural and educational cooperation; and (c) universal respect for, and observance of, human rights and fundamental freedoms for all without distinction as to race, sex, language, or religion.

Although the word 'civilization' is not used here, and indeed could not be used because of its lingering objectionability to peoples who for so long had laboured under the stigma of being treated as uncivilized, that is more or less how a nineteenth-century international lawyer or colonial administrator would have understood the concept. Consider, for example, John Stuart Mill's definition of the concept, which I quoted earlier but deserves to be recalled at this point:

a country rich in the fruits of agriculture, commerce and manufactures, we call civilized ... Wherever ... we find human beings acting together for common purposes in large bodies, and enjoying the pleasures of social intercourse, we term them civilized ... We ... call a people civilized, where the arrangements of society, for protecting the persons and property of its members, are sufficiently perfect to maintain peace among them.[33]

The fit is by no means perfect, but I submit that there is enough of a resemblance to make it very clear what was the source of these purposes of the UN system.

But these variations on the old idea of civilization were not the only goals that the United Nations set for itself. The Preamble also asserted the equality of 'nations large and small', and the UN's members committed themselves 'to practice tolerance and live together in peace with one another as good neighbours'. As one would expect, this goal was encapsulated in the founding principles of the organization as laid out in Article 2: that the organization is based on the principle of sovereign equality; and that, apart from the limitation on the use of force and the need to maintain international peace and security, 'Nothing contained in the present Charter shall authorize the United Nations to intervene in matters which are essentially within the domestic jurisdiction of any state.' It is obvious where this part of the Charter comes from: with the exception of the restriction on the use of force, these assertions are clearly the legacy of the 'Westphalian system' and the society of states. In the UN

---

[33] John Stuart Mill, 'Civilization', in Mill, *Collected Works, Volume 18: Essays on Politics and Society* (London: Routledge, 1997), p. 120.

system, in other words, states are all understood to be sovereign, in the sense that they are all equal and possess an inviolable right to territorial integrity and political independence. As a report by a Special Committee of the General Assembly later argued, this logically implies that every state 'has the right freely to choose and develop its political, social, economic and cultural systems'.[34] That old adage of orthodox international society theorists, never mind that it is more Augbsurgian than Westphalian, springs to mind: *cuius regio, eius religio*.

It should be obvious how serious a dilemma this duality of purpose presents. On the one hand, the United Nations as an organization and all its members are dedicated to promoting what can only be called civilization: economic and social progress, collaborative social intercourse, and respect for the fundamental human rights of individuals. On the other, the United Nations as an organization and all its members are dedicated to promoting what can only be called toleration: respect for all states' equal and independent territorial sovereignty, and for their right to develop whatever kind of political, social, economic and cultural system they choose. As I have argued in this book, these have long been the central purposes that have defined order in modern world politics. In that sense, it is unremarkable to find both of them being articulated as fundamental purposes and principles of the United Nations. What is remarkable, however, is to find them being asserted together, at the same time, and for all peoples. That represents a novel departure for international order, and while all would probably agree (I certainly would) that the abandonment of racial discrimination as a principle of international law has been a progressive development, the legacy is a pattern of order in the world today that is global, but divided.

Over the last fifty years, these divisions have expressed themselves in a number of specific questions about the content of international law and the structure of international organization, both at the global and regional levels. The United Nations' ability to interpret, and in some cases substantially change, what is 'essentially within' the domestic jurisdiction of any individual state means, for example, that 'a new content has been given to the obligations and legal competence of states through the medium of the Charter'.[35] In effect, the United Nations has acquired a competence to redefine what state sovereignty actually means in many different circumstances, and this represents a significant compromise of

---

[34] Goodrich *et al.*, *Charter of the United Nations*, p. 40.
[35] Ian Brownlie, *Principles of Public International Law* (Oxford: Clarendon Press, 1990), p. 295, and for a very good analysis of how this happened, see Rosalyn Higgins, *The Development of International Law through the Political Organs of the United Nations* (London: Oxford University Press, 1963).

the decentralized, voluntaristic pattern of order that is supposed to obtain in the society of states. This process of the partial centralization of authority, and the emergence of 'community-oriented' procedures at the expense of 'sovereignty-oriented' ones,[36] has gone even further in some regional organizations, most notably in the European Union. The growing supranational authority of European bodies, especially when coupled with the articulation of notions of 'subsidiarity' and 'European citizenship' in the Maastricht and Amsterdam Treaties, has led some scholars to suggest that 'Europe may well become a model of post-Westphalian political organization' where political authority is de-territorialized, and where sovereignty is 'pooled' or 'divided' among states in an effort to maximize the presumed economic benefits of integration.[37]

Another controversial feature of the UN Charter is its assertion that all human beings have certain fundamental and inalienable rights. Again, this breaches what Hedley Bull described as the 'conspiracy of silence' about individuals' rights that is one consequence of the acceptance of toleration and mutual independence in the European society of states.[38] According to one international lawyer, W. Michael Reisman, this represents a fundamental challenge to the compact of coexistence embodied in the principle of respect for state sovereignty: 'By shifting the fulcrum of the system from the protection of sovereigns to the protection of people, [the principle of human rights] works qualitative changes in virtually every other component' of the international legal order.[39] While few would go so far as to claim that individuals now have an equivalent kind of international personality to that traditionally possessed by states, the idea that all people have certain rights as human beings weakens the ability of

---

[36] These phrases are taken from Richard Falk, 'The Interplay of Westphalia and Charter Conceptions of International Legal Order', in Falk, Friedrich Kratochwil and Saul Mendlovitz (eds.), *International Law: A Contemporary Perspective* (London: Westview Press, 1985), p. 123.

[37] For discussions of the international political and legal dimensions of this development, see David Held, *Democracy and the Global Order: From the Modern State to Cosmopolitan Governance* (Cambridge: Polity Press, 1995), and Andrew Linklater, *The Transformation of Political Community* (Cambridge: Polity Press, 1998), especially ch. 6. For an analysis of the continuing tensions between intergovernmentalism and supranationalism within the EU framework, see Helen Wallace, 'Deepening and Widening: Problems of Legitimacy for the EC', in Soledad Garcia (ed.), *European Identity and the Search for Legitimacy* (London: Pinter, 1993). Interestingly, the division of sovereignty in the EU has been quite different from the normal practice that characterized imperial systems, in the sense that European states have largely retained their external sovereignty, while losing much of their internal sovereignty; precisely the reverse of the situation in which the Indian Native States were placed.

[38] Hedley Bull, *The Anarchical Society: A Study of Order in World Politics* (London: Macmillan, 1977), p. 83.

[39] W. Michael Reisman, 'Sovereignty and Human Rights in Contemporary International Law', *American Journal of International Law*, 84 (1990), 872.

states to claim that their sovereignty provides them with an inviolable jurisdiction over their domestic territory and population. As John Vincent puts it, 'there is now an area of domestic conduct in regard to human rights . . . that is under the scrutiny of international law. This does not issue a general licence for intervention . . . But it does expose the internal regimes of all the members of international society to the legitimate appraisal of their peers.'[40] Another international lawyer, Thomas Franck, interprets these changes in terms of a general 'democratic entitlement' that has been established in international law, reflecting the extreme degree to which internationally defined legal standards now qualify the supposed right of all states to a territorially sovereign domestic jurisdiction within which they can develop whatever kind of political and legal arrangements they choose.[41]

Conclusion

What I have tried to do in this chapter is to show how we have moved from a world that was clearly divided between two distinct patterns of international order, each with its own core purpose and separated by a discriminatory distinction between civilized and uncivilized nations, to a world that possess a single, global structure of political and legal order but is riven by contradictions because we have not resolved the fundamental modern dichotomy about what order in world politics is for. The crucial development that took place between 1914 and 1945 was the erosion of the thesis that different peoples should conduct their international relations in different ways, depending on the level of civilization they had achieved. As orthodox scholars have long argued, the basic Westphalian principle of toleration, with its associated norm that the world is composed of states who should all respect each other's territorial sovereignty, has effectively been globalized. To this already well-established claim, I have sought to add a new point: that, at the same time, the basic principle of extra-European order that civilization should be promoted, with its associated norm of the division of sovereignty across territorial boundaries, has also been globalized. The contemporary pattern of international order embodies two distinct normative principles: that the sovereign independence of states should be respected, so as to encourage the toleration

---

[40] Vincent, *Human Rights*, p. 152.

[41] Gregory Fox, 'The Right to Political Participation in International Law', *Yale Journal of International Law*, 17 (1992), 539–607, and Thomas Franck, 'The Emerging Right to Democratic Governance', *American Journal of International Law*, 86 (1992), 46–91. For a more cautious treatment, which makes the continuing importance of toleration and reciprocal recognition to this equation much clearer, see Brad Roth, *Governmental Illegitimacy in International Law* (Oxford: Clarendon Press, 1999).

of political and cultural differences; and that their sovereignty should be divided, so as to facilitate the promotion of civilization.

It is obvious that, unless we are prepared to accept either perennial instability or some kind of *de facto* discrimination operating below the official, formal level of international law, we need to find some way of reconciling the two contrasting goals of order in world politics today. We need to find, in other words, some way of articulating the idea of a civilized world that is fully cognisant of the need to tolerate different peoples and cultures. That is certainly the avowed aim of a host of political theorists, international legal experts, diplomats and statesmen today, and has indeed been a feature of the liberal vision of civilization ever since doubts about late nineteenth-century discriminatory theories began to be deeply felt. This project can, in essence, be seen as an attempt to save the modern way of organizing international politics from its own contradictions, without resort to the discriminatory and inegalitarian arguments which kept it afloat for a century or more. We may have little choice but to take on that project, since we may well have no readily available alternative schemes of international political and legal order available at present, but we should at least not undertake it with the illusion that we are doing anything but trying to patch up an order that emerged in an *ad hoc* way as Europeans struggled to gain control of the lands and commerce of the non-European world, and has since developed along lines that most of us, I am sure, would find highly objectionable.

Conclusion

The main critical point I have made in this book is that orthodox theories of order in modern world politics are inadequate because their analysis of the development of modern international order is too narrowly concentrated on the European states-system. While they have given some excellent descriptions of how that system operates, and especially how its members have collectively formed an international society based on the principle of respect for each other's sovereign equality and independence, orthodox theorists have almost completely ignored the way in which Europeans behaved beyond Europe, and therefore have failed to provide a proper analysis of the principles that have structured their relations with non-European peoples since the seventeenth century. Moreover, because they adopted a mistaken interpretation of the 'Grotian tradition' of international legal thought, and because their theory of the society of states is now popularly believed to represent that tradition, one of the principal examples of modern legal thinking about the characteristic features of international order beyond Europe has been cast into obscurity, making it much harder to recover a proper sense of what was going on in that part of the world.

The bulk of my argument has been devoted to trying to give an account of the pattern of international political and legal order that developed in the world beyond Europe, my goal being to supplement, rather than replace, the orthodox theory of order in the European states-system. I began with an analysis of Hugo Grotius's theory of the law of nations, and showed that Grotius developed two core propositions about the rights that public authorities and private individuals possess in the law of nations: first, that the sovereign prerogatives held by public authorities are divisible from one another; and secondly, that private individuals can acquire property rights in the law of nations under certain specific circumstances. I explained that, contrary to popular belief, these were not reflections of a nostalgic medievalism or an idealistic utopianism in Grotius's thought, soon to be superseded by more modern and more pragmatic scholarship on the balance of power and positive international law. Both of Grotius's core ideas were picked up and developed further by subsequent theorists of the law of nations, and remained prominent in modern international legal thought at least until the early twentieth century. Grotius's views on sovereignty and individuals' rights came to be employed, however, within the context of a radically different methodological and philosophical approach to the study of international law. Grotius himself believed that he was describing a universal normative order, applicable to all peoples, including Europeans. During the eighteenth and nineteenth centuries, international lawyers began to accept the increasingly obvious fact that European states were following one legal code in their relations among themselves, and a different one in their relations with other peoples. The specific Grotian propositions about the content of the law of nations became most closely associated with the latter pattern of legal order, and a discriminatory distinction between 'civilized' and 'uncivilized' peoples began to be employed to rationalize the differences between the two legal codes.

I have also tried to explain how the extra-European pattern of international order operated and why it developed in such a different way from the European states-system. In Europe, as absolutist monarchs gradually consolidated their grip on their own dynastic possessions, they increasingly adopted a practice of mutual recognition among themselves. In part, they wanted to undermine the international status of other sub or suprastate actors, but once this had been achieved they maintained the practice both so as to provide a foundation for resisting potentially hegemonic members of the society of states and to reduce the risks that a conflict among themselves might arise because of political or cultural differences. International circumstances were very different beyond Europe: here, European states' primary interest was to maximize their economic opportunities through the control of trade. In North America, this largely involved the establishment of colonial settlements; in the East Indies, it principally involved making exclusive trading agreements with indigenous rulers, and in time the acquisition of sovereign prerogatives from those rulers so as to give European trading corporations legitimate authority to use violence to protect their monopolies and extract even more revenue through new taxation systems. In both cases, international relations involved the division of sovereignty between different public authorities and the assertion of individuals' rights to appropriate unoccupied, uncultivated or unimproved land.

While the goal of profit and revenue maximization never went away, as the extra-European pattern of order was consolidated during the eighteenth and nineteenth centuries another goal began to assume equal importance: the project of bringing the benefits of 'civilization' to uncultivated wildernesses and 'backward' peoples. The project of civilization had two main components: the promotion of economic and technological progress, and the establishment of good government in a more political and judicial sense. This new mission developed in parallel with the new international political and legal theories that discriminated between Europeans or whites and the rest of the world, and which now provided a potent justification for the increasingly systematic treatment of the sovereignty of indigenous rulers as divisible, and for the massive interventions through which colonial administrators developed new property systems and corrected what they saw as corruption, despotism or maladministration. By the late nineteenth century, there was a very clear division in the world between two different patterns of political and legal order. Within Europe, international order was supposed to provide for peaceful coexistence in an anarchic and plural world by encouraging toleration: the fundamental norm governing relations between European states was therefore the reciprocal recognition of each state's equality and independence with regard to its territorial sovereignty. Beyond Europe, international order was intended to promote civilization: the fundamental norm governing relations between European states and non-European peoples was that the latter were backward and that some of the sovereign prerogatives of indigenous rulers ought to be held by more advanced Europeans in order to introduce the economic, political and judicial benefits of civilized life.

The final step in my argument was to explain how this division of the world into two patterns of political and legal order has collapsed, to be replaced by a single global order. The pivotal development here was the gradual erosion of the discriminatory distinction between European peoples as civilized and non-European peoples as backward. Although I do not want to disrespect the formidable efforts that the latter made to secure their recognition on the world stage, nor the assistance given to them by the Soviet Union and other communist states, I think that, nevertheless, the most decisive development here was the decline in the self-assurance of the Europeans themselves; to paraphrase Lenin, revolutionary changes happen when the old regime decides it cannot continue to go on in the same old way. The experience of the two wars against Germany, and especially the struggle against the Nazi version of the doctrine of white supremacy, led the major European powers to question their belief in their destiny as the bringers of civilization to the rest of the world. What replaced the old doctrine, however, was not a rejection of civilization as such, so much as the idea that it had to be pursued within the context of a more tolerant global order. The construction of the UN system represented an attempt to bring the two major purposes of modern international order together in a single political and legal framework that would be founded on the principle of reciprocal respect for the territorial sovereignty of *all* peoples, but would nevertheless continue to work to promote the goals of economic and technological progress, good government and individuals' rights that would bring about a more civilized world.

For all its noble intentions, the attempt to construct a global order on those terms has left us with a host of questions about how international affairs should be conducted. Toleration and civilization were fundamentally different purposes of international order, and the effort to realize both at the same time has led to serious tensions, or even contradictions, in the internal structure of the contemporary international political and legal framework. Precisely how should the line be drawn between the rights of states to an inviolable domestic jurisdiction and the role that international organizations are supposed to play in protecting the rights of citizens against their own governments? How many of their sovereign prerogatives should states be required to give up to global or regional organizations in order to secure the benefits of economic and technological development? How far should international organizations go in trying to promote good government within states? Do all nations deserve to have their right to self-determination recognized, or should recognition be made contingent on the establishment of a particular kind of government that fits in with long-standing ideas about civilized administration and judicial practice?

Scholars have been grappling with precisely these problems for the last fifty years. But in my view far too much of the current literature has treated them in a way that obscures their origins, and therefore makes it hard to appreciate precisely what is at stake in the dilemmas that we face. What is particularly damaging is the persistent tendency to think about the contradictory nature of contemporary political and legal order in terms of the emergence of a new kind of 'post-Westphalian' order, which is gradually superseding the old society of states. I think that that point of view is completely wrong. The pattern of order that is challenging the idea of state sovereignty today is as old as the society of states itself, and there is nothing new about the notion that the sovereignty of states should be compromised by a higher structure of international organization that facilitates the promotion of economic progress, good government and individuals' rights. Indeed, if anything *is* new about the world we live in today, it is not so much the assertion of these 'post-Westphalian' principles as goals of international order but the increasing importance of the 'Westphalian' principle of toleration in relations between European and non-European states. To suggest that the 'Westphalian system' is

collapsing is to give that system an importance that it had never had in
the past, except if one myopically concentrates on the historical experience of European states, and it is to misread the role that its core goal
of promoting toleration has played in the construction of a global order
during the twentieth century. The increasingly popular suggestion that
we are witnessing the emergence of a 'new medievalism' is similarly unhelpful: the world we live in today is trapped within a dichotomy that,
with the subtraction of pseudo-scientific theories of racial discrimination,
is unambiguously modern.

Moreover, by exaggerating the novelty of the idea of civilization as a
goal of international order today, much of the contemporary scholarship
gives that idea a pristine moral quality that it really does not deserve. It
is too easy to suppose that, because these are 'new' dimensions of international order, they represent a step towards the realization of some
idealistic or utopian vision for world politics. I ought to make it clear that
I am not suggesting that the current project of building a global civilization is automatically tainted just because it was associated in the past with
European imperialism. Nevertheless, the adoption of a deeper historical
perspective inevitably raises some awkward questions about the civilizing
mission to which international order is currently dedicated, and it is not
a proper response simply to pretend that those questions do not exist because the idea of human rights was only asserted in international relations
after 1945, or because the division of sovereignty in contemporary international organizations is an unprecedented phenomenon. Personally,
I have a great deal of sympathy with both the promotion of human rights
and the further development of supranational organizations, but I think
that their defenders should still face up to the long and not always attractive history of these features of order in modern world politics, and
perhaps moderate some of their enthusiasm accordingly.

The fundamental question that we face today is whether it is possible to pursue both of the purposes of modern international order, as the
UN system tries to do, without ultimately being forced either to choose
between them or to return to something like the discriminatory way of re-
solving their mutual contradictions that characterised nineteenth-century
scholarship and diplomatic practice: can we still have the modern patterns of order in world politics with a post-modern method of making
them coherent? I realize that this is an extremely difficult question, and
the analysis I have presented here is merely intended to demonstrate its
long-standing seriousness for experts on international relations, rather
than point to any easy solutions. But the only hope of finding a solution
to contemporary problems is to realize how complex and enduring they
are, rather than explaining them away by pretending that we are now

confronted with a novel dilemma that never occurred to anyone in the past. That is a form of escapism that promises nothing; indeed, it runs the risk that we will just end up repeating the same demands for new thinking that have been made by political and legal theorists for at least a hundred years. The starting-point for understanding what kind of world order we have today, and what the possibilities are for the future, is to understand the bifurcated, contradictory and discriminatory nature of international order in the past. As I have shown here, we cannot do that if we continue to accept the tired old conventional wisdoms about the Westphalian system and the 'anarchical society' of sovereign states. The new study of order in world politics that I have presented here may not be perfect, and I fully expect that it could be extended and refined in all sorts of ways, but at least it is a start in trying to develop a better appreciation of the challenges that are our legacy from the modern world.

Bibliography

Alexandrowicz, Charles, *An Introduction to the History of the Law of Nations in the East Indies*, Oxford: Clarendon Press, 1967.

'Empirical and Doctrinal Positivism in International Law', *British Year Book of International Law*, 47 (1974–75), 286–9.

Angelino, A.D.A. de Kat, *Colonial Policy*, trans. G. Renier, 2 vols., The Hague: Martinus Nijhoff, 1931.

Appleby, Joyce, *Liberalism and Republicanism in the Historical Imagination*, Cambridge, MA: Harvard University Press, 1992.

Arasaratnam, Sinnappah, *Dutch Power in Ceylon, 1658–1687*, Amsterdam: Djambatan, 1958.

'Dutch Sovereignty in Ceylon: A Historical Study of its Problems', *Ceylon Journal of Historical and Social Studies*, 1 (1958), 105–21.

'The Kingdom of Kandy: Aspects of its External Relations and Commerce', *Ceylon Journal of Historical and Social Studies*, 3 (1960), 109–27.

Arneil, Barbara, *John Locke and America: The Defence of English Colonialism*, Oxford: Clarendon Press, 1996.

Ashton, S.R., *British Policy Towards the Princely States, 1905–1939*, London: Curzon Press, 1982.

Austin, John, *Lectures on Jurisprudence, or The Philosophy of Positive Law*, 4th edn, London: John Murray, 1879.

Bachman, Van Cleaf, *Peltries or Plantations: The Economic Policies of the Dutch West India Company in New Netherland, 1623–1639*, Baltimore: Johns Hopkins University Press, 1969.

Bailyn, Bernard, *The Ideological Origins of the American Revolution*, Cambridge: Belknap Press, 1967.

Bar, L. von, *The Theory and Practice of Private International Law*, 2nd edn, trans. G.R. Gillespie, Edinburgh: William Green, 1892.

Bayly, C.A., 'Creating a Colonial Peasantry: India and Java, *c.* 1820–1880', *Itinerario*, 11 (1987), 93–106.

Bayly, C.A. and Kolff, D.H.A. (eds.), *Two Colonial Empires: Comparative Essays on the History of India and Indonesia*, Lancaster: Martinus Nijhoff, 1986.

Belch, Stanislaus F., *Paulus Vladimiri and his Doctrine Concerning International Law and Politics*, 2 vols., London: Mouton, 1965.

Bell, Clive, *Civilization: An Essay*, London: Chatto and Windus, 1929.

Bellamy, Richard and Castiglione, Dario, 'Building the Union: The Nature of Sovereignty in the Political Architecture of Europe', *Law and Philosophy*, 16 (1997), 421–45.

Bethel, Slingsby, *The Interest of Princes and States*, London: John Wickins, 1680.

Biersteker, Thomas and Weber, Cynthia (eds.), *State Sovereignty as Social Construct*, Cambridge: Cambridge University Press, 1996.

Bodin, Jean, *On Sovereignty: Four Chapters from the Six Books of the Commonwealth*, ed. and trans. Julian Franklin, Cambridge University Press, 1992.

Booth, Anne, O'Malley, W.J. and Weidemann, Anna (eds.), *Indonesian Economic History in the Dutch Colonial Era*, New Haven: Yale University Southeast Asia Studies, 1990.

Borschberg, Peter, 'Grocio y el Contracto Social: Un Estudio Preliminario de las Inéditas *Theses LVT*, *Revista de Estudios Políticos*, forthcoming.

Bourne, Kenneth, Watt, D. Cameron and Partridge, Michael (eds.), *British Documents on Foreign Affairs*, part 2, series J, vol. X, University Publications of America, 1995.

Braudel, Fernand, *A History of Civilizations*, trans. Richard Mayne, London: Penguin, 1994.

Brewer, John, *The Sinews of Power: War, Money and the English State, 1688–1783*, London: Unwin Hyman, 1989.

Brierly, J.L., 'The Shortcomings of International Law', *British Year Book of International Law*, 5 (1924), 4–16.

Bromley, J.S. and Kossmann, E.H., *Britain and the Netherlands: Volume 5, Some Political Mythologies*, The Hague: Martinus Nijhoff, 1975.

Brown, Chris, *International Relations Theory: New Normative Approaches*, Brighton: Harvester Wheatsheaf, 1984.

Brown, Philip Marshall, 'Editorial Comment: Reserved International Rights', *American Journal of International Law*, 38 (1944), 281–3.

Brownlie, Ian, *Principles of Public International Law*, Oxford: Clarendon Press, 1990.

Buckland, W.W., *A Manual of Roman Private Law*, 2nd edn, Cambridge University Press, 1947.

Buckle, Stephen, *Natural Law and the Theory of Property: Grotius to Hume*, Oxford: Clarendon Press, 1991.

Bull, Hedley, *The Anarchical Society: A Study of Order in World Politics*, London: Macmillan, 1977.

The Hagey Lectures, University of Waterloo, *Mimeo*, 1984.

Bull, Hedley and Watson, Adam (eds.), *The Expansion of International Society*, Oxford: Clarendon Press, 1984.

Bull, Hedley, Kingsbury, Benedict and Roberts, Adam (eds.), *Hugo Grotius and International Relations*, Oxford: Clarendon Press, 1992.

Burch, Kurt, *'Property' and the Making of the International System*, Boulder: Lynne Reinner, 1998.

Burchill, Scott, Linklater, Andrew *et al.*, *Theories of International Relations*, London: Macmillan, 1995.

Burger, Thomas, *Max Weber's Theory of Concept Formation: History, Laws and Ideal Types*, Durham: Duke University Press, 1976.

Burns, J.H. (ed.), *The Cambridge History of Political Thought, 1450–1700*, Cambridge University Press, 1991.

Butterfield, Herbert, *Man on his Past*, Cambridge University Press, 1955.

The Origins of History, ed. Adam Watson, London: Eyre Methuen, 1981.

Butterfield, Herbert and Wight, Martin (eds.), *Diplomatic Investigations: Essays on the Theory of International Politics*, London: George Allen and Unwin, 1966.

Callahan, Michael, *Mandates and Empire: The League of Nations and Africa, 1914–1931*, Brighton: Sussex Academic Press, 1999.

Camilleri, Joseph and Falk, Jim, *The End of Sovereignty? The Politics of a Shrinking and Fragmenting World*, Aldershot: Elgar, 1992.

Campbell, John, *The Present State of Europe, Explaining the Interests, Connections, Political and Commercial Views of its Several Powers*, 3rd edn, London: Longman, 1752.

Canny, Nicholas (ed.), *The Oxford History of the British Empire, Volume 1: The Origins of Empire*, Oxford University Press, 1998.

Cayton, Andrew, *The Frontier Republic: Ideology and Politics in the Ohio Country, 1780–1825*, Kent State University Press, 1986.

Cheyney, Edward, 'The Manor of East Greenwich in the County of Kent', *American Historical Review*, 11 (1906), 29–35.

Cohn, Bernard, 'From Indian Status to British Contract', *Journal of Economic History*, 21 (1961), 613–28.

Davis, George, *The Elements of International Law with an Account of its Origins, Sources and Historical Development*, 2nd edn, New York: Harper, 1900.

Day, Clive, *The Policy and Administration of the Dutch in Java*, revised edn, Kuala Lumpur: Oxford University Press, 1966.

Dekker, C., 'The Representation of the Freeholders in the Drainage Districts of Zeeland West of the Scheldt during the Middle Ages', *Acta Historiae Neerlandicae*, 8 (1975), 1–30.

Deudney, Daniel, 'The Philadelphian System: Sovereignty, Arms Control, and Balance of Power in the American States-Union, circa. 1787–1861', *International Organization*, 49 (1995), 191–228.

Dicey, A.V., *A Digest of the Law of England with Reference to the Conflict of Laws*, London: Stevens, 1896.

Dickinson, Edwin Dewitt, 'The Analogy between Natural Persons and International Persons in the Law of Nations', *Yale Law Journal*, 26 (1916–17), 564–91.

Donaldson, Thomas, *The Public Domain: Its History, with Statistics*, New York: Johnson Reprint Corporation, 1970.

Donnelly, Jack, *International Human Rights*, 2nd edn, Boulder: Westview Press, 1998.

Dugard, John, *Recognition and the United Nations*, Cambridge: Grotius Publications, 1987.

Duggan, S.P., *The League of Nations*, Boston, 1919.

Dumont, Jean, *Les Soupirs de l'Europe, Or the Groans of Europe at the Prospect of the Present Posture of Affairs*, trans. anon., 1713.

Corps Universel Diplomatique du Droit des Gens ... depuis le Regne de l'Empereur Charlemagne, 6 vols., Amsterdam, 1726.

Dunne, Timothy, *Inventing International Society: A History of the English School*, London: Macmillan, 1998.

Elias, Norbert, *The Civilizing Process: Sociogenetic and Psychogenetic Investigations*, trans. Edmund Jephcott, revised edn, Oxford: Blackwell, 2000.

Elson, R.E., *Village Java under the Cultivation System, 1830–1870*, Sydney: Allen and Unwin, 1994.

Etcheson, Nicole, *The Emerging Midwest: Upland Southerners and the Political Culture of the Old Northwest*, Bloomington: Indiana University Press, 1992.

Everitt, Alan, *Continuity and Colonisation: The Evolution of Kentish Settlement*, Leicester University Press, 1986.

Fachiri, Alexander, 'Expropriation and International Law', *British Year Book of International Law*, 6 (1925), 159–71.

Falk, Richard, Kratochwil, Friedrich and Mendlovitz, Saul (eds.), *International Law: A Contemporary Perspective*, London: Westview Press, 1985.

Fasseur, Cornelis, *The Politics of Colonial Exploitation: Java, the Dutch and the Cultivation System*, trans. R.E. Elson and Ary Kraal, Ithaca: Cornell University Press, 1992.

Fleming, D.F., *The United States and the League of Nations, 1918–1920*, New York: Russell and Russell, 1932.

Force, Peter (ed.), *Tracts and Other Papers, Relating Principally to the Origin, Settlement and Progress of the Colonies in North America*, 4 vols., Washington: Peter Force, 1836–46.

Fox, Gregory, 'The Right to Political Participation in International Law', *Yale Journal of International Law*, 17 (1992), 539–607.

Franck, Thomas, 'The Emerging Right to Democratic Governance', *American Journal of International Law*, 86 (1992), 46–91.

Garcia, Soledad (ed.), *European Identity and the Search for Legitimacy*, London: Pinter, 1993.

Gates, Paul Wallace, *The Jeffersonian Dream: Studies in the History of American Land Policy and Development*, Albuquerque: University of New Mexico Press, 1996.

Gelderen, Martin van, *The Political Thought of the Dutch Revolt, 1555–1590*, Cambridge University Press, 1992.

Gentz, Friedrich von, *On the State of Europe Before and After the French Revolution; Being an Answer to the Work Entitled De l'État de la France à la Fin de l'An VIII*, trans. John Charles Herries, 2nd edn, London: Hatchard, 1803.

Gierke, Otto von, *Natural Law and the Theory of Society*, trans. Ernest Barker, Boston: Beacon Press, 1957.

Gobineau, Arthur, *The Inequality of Human Races*, trans. Adrian Collins, New York: Howard Fertig, 1967.

Gong, Gerrit, *The Standard of Civilization in International Society*, Oxford: Clarendon Press, 1984.

Goodrich, Leland M., Hambro, Edvard and Simons, Anne Patricia, *Charter of the United Nations: Commentary and Documents*, 3rd edn, New York: Columbia University Press, 1969.

Goonewardena, K.W., *The Foundation of Dutch Power in Ceylon, 1638–1658*, Amsterdam: Djambatan, 1958.

'A New Netherland in Ceylon: Dutch Attempts to Found a Colony During the First Quarter-Century of their Power in Ceylon', *Ceylon Journal of Historical and Social Studies*, 2 (1959), 203–44.

Green, L.C. and Dickason, Olive, *The Law of Nations and the New World*, Edmonton: University of Alberta Press, 1989.

Grotius, Hugo, *De Jure Belli ac Pacis Libri Tres*, trans. Francis Kelsey *et al.*, Oxford: Clarendon Press, 1925.

The Jurisprudence of Holland, trans. R.W. Lee, Oxford: Clarendon Press, 1926.

'*Commentarius in Theses XI*': *An Early Treatise on Sovereignty, the Just War and the Legitimacy of the Dutch Revolt*, trans. Peter Borschberg, Berne: Peter Lang, 1994.

De Jure Praedae Commentarius, trans. Gwladys Williams, Buffalo: William S. Hein, 1995.

Grotius Society, 'The Future of International Law', *Transactions of the Grotius Society*, 28 (1941), 289–91.

Hall, William Edward, *A Treatise on International Law*, 2nd edn, Oxford: Clarendon Press, 1884.

Hamilton, Neil, *America Began at Greenwich*, London: Poseidon Press, 1976.

Hankins, Frank, *The Racial Basis of Civilization: A Critique of the Nordic Doctrine*, New York: Knopf, 1926.

Hargrove, Eugene C., 'Anglo-American Land Use Attitudes', *Environmental Ethics*, 2 (1980), 121–48.

Harris, Marshall, *Origins of the Land Tenure System in the United States*, Ames: Iowa State College Press, 1953.

Hart, Marjolein 't, *The Making of a Bourgeois State: War, Politics and Finance during the Dutch Revolt*, Manchester University Press, 1993.

Hauterive, Alexandre Maurice Blanc de Lanautte, *De l'Etat de la France à la Fin de l'An VIII*, Paris: Henrics, 1800.

Haynes, Sam and Morris, Christopher (eds.), *Manifest Destiny and Empire: American Antebellum Expansion*, College Station: Texas A&M University Press, 1997.

Heeren, A.H.L., *Manual of the History of the Political System of Europe and its Colonies, from its Formation at the Close of the Fifteenth Century to its Re-Establishment upon the Fall of Napoleon*, trans. from 5th German edn, 2 vols., Oxford: D.A. Talboys, 1834.

Heffter, A.G., *Le Droit International Public de L'Europe*, trans. from 3rd German edn Jules Bergson, Paris: Cotillon, 1857.

Held, David, *Democracy and the Global Order: From the Modern State to Cosmopolitan Governance*, Cambridge: Polity Press, 1995.

Henshall, Nicholas, *The Myth of Absolutism: Change and Continuity in Early Modern European Monarchy*, London: Longman, 1992.

Herman, Arthur, *The Idea of Decline in Western History*, New York: Free Press, 1997.

Hershey, Amos, *The Essentials of International Public Law*, New York: Macmillan, 1912.

Hibbard, Benjamin Horace, *A History of the Public Land Policies*, New York: Peter Smith, 1965.

Higgins, Rosalyn, *The Development of International Law through the Political Organs of the United Nations*, Oxford University Press, 1963.

Houben, V.J.H., 'Native States in India and Indonesia: The Nineteenth Century', *Itinerario*, 11 (1987), 107–34.

Hovden, Eivind and Keene, Edward (eds.), *The Globalization of Liberalism*, London: Palgrave, 2001.

Hyman, Harold, *American Singularity: The 1787 Northwest Ordinance, the 1862 Homestead and Morrill Acts, and the 1944 G.I. Bill*, Athens: University of Georgia Press, 1986.

Jackson, Robert, *Quasi-States: Sovereignty, International Relations and the Third World*, Cambridge University Press, 1990.

Jefferson, Thomas, *Papers of Thomas Jefferson*, ed. Julian Boyd *et al.*, 25 vols., Princeton University Press, 1950.

Katzarov, Konstantin, *The Theory of Nationalisation*, The Hague: Martinus Nijhoff, 1964.

Keith, Arthur Berriedale, *The Sovereignty of the British Dominions*, London: Macmillan, 1929.

Kennedy, David, 'Primitive Legal Scholarship', *Harvard International Law Journal*, 27 (1986), 1–98.

Kidd, Benjamin, *The Control of the Tropics*, London: Macmillan, 1898.

Principles of Western Civilization, New York: Macmillan, 1902.

Klüber, Jean Louis, *Droit des Gens Modernes de L'Europe*, 2 vols., Stuttgart: Cotta, 1819.

Koch, C.W., *Table des Traités entre la France et les Puissances Étrangères, depuis la Paix de Westphalie jusqu'à nos Jours*, 2 vols., Basle: Decker, 1802.

History of the Revolutions in Europe, incl. additions by F. Schoell, trans. Andrew Chrichton, 3 vols., Constable's Miscellany, vols. 33–5, Edinburgh: Constable, 1828.

Koch, C.W. and Schoell, Frederic, *Histoire Abrégé des Traités de Paix, entre les Puissances de l'Europe, depuis la Paix de Westphalie*, revised edn, Paris: Gide, 1817.

Koebner, Richard, *Empire*, New York: Grosset and Dunlap, 1965.

Koskenniemi, Martti, *From Apology to Utopia: The Structure of International Legal Argument*, Helsinki: Finnish Lawyers' Publishing Co., 1989.

Kossmann, E.H. and Mellink, A.F. (eds.), *Texts Concerning the Revolt of the Netherlands*, Cambridge University Press, 1974.

Kuitenbrouwer, Maarten, *The Netherlands and the Rise of Modern Imperialism: Colonies and Foreign Policy, 1870–1902*, New York: Berg, 1991.

Lang, Daniel, *Foreign Policy in the Early Republic: The Law of Nations and the Balance of Power*, Baton Rouge: Louisiana State University Press, 1985.

Lansing, Robert, 'Some Legal Questions of the Peace Conference', *American Journal of International Law*, 13 (1919), 631–50.

'Notes on World Sovereignty', *American Journal of International Law*, 15 (1921), 13–27.

Lauterpacht, Hersch, *International Law: The Collected Papers of Hersch Lauterpacht*, ed. E. Lauterpacht, 4 vols., Cambridge University Press, 1970.

Lawrence, T.J., *Essays on Some Disputed Questions of International Law*, London: George Bell, 1885.

The Principles of International Law, 3rd edn, Boston: D.C. Heath, 1905.

Lebovics, Herman, 'The Uses of America in Locke's *Second Treatise on Government*', *Journal of the History of Ideas*, 47 (1986), 567–81.

Leibniz, Gottfried Wilhelm, *The Political Writings of Leibniz*, ed. and trans. Patrick Riley, Cambridge University Press, 1972.

Leibowitz, Arnold, *Defining Status: A Comprehensive Analysis of United States Territorial Relations*, London: Martinus Nijhoff, 1989.

Leonard, Frederic, *Recueil des Traitez de Paix . . . depuis pres de Troi Siecles*, 6 vols., Paris, 1693.

Lindley, M.F., *The Acquisition and Government of Backward Territory in International Law: Being a Treatise on the Law and Practice Relating to Colonial Expansion*, London: Longmans, 1926.

Linklater, Andrew, *The Transformation of Political Community*, Cambridge: Polity Press, 1998.

Lisola, François Paul de, *The Buckler of State and Justice*, London: James Fisher, 1667.

Lister, Frederick K., *The European Union, the United Nations and the Revival of Confederal Governance*, Westport: Greenwood Press, 1996.

Lockridge, Kenneth, *Settlement and Unsettlement in Early America: The Crisis of Political Legitimacy before the Revolution*, Cambridge University Press, 1981.

Lorimer, James, *The Institutes of the Law of Nations: A Treatise of the Jural Relations of Separate Political Communities*, 2 vols., Aalen: Scientia Verlag, 1980, reprint of the 1883 Edinburgh edition.

Lyon, Bryce, 'Medieval Real Estate Developments and Freedom', *American Historical Review*, 63 (1957), 47–61.

Lyons, Gene and Mastanduno, Michael (eds.), *Beyond Westphalia? State Sovereignty and International Intervention*, Baltimore: Johns Hopkins University Press, 1995.

Maine, Henry Sumner, *Ancient Law*, London: John Murray, 1861.

Village Communities in the East and West, London: John Murray, 1871.

International Law: The Whewell Lectures of 1887, 2nd edn, London: John Murray, 1915.

Malawer, Stuart, *Imposed Treaties and International Law*, Cambridge: Hein, 1977.

Mann, Thomas, *Reflections of a Nonpolitical Man*, trans Walter Morris, New York: Frederick Ungar, 1983.

Manning, William, *Commentaries on the Law of Nations*, London: Sweet, 1839.

Mapel, David and Nardin, Terry (eds.), *International Society: Diverse Ethical Perspectives*, Princeton University Press, 1998.

Marshall, P.J. (ed.), *The Oxford History of the British Empire, Volume 2: The Eighteenth Century*, Oxford University Press, 1998.

Martel, Gordon (ed.), *American Foreign Relations Reconsidered*, London: Routledge, 1994.

Martens, G.F. de, *Summary of the Law of Nations, Founded on the Treaties and Customs of the Modern Nations of Europe*, trans. William Cobbett, Philadelphia, 1795.

Masselman, George, *The Cradle of Colonialism*, London: Yale University Press, 1963.

Mayall, James, *Nationalism and International Society*, Cambridge University Press, 1990.

Meron, Theodore, *Human Rights and Humanitarian Norms as Customary International Law*, Oxford: Clarendon Press, 1989.

Mill, John Stuart, *Collected Works, Volume 18: Essays on Politics and Society*, London: Routledge, 1977.

Collected Works, Volume 30: Writings on India, London: Routledge, 1990.

Mills, Mark Carter, 'The Mandatory System', *American Journal of International Law*, 17 (1923), 50–62.

Montesquieu, *The Spirit of the Laws*, trans. Thomas Nugent, New York: Harper, 1966.

Moor, Jap de and Rothermund, Dietmar (eds.), *Our Laws, Their Lands: Land Laws and Land Use in Modern Colonial Societies*, Münster: Lit, 1994.

Muldoon, James, *Popes, Lawyers and Infidels: The Church and the Non-Christian World, 1250–1550*, Philadelphia: University of Pennsylvania Press, 1979.

Empire and Order: The Concept of Empire, 800–1800, London: Macmillan, 2000.

Murray, Gilbert, *From the League to UN*, Westport: Greenwood Press, 1988.

Nissenson, S.G., *The Patroon's Domain*, New York: Columbia University Press, 1937.

Noel-Baker, Philip, 'The Doctrine of Legal Equality of States', *British Year Book of International Law*, 4 (1923–24), 1–20.

The Present Juridical Status of the British Dominions in International Law, London: Longmans, 1929.

Northedge, Fred, *The League of Nations: Its Life and Times, 1920–1946*, Leicester University Press, 1986.

Nussbaum, Arthur, *A Concise History of the Law of Nations*, New York: Macmillan, 1947.

Olivecrona, Karl, 'Appropriation in the State of Nature: Locke on the Origin of Property', *History of Ideas*, 35 (1974), 211–30.

'Locke's Theory of Appropriation', *Philosophical Quarterly*, 24 (1974), 220–34.

Onuf, Nicholas, *The Republican Legacy in International Politics*, Cambridge University Press, 1998.

Onuf, Peter and Onuf, Nicholas, *Federal Union, Modern World: The Law of Nations in an Age of Revolutions, 1776–1814*, Madison House, 1993.

Oppenheim, L., *International Law: A Treatise*, 2nd edn, 2 vols., London: Longmans, Green and Co., 1912.

Oresko, Robert, Gibbs, G.C. and Scott, H.M. (eds.), *Royal and Republican Sovereignty in Early Modern Europe*, Cambridge University Press, 1997.

Paassen, Pierre van and Wise, James (eds.), *Nazism: An Assault on Civilization*, New York: Harrison Smith, 1934.

Pagden, Anthony, *Lords of all the World: Ideologies of Empire in Spain, Britain and France, 1500–1800*, New Haven: Yale University Press, 1995.

Patterson, Thomas, *Inventing Western Civilization*, New York: Monthly Review Press, 1997.

Pelzer, Karl, *Pioneer Settlement in the Asiatic Tropics: Studies in Land Utilization and Agricultural Colonization in Southeastern Asia*, New York: American Geographical Society, 1945.

Phillimore, Robert, *Commentaries upon International Law*, 2nd edn, 2 vols., London: Butterworths, 1871.

Pletcher, David, *The Diplomacy of Annexation: Texas, Oregon and the Mexican War*, Columbia: University of Missouri Press, 1973.

Pomerance, Michla, *Self-Determination in Law and Practice*, London: Martinus Nijhoff, 1982.

Postan, M.M. (ed.), *The Agrarian Life of the Middle Ages*, 2nd edn, Cambridge University Press, 1966.

Pütter, Johann Stephan, *An Historical Development of the Present Political Constitution of the Germanic Empire*, trans. Josiah Dornford, 3 vols., London, 1790.

Reisman, W. Michael, 'Sovereignty and Human Rights in Contemporary International Law', *American Journal of International Law*, 84 (1990), 866–76.

Rink, Oliver, *Holland on the Hudson: An Economic and Social History of Dutch New York*, Ithaca: Cornell University Press, 1986.

Roelofsen, Cornelis, 'Grotius and the "Grotian Heritage" in International Law and International Relations: The Quarcentenary and its Aftermath', *Grotiana*, 11 (1990), 6–28.

'Grotius and the Development of International Relations Theory: The "Long Seventeenth Century" and the Elaboration of a European States System', *Grotiana*, 18 (1997), 97–120.

Rohan, Henri, Duc de, *A Treatise of the Interests of the Princes and States of Christendom*, trans. 'H.H.', Paris: Thomas Brown, 1640.

Roosevelt, Theodore, 'Mr. Roosevelt's Nobel Address on International Peace', *American Journal of International Law*, 4 (1910), 700–3.

Rosenberg, Justin, *The Empire of Civil Society: A Critique of the Realist Theory of International Relations*, London: Verso, 1994.

Roth, Brad, *Governmental Illegitimacy in International Law*, Oxford: Clarendon Press, 1999.

Rousseau, Jean-Jacques, *The Social Contract and other Later Political Writings*, trans. Victor Gourevitch, Cambridge University Press, 1997.

Ruggie, John Gerard, *Constructing the World Polity: Essays in International Institutionalization*, London: Routledge, 1998.

Saint-Prest, Jean-Yves de, *Histoire des Traités de Paix...depuis la Paix de Vervins*, 2 vols., Amsterdam, 1725.

Schmutzer, Eduard, *Dutch Colonial Policy and the Search for Identity in Indonesia, 1920–1931*, Leiden: E.J. Brill, 1977.

Sever, Adrian (ed.), *Documents and Speeches on the Indian Princely States*, 2 vols., Delhi: B.R. Publishing, 1985.

Shaw, Malcolm, *Title to Territory in Africa: International Legal Issues*, Oxford: Clarendon Press, 1986.

Skinner, Quentin, *The Foundations of Modern Political Thought, Volume 2: The Age of Reformation*, Cambridge University Press, 1978.

Somervell, D.B., 'The Indian States', *British Year Book of International Law*, 11 (1930), 55–62.

Spruyt, Hendrijk, *The Sovereign State and its Competitors: An Analysis of Systems Change*, Princeton University Press, 1997.

'S.W.', *A General Collection of Treatys...from 1648 to the Present*, 4 vols., London, 1710–32.

TeBrake, William H., *Medieval Frontier: Culture and Ecology in Rijnland*, College Station: Texas A&M University Press, 1985.

Toynbee, Arnold, *A Study of History*, 11 vols., Oxford University Press, 1954.

Tuck, Richard, *Natural Rights Theories: Their Origin and Development*, Cambridge University Press, 1977.

   Philosophy and Government, 1572–1651, Cambridge University Press, 1993.

   The Rights of War and Peace: Political Thought and the International Order from Grotius to Kant, Oxford University Press, 1999.

Tully, James, *An Approach to Political Philosophy: Locke in Contexts*, Cambridge University Press, 1993.

Turner, Frederick Jackson, *The Frontier in American History*, Tucson: University of Arizona Press, 1986.

Twiss, Travers, *The Law of Nations Considered as Independent Political Communities: On the Rights and Duties of Nations in Time of Peace*, Oxford University Press, 1861.

Tylor, Edmund, *Primitive Culture: Researches into the Development of Mythology, Philosophy, Religion, Language, Art and Custom*, 2 vols., London: John Murray, 1920.

UN, *Public Papers of the Secretaries-General of the United Nations, Volume 1: Trygve Lie, 1946–1953*, New York: Columbia University Press, 1969.

UNCIO, *Documents of the United Nations Conference on International Organization at San Francisco*, 22 vols., London: UN Information Organization, 1945.

Vandenbosch, Amry, *The Dutch East Indies: Its Government, Problems and Politics*, 3rd edn, Berkeley: University of California Press, 1944.

Vattel, Emerich de, *The Law of Nations or the Principles of Natural Law Applied to the Conduct and to the Affairs of Sovereigns*, trans. C.G. Fenwick, Washington: Carnegie Institution, 1916.

Ven, G.P. van de, *Man-Made Lowlands: History of Water Management and Land Reclamation in the Netherlands*, 2nd edn, Utrecht: Uitgeverij Matrijs, 1994.

Vermeulen, Ben, 'Discussing Grotian Law and Legal Philosophy: Marginal Notes to Some Recent Articles on Grotius', *Grotiana*, 6 (1985), 84–92.

Vincent, R.J., *Human Rights and International Relations*, Cambridge University Press, 1986.

Vinogradoff, Paul, *Outlines of Historical Jurisprudence*, 2 vols., London: Oxford University Press, 1920.

Vitoria, Franciscus de, *De Indis et De Jure Belli Reflectiones*, trans. John Pawley Bale, Washington: Carnegie Institution of Washington, 1917.

Vollenhoven, C. van, 'Holland's International Policy', *Political Science Quarterly*, 34 (1919), 193–209.

Voltaire, *Political Writings*, trans. David Williams, Cambridge University Press, 1994.

Vries, Jan de, *The Dutch Rural Economy in the Golden Age, 1500–1700*, London: Yale University Press, 1974.

Ward, Robert Plumer, *An Enquiry into the Foundation and History of the Law of Nations in Europe*, 2 vols., London: Butterworth, 1795.

Watson, Adam, 'Hedley Bull, States Systems and International Societies', *Review of International Studies*, 13 (1987), 147–53.

'Systems of States', *Review of International Studies*, 16 (1990), 99–109.

The Evolution of International Society, London: Routledge, 1992.

Weber, Max, *The Protestant Ethic and the Spirit of Capitalism*, trans. Talcott Parsons, London: Routledge, 1930.

The Methodology of the Social Sciences, trans. E. Shils and H. Finch, New York: Free Press, 1949.

Weinberg, Albert, *Manifest Destiny: A Study of Nationalist Expansionism in American History*, Baltimore: Johns Hopkins University Press, 1935.

Westlake, John, *Chapters on the Principles of International Law*, Cambridge University Press, 1894.

The Collected Papers of John Westlake on Public International Law, Cambridge University Press, 1914.

Wheaton, Henry, *History of the Law of Nations in Europe and America; from the Earliest Times to the Treaty of Washington*, New York: Gould, Banks and Co., 1845.

Elements of International Law, 6th edn, revised William Beach Lawrence, London: Sampson Low, 1857.

Wight, Martin, *The Gold Coast Legislative Council*, London: Faber and Faber, 1947.

British Colonial Constitutions, Oxford: Clarendon Press, 1952.

Systems of States, Leicester University Press, 1977.

International Theory: The Three Traditions, Leicester University Press, 1991.

Williams, E.T., 'The Conflict between Autocracy and Democracy', *American Journal of International Law*, 32 (1938), 663–79.

Wilson, Robert (ed.), *International and Comparative Law of the Commonwealth*, Durham: Duke University Press, 1968.

Woolsey, L.H., 'Editorial Comment: A Pattern of World Order', *American Journal of International Law*, 36 (1942), 621–8.

Index

162